PRAISE FOR *THE CUSTOMER-MARKETING HANDBOC*

'I love this book! Fab Giovanetti has used her impressive knowledge and deep experience to write a modern manual, full of practical and actionable advice, that is a must-have for all marketers. She shows how marketing never stops, how it is always evolving and, ultimately, why it should always focus on the customer to build long-term relationships. Highly recommended reading!'
Gus Bhandal, Founder, The M Guru, the LinkedIn-first digital marketing agency

'It's the blend of real marketing strategies, broken down into steps you can take, that makes this book so powerful. Fab Giovanetti has created something that will stand the test of time. It's sharp, brilliantly written and full of high-level strategy paired with real-world examples so you can inject it straight into your marketing.'
Jess Bruno, content strategist

'Fab Giovanetti provides a personal, and even intimate update on the foundations of brand marketing. A fun read!'
Mark Schaefer, author of *Audacious: How humans win in an AI marketing world*

'This book reminded me why I love marketing. It brings our focus back to what truly matters: people. It's the perfect mix of psychological theories, relatable examples and moments that make you stop and reflect. A refreshing, clarifying read.'
Miruna Dragomir, CMO, Planable

'Fab Giovanetti masterfully combines behavioural psychology with practical marketing frameworks that actually work. As a product onboarding consultant, I especially appreciate the chapters on personalization and trust-building – concepts that directly translate to better user activation and retention. This handbook bridges the gap between theory and implementation better than any marketing book I've read.'
Ramli John, Founder, Delight Path

'Wow, this is a very good marketing book. A very, very good marketing book. Thoughtful, smart and thorough. I felt Fab Giovanetti really speaking to me (helped by all the food-themed references and stories which, by the way, I am here for). I loved the focus on marketing to hearts, to our craving for community and connection and how budget limitations, tiny teams and tight timelines can boost creativity.'

Sophie Cross, Founder and Editor, *Freelancer Magazine*

The Customer-Driven Marketing Handbook

Building marketing plans that capture and convert

Fab Giovanetti

KoganPage

First published in Great Britain and the United States in 2026 by Kogan Page Limited

Kogan Page
Kogan Page Ltd, 2nd Floor, 45 Gee Street, London EC1V 3RS, United Kingdom
Kogan Page Inc, 8 W 38th Street, Suite 902, New York, NY 10018, USA
www.koganpage.com

EU Representative (GPSR)
Authorised Rep Compliance Ltd, Ground Floor, 71 Baggot Street Lower, Dublin D02 P593, Ireland
www.arccompliance.com

Kogan Page books are printed on paper from sustainable forests.

© Fab Giovanetti, 2026

The moral rights of the author have been asserted in accordance with the Copyright, Designs and Patents Act 1988.

ISBNs
Hardback   978 1 3986 2243 2
Paperback   978 1 3986 2242 5
Ebook   978 1 3986 2244 9

British Library Cataloguing-in-Publication Data
A CIP record for this book is available from the British Library.

Library of Congress Control Number
2025034519

Typeset by Integra Software Services, Pondicherry
Printed and bound by CPI Group (UK) Ltd, Croydon CR0 4YY

To Michael – my partner in everything – and our little girl, Florence, who has been with me through every word, every idea, every moment of this journey. You make every chapter of life better.
And to our students – past, present and future. You are the reason I believe in better marketing and in better ways of doing things. Thank you for trusting me to be part of your journey. Watching you grow, challenge norms and build with heart has been one of the greatest privileges of my life.
This book is for all of you.

CONTENTS

ABOUT THE AUTHOR

Fab Giovanetti is an award-winning author, entrepreneur and marketing consultant. As the CEO and head teacher of Alt Marketing School, she supports individuals to make a positive impact through their marketing efforts. Based in Cambridge, UK she has featured in The Next Web, Business Insider and Forbes, amongst others and has been nominated as one of the 50 Digital Women to Watch as well as one of the Top 100 Marketers in 2023 by Growth Daily and in the Top 100 Marketing Influencers Index of 2023.

ACKNOWLEDGEMENTS

Writing a book is never a solo effort and I am deeply grateful to all the people who made this one possible.

To my husband, Michael – your love, patience and encouragement carried me through every stage of this journey. Thank you for being my anchor and my biggest champion.

I cannot believe this journey has been shared with our little Florence straight from the womb, who has been with me every step of the way as I wrote this book – you've already changed my world in the most beautiful ways.

To our students – you are the heartbeat of everything we do. Your passion, your curiosity and your drive to make marketing better continue to inspire me every single day.

How could I forget our incredible team at Alt Marketing School? A bunch of freelancers with a heart of gold: Lisa and Anu – thank you for keeping the school thriving while I split my heart (and time) between writing and leading. Your dedication, care and resilience mean more than words can say.

To all of our teachers at Alt Marketing School – your insights, generosity and example have shaped this community into what it is today. You've inspired me to keep pushing, keep learning and keep showing up.

Finally, a special thanks goes to the team at Kogan Page – thank you for believing in me and in this project. Special thanks to Donna Goddard for reaching out, encouraging me to dive into another book and for seeing potential when I needed it most. And to Bobbi-Lee Wright for your editing expertise and the kind, steady words of encouragement that helped me keep going.

And finally, heartfelt thanks to our three featured interviewees – Dan Nelken, Charlie Terry and Tania Gerard – for lending your insights, your stories and your brilliance to this project. Your contributions helped bring this book to life in ways I will always be grateful for.

Thank you for being part of this journey.

And, as always – don't forget to be kind to yourselves and others, and never stop learning. Because practice makes progress.

Introduction

Navigating the new marketing landscape

Have you ever had a first date that goes really well? And by 'really well' I mean the conversation is flowing, you've got similar interests, maybe they're making you laugh or they're asking just the right questions. You're having the time of your life, enjoying the meal if you had one, or whatever activity you've chosen together. Then, right at the end of the date, they look at you, go down on one knee and ask, *'Will you marry me?'*

What would you say to that?

I've asked this question to over 500 students in the past seven years. I share this scenario with them and I love asking it because I believe it's incredibly relevant to what marketing is, what it stands for and what it's about. More often than not, the students reply that they wouldn't say *'Yes'* to a marriage proposal after a first date – and, personally, I'd say that's pretty wise.

In a similar vein, great marketing takes time.

The truth is, marketing has become a relationship-building journey, and to make it efficient and effective we have to understand humans. Just like most people wouldn't commit to something on a first interaction – no matter how charming, funny and compatible it might seem – the same goes for marketing. Our customers want to connect, relate and understand how we, as marketers, along with the companies we represent, can enrich their lives and build a meaningful relationship moving forward.

Customer-driven is more than a buzzword. It can be a way of shaping every step of your strategy. The beauty of a customer-driven approach is its timelessness, rooted in psychology and human interaction.

In a world where trends and platforms come and go – where hacks and tactics age faster than the yoghurt you might have in your fridge (big fan of coconut yoghurt myself) – it's reassuring to know that some strategies are timeless because they put people first. This approach can make our jobs as marketers so much easier. The question is, what makes customer-driven marketing, well, driven by customers?

A deep dive into customer-driven marketing

> Customer-driven starts with putting people first, which means considering how you want to be perceived and how your audience connects with you.

Are you a LEGO fan? My husband is a huge fan – so much so that part of my dowry was made from LEGO blocks. Whether or not you're a fan (which, by the way, LEGO has a term for: Adult Fans of LEGO – AFOL), you've probably been around someone who loves the brand and everything it stands for.

One thing LEGO has always done well is understand its customers. A brilliant example of this customer-driven approach comes from a simple yet clever billboard campaign.

If LEGO had to explain what they do, they could say they've been 'selling construction toys since 1932'. But that's not nearly as relatable, is it? What does LEGO do? Among other things, LEGO has been destroying parents' feet since 1932. That was the actual copy from one of their billboards.[1]

It's such a relatable message and it perfectly shows how LEGO puts the customer's experience, interests and quirks at the centre of its approach. This connection spans across generations, from the youngest LEGO fans to the adults and parents, who – let's be honest – will often be caught off guard by stray LEGO pieces!

Hopefully, this example reminds you, dear reader, that often we'll be starting small when it comes to making a change.

There's often pressure to overhaul your marketing strategy to be 'customer-driven', but it's simpler than that. Customer-driven starts with putting people first, which means considering how you want to be perceived and how your audience connects with you.

Over the past five years, we've seen this approach rise alongside major shifts in technology, global events and – crucially – consumer behaviour. As marketers, we've learned to humble ourselves and treat customers with the respect they deserve – it is important that we give our audience more credit.

Like the geek that I am, when seeing shifts so monumental, I have to ask myself: why right now?

It could be that this shift was accelerated by our collective focus change during the pandemic, yet one of the biggest shifts affecting our customers' decisions is their heightened awareness of the impact of their purchases.

And yes, while marketing is not only about selling, it is still a relation-ship-building exercise with a goal in mind. At the end of this journey, our version of going down on one knee with a ring might look less romantic – perhaps a card reader or an invoice ready to sign. And as consumers are more thoughtful than ever about the impacts of their purchases, we as brands and marketers need to consider what our customers truly care about, what we care about and how to communicate the difference we're making to get them to commit.

For example, with the rise in remote work, customers interact with brands across more channels than ever, all while longing for community and connection. Think back to the Covid-19 pandemic: that forced isolation highlighted just how much people crave community. Now, customers want to engage with brands that share their values and get them.

Even more so, the pandemic had an impact on customers of all ages and backgrounds: for example, it led to wider adoption of technology across all age groups. Over 68 per cent of older adults indicated they would continue using these technologies post-pandemic.[2]

With the rise of online shopping and curiosity at an all-time high, building trust has become one of the most valuable currencies. As our audiences can now access opinions, reviews and word-of-mouth, trust is only growing in importance.

Customer-driven means amplifying small special moments and unique ways to have our people think back and say '*You are literally reading my mind!*' Picture a parent stepping on a LEGO piece at 3 a.m. on the way to the bathroom – a small but universally relatable moment for many parents with kids. Moments like these connect people to a brand because they're authentic, recognizable experiences. As consumers, we're more motivated than ever to build meaningful relationships and find brands that resonate with us. By putting customers' needs, desires and pain points first, we can only strengthen our marketing strategy.

Why you should start marketing to hearts

One of the most impactful changes I made in the customer journey for Alt Marketing School is probably one of the smallest – and maybe not the most scalable – changes I've implemented. And, honestly, it brings me so much joy every time I do it. I still remember a message from a new student: 'I just watched your video, and at first I thought it was a generic welcome. Then I realized you said my name and shared specific tips on making the most of the platform, and I realized this video was made just for me. I felt so special.'

Yes, we send a welcome video to every new student who joins our positive impact marketing certification. It may not be the most scalable or efficient choice, especially for someone like me who's known for loving systems and efficiency. And, sure, there are tools out there that could generate personalized videos at scale if I wanted. I'd like to add, they are scarily good at doing so too.

Yet, everything I teach comes back to marketing to hearts. And marketing to hearts is about finding those golden moments where a human touch still matters. These are the moments where people feel seen and genuinely valued. It's telling that expectations are often so low when it comes to truly surprising and delighting customers. So much of what we see feels impersonal, even when it's meant to be direct. But, as marketers, when we make that shift – taking the time to genuinely learn how we can serve our people better – every step in that relationship can be infused with these small, heartfelt touches that make the experience truly special.

I know you may be wondering, *'But Fab, I don't have the time, budget or resources to do this.'* And this, my dear reader, is the moment where I remind you that, to make your strategy customer-driven, you'll need to make some key changes to your mindset.

Here's a little truth I've learned after a decade of working with startups, including my own self-funded ventures: a slim budget, very often non-existent, is the reality for so many of us. Whether it's budget, team power or even just time, working within constraints is a skill that makes us sharper, scrappier and ultimately more creative. Some of my best ideas were born out of budgets so tight they practically vanished into thin air. Because when you're forced to make every penny (or minute) count, that's when the real magic happens.

Want proof? Here are three constraints that can boost your creativity:

- **Budget limitations:** A small budget makes you resourceful, encouraging partnerships, bartering or tapping into untapped resources like user-generated content that might go overlooked with a bigger budget.

- **Tiny teams:** When you're working solo or with a small team, you start to think cross-functionally. A lean team challenges you to pick up new skills, learn faster and get creative with collaboration tools.

- **Tight timelines:** Limited time helps you cut out the fluff and focus on what truly matters. When every minute counts, you're forced to work smarter, not harder, leading to faster, punchier results.

As clichéd as it may sound, less really is more. Time to get scrappy, get inventive and be bold enough to pursue weird and wonderful ideas. Because the most weird and wonderful ideas tend to be the ones that work best when it comes to infusing a human touch into your marketing. And when you make this shift – putting the relationship with your customers first – it doesn't mean following the old adage that 'the customer is always right'.

Personally, I've never quite agreed with that, perhaps because I spent a few years working in hospitality before becoming a marketer. So, in true Fab style, I like to spin the way we look at this. I do believe that the customer should always be heard and seen. And when they're not right, it's an opportunity to start a dialogue to find ways to make things better for each party. This mindset is one of openness, of making decisions aligned with your values and of serving the purposes your products or services fulfil for customers – with a sprinkle of kindness added in.

If you need another reason to embrace a customer-driven approach, remember that it's an approach that speaks not only to our rational side but also to the warm, fuzzy side. This makes it timelessly effective, reaching results that last beyond the next algorithm update.

My promise to you, dear reader, is that by following the path laid in this book, one of the biggest benefits you'll see from this approach is increased retention, loyalty and advocacy. Since the cost of acquiring a new customer is far higher than that of retaining someone who already loves you, nurturing superfans is a milestone in itself. And results, of course, matter to us as marketers. The efforts we put in must yield fruit, especially when juggling eight or nine campaigns at a time.

As marketers, we're always busy – and yes, sending individual videos to each new student can be time-consuming. Yet I know it's the very thing that prompts students to share their experiences with others, because they feel a personal connection. So, the time I invest in this simple activity consistently brings a return. I don't have to try new tactics or create complex strategies to turn these new customers into advocates. It's something I can replicate time and again, with success each time.

And that timelessness of relationship-building touch points? It's one of the best ways to simplify a solid strategy, even in a world of constantly changing platforms and trends.

But then again, I hear you – is there really nothing I can do to make the process easier? You may not be surprised to hear I have a few aces up my sleeve.

Why a customer-driven marketing strategy saves time in the long run

Once, I had the pleasure of interviewing Dan Nelken on the Alt Marketing School podcast. Dan is a phenomenal author, world-class copywriter, speaker and genuinely amazing human.[3]

One of my favourite questions to ask guests like Dan is, 'What's the most underrated tool in your work?' Now, I was ready for a list of frameworks with catchy acronyms – marketers do love those, don't we? Maybe something like the AIDA or FAB framework, or even an online tool for writing and proofreading. But Dan's answer surprised me: he said, 'Systems.'

And systems are at the core of any successful and repeatable strategy. When we think about how a customer-driven marketing strategy can save time, especially when we're juggling a hundred things at once, systems and processes are exactly what make it possible. Plus, the right systems allow us to focus on what matters most.

A lot of customer-driven strategy is standing on the practice of understanding customer needs and preferences so that we can create campaigns that are highly targeted and minimize time spent on less effective tactics. And with deeper insights into consumer behaviour, decisions come quicker, adjustments are easier and there's less trial and error along the way. Improved retention rates mean we can invest less time and resources in constantly acquiring new customers, freeing us up to focus on high-impact areas that only humans can address.

Streamlining processes isn't just beneficial operationally. In fact, it also makes you a more experienced, influential marketer, someone who can work smarter, not just harder.

As you'll see throughout this book, I'm a big advocate for systems and efficiency. Building better systems can be a transformative part of your customer-driven journey. But here's the truth: without effective systems, these benefits won't come easily. So, how do we build them?

- **Mapping workflows with the customer journey in mind:** A customer-driven strategy starts by thoroughly understanding the customer journey. When the customer comes first, identifying bottlenecks and unnecessary steps becomes much simpler. We can better evaluate areas for improvement that align directly with what customers want and need.

- **Standardizing and creating reusable templates:** By building timeless strategies, we can also start standardizing our work. Templates and standard operating procedures (SOPs) allow us to revisit and reuse frameworks for campaign planning and content creation, making it faster and easier to maintain a consistent approach. In larger teams, SOPs help clarify roles and ensure each person knows their part in the customer journey.

- **Automating repetitive tasks:** Once workflows are established, it becomes easier to identify tasks that can be automated. With the right tools in place, automations free us from repetitive processes, allowing us to focus on more strategic elements. However, this automation can only succeed if we've first mapped, standardized and streamlined our workflows around the customer journey.

- **Building a centralized knowledge base:** When a strategy is rooted in customer understanding, it creates a rich knowledge base that can be revisited whenever needed. Organizing this information allows us to have a go-to resource for insights on customer behaviours, preferences and needs, which helps inform future strategies.
- **Setting data-driven success metrics:** A customer-driven approach provides a clear foundation for setting meaningful success metrics. With a rich data pool, we can evaluate what's working and what isn't based on customer-centric outcomes, allowing for more informed discussions and strategic decisions across teams.

A major benefit of these systems and processes is improved collaboration. Breaking down silos allows us as marketers to both give and receive support from other teams, enhancing the overall customer experience. When we're constantly learning from our customers, we're continuously revisiting and adapting to their shifting behaviours, habits and needs, ensuring we stay relevant and responsive.

Ultimately, the long-term benefits of a customer-driven strategy are immense. Yet, systems can look different to different people, which is exactly why we'll be covering lots of the examples in the above list in this book.

With streamlined systems and (hopefully) a wealth of data, you'll have the insights and processes needed to keep building on your successes, saving time and creating impact with every step.

The power of community in modern marketing

> Just because you posted something doesn't mean your audience owes you a share, a comment or a like.

I've been thinking a lot about this, and there's a harsh truth we don't consider enough as marketers: just because you posted something doesn't mean your audience owes you a share, a comment or even a like. In fact, it's the other way around – we are the ones who owe them everything. We owe them growth, impact and the results we bring to brands and clients.

This truth explains even better why a customer-driven and community-centred approach is essential in this new era of marketing.

In a world where some marketers still believe their followers will accept bland, inauthentic or clickbait content, it's refreshing to see brands building content and strategies that genuinely resonate – strategies that inspire, surprise or even make audiences laugh. Community is an essential part of a customer-driven strategy, but it's not limited to large brands with big budgets. It's a foundational part of any great strategy, and throughout this book we'll explore specific ways to build and nurture community in our marketing. Community marketing has the power to completely shift the way we look at customer experience, allowing us to rely less on paid ads and fleeting trends.

Private spaces are the future. Broadcast channels, WhatsApp communities and Substack make intimate engagement on social media more accessible than ever, and the brands who'll last are the ones prioritizing building there.

Ultimately, our audiences crave genuine connection and interactions, which foster the kind of emotional bonds that lead to long-term customer relationships. A strong community can even help create brand ambassadors who boost visibility through word-of-mouth marketing.

And if we come back to the basics of understanding customer needs, an active community provides invaluable insights into customer preferences, helping us shape better products and services.

Private spaces and community engagement

Building community doesn't have to be a massive lift from the start. It goes even beyond building memberships or community spaces – it should start with nurturing an audience that feels truly seen and appreciated by your brand.

Another valuable lesson in community marketing, which we see as the foundation of a customer-driven approach, is to listen and learn. By going beyond product reviews and actively engaging in social listening, we can meet our customers where they are and improve our offerings. This builds brand trust and loyalty.

Take Airbnb, which took this concept to new heights in 2023 by announcing over 50 updates aimed at improving customer experience – all shaped by extensive user feedback.[4] They've honed a system for gathering insights, employing multiple approaches to stay in tune with what their community values most:

1 **Online surveys and in-app feedback:** After each stay, Airbnb regularly prompts both guests and hosts for feedback, gathering valuable insights about their experiences.

2 **Community forums:** These forums allow users to suggest new features and report issues, creating a direct line of interaction between Airbnb and its community.

3 **Customer support channels:** Every interaction with customer support is a chance to learn, and feedback gathered here is used to identify areas where the service could be improved.

Consumer behaviour is shifting and people want brands that talk to them, not at them. This shift invites us to build spaces where people can share their voices, feel heard and see that they're valued. A great example of this is the shift towards community-driven experiences rather than influencer-centric campaigns.

For example, in summer 2024 the beauty brand Refy invited their community on a special trip to Mallorca, putting customers and loyal fans at the heart of their brand experience. Not only did this provide heaps of beautifully raw, organic and inspiring content from real customers, but it also gave back to the loyal community Refy built – with the added bonus of a viral social media sensation.[5]

Community marketing isn't just for product-driven brands, either. From brands becoming lifestyle inspirations to business-to-business (B2B) companies acquiring publications (like HubSpot with The Hustle),[6] the opportunities to build community-driven, customer-centric marketing are endless. The case study of The Hustle clearly shows how HubSpot asked itself the questions 'What does our target audience really want to learn about and why? How can we help them beyond what we offer as customer relations management software?'

Another fantastic example of this is Lululemon, a brand that's seen incredible growth by building community in a unique, offline way.[7] Rather than focusing solely on digital platforms, Lululemon invests in local communities, nurturing connections that thrive in real life. They build relationships with local leaders – yoga instructors, fitness studio owners and other wellness influencers – through sponsorships and collaborative partnerships.

What's refreshing is that Lululemon empowers each store to lead these connections on their own, trusting local teams to foster relationships authentically instead of controlling them from a central HQ. This decentralized approach allows connections to flourish naturally, with locals engaging face-to-face and building a community that feels genuine and deeply rooted in shared values.

The role of AI in customer-driven approaches

I am a huge music lover, a passion that stems from my years as a music journalist before transitioning into a full marketing background. My relationship with Spotify has been both complex and relatively loyal, largely due to one of their most exciting campaigns – Spotify Wrapped.[8]

Every year, this campaign fills me with the same excitement as Christmas. It is a perfect example of how two things can be true at once: customer-driven campaigns can focus deeply on human interests and passions, and at the same time they can rely on artificial intelligence (AI) to make it all happen.

Spotify Wrapped takes what could be considered dull data – like the minutes spent streaming music – and transforms it into something personal, fun and engaging. The campaign creates personalized content for each user, making them feel as though they're receiving something made just for them. This approach is as customer-driven as it gets, highlighting the personal connection between Spotify and each listener.[9]

While not every brand has the resources to create such a customized report, AI offers us a way to analyse vast amounts of data, build richer customer profiles and tailor offers based on preferences and behaviours. Just as Spotify has its own system, there are countless tools (many of which we'll explore throughout this book) that enable brands to build this level of personalization.

Beyond campaigns, AI has transformed other critical areas, like customer support – a function often perceived as separate from marketing but fundamentally tied to it. Providing timely, accurate answers to customers' questions builds trust and strengthens relationships. And with customers asking questions across every possible channel, including marketing ones, AI has made it possible to offer round-the-clock support, helping customers feel seen and valued whenever they need help.

Another strength of AI lies in its ability to analyse customer feedback and detect recurring issues, which helps improve retention by preventing churn. For example, AI can examine customer interactions and detect sentiment, highlighting common themes and issues that might otherwise go unnoticed.

User cases like this let us address potential problems early, creating better customer experiences. Then, humans can step in to add those thoughtful, personal touchpoints that elevate the experience even further.

If I haven't sold you on AI and automation yet, let me add one last cherry on top. Given my obsession with systems and processes, I prioritized automating routine tasks and streamline processes, helping me reduce budget constraints and operational costs. Freeing up time and resources allows you to focus more on human-to-human interactions that make your customer journey truly special.

As I always say, knowledge is power. Understanding the role of AI and where it fits into your unique marketing strategy is key. There's no one-size-fits-all approach, but just because we are talking about customer-driven and human approaches, it does not mean we cannot get a little help from our AI friends, supporting our human-to-human focus in ways that make marketing both efficient and meaningful.

No cheat codes: Developing your marketing muscle

> If one person takes the time to watch a video, comment on your post or engage in any meaningful way, you've made an impact at least on one person's day.

I was part of a Q&A with some brilliant young marketers. After 15 years in the field, I heard a question that really stood out: 'What's the cheat code? How do you win the race in marketing?'

This book is about customers and human connections, and ultimately about answering that question. And to answer it truthfully – like everything I'll share with you in these pages – it's going to come from an honest perspective. Because, especially for strategies built with customers in mind, there is no cheat code.

Yes, in that moment, I could've given tips, quick tricks or shiny shortcuts, and I could give those to you too. But that's not what great marketing is.

As marketers, we suffer from a condition I like to call 'viralitis'. Viralitis is the urge to see fast results, to create content that immediately 'pops' with big numbers and to achieve success that we can showcase. This pressure comes not only from our marketing goals but also from consuming content online, where we see others sharing their big wins and flashy metrics.

But here's a reframe I want you to consider: if one person takes the time to watch a video, comment on your post or engage in any meaningful way, you've made an impact at least on one person's day. Multiply that by 100 and you've reached 100 people who have committed time and attention to your work. That's huge – a real success in community-building.

Yet, viralitis often blinds us to these small but significant wins, stopping us from practising the patience essential to letting a customer-centric strategy unfold naturally.

A true customer-centric approach means making time, giving your strategy room to breathe and trusting that your audience will come to you in their own time. Sure, we could build strategies solely on tactics, but honestly? That's not how you get lasting results. That's not how you see a difference in your strategy. For me, there's no shortcut to building a strong, customer-driven marketing strategy.

Real confidence, mindset and mastery come from experience, hard work and a whole lot of curiosity. Those are the qualities that will make you a better marketer, ones that will shape a customer-centric approach.

I wouldn't be where I am today, passionate about creating strategies that are inherently human, empathetic and kind, if I hadn't taken time, shown commitment and, most importantly, had the patience to make mistakes along the way.

Oh, and don't be mistaken. While this book can help you avoid some of the mistakes I made, it's not about skipping the line. I'll still be encouraging you to try things for yourself, learning from them and staying curious about what works and what doesn't.

It's about being willing to ask more questions and making things better for your audience and customers. What you can rest assured about is that I'll be on the sidelines cheering you on – it's kind of my thing.

This approach may not bring instant, viral-worthy results or LinkedIn glory, but it's the kind that sticks. This is how my students and clients have achieved sustainable, exciting results over the past fifteen years.

Experience rather than cheat codes, hey?

To my surprise, this answer at the Q&A resonated with the room. And the reason I'm sharing this with you is that, deep down, we all know there's no magic shortcut to success. We know we need to be curious and willing to dive deeper.

So, consider this book a chance to dive deeper, to take your time, to trust the process, to experiment and to keep showing up. The lessons, wins and confidence you'll gain? They'll come with every hour you put into your work, with each new idea you try and with every customer interaction that brings a smile and a super fan ready to recommend you to their friends. That's where real success lies.

KEY POINTS

- Marketing has evolved into a relationship-building journey that requires understanding humans and their needs. Customer-driven marketing is timeless and rooted in psychology and human interaction.

- The pandemic accelerated shifts in consumer behaviour, including increased awareness of purchase impacts and desire for community.

- Trust has become a valuable currency in marketing due to wider technology adoption and access to information.

- Marketing to hearts involves creating authentic, recognizable experiences that resonate with customers.

- Constraints in budget, team size and time can boost creativity and lead to innovative marketing solutions.

- A customer-driven approach can save time in the long run through improved retention, loyalty and advocacy.

- Implementing systems and processes is crucial for executing an effective customer-driven marketing strategy.

- Building and nurturing community is essential in modern marketing, fostering genuine connections and long-term relationships.

Notes

1 u/TheRealRandyMarsh7. Lego: Destroying parents' feet since 1952, Reddit, 26 August 2014. www.reddit.com/r/funny/comments/3i9h8d/lego_destroying_parents_feet_since_1952/ (archived at https://perma.cc/GTR5-TT2P)

2 J H A Wong et al. Association of individual health literacy with preventive behaviours and family well-being during Covid-19 pandemic: Mediating role of

family information sharing, *International Journal of Environmental Research and Public Health*, 2020, 17 (23), 8838. www.mdpi.com/1660-4601/17/23/8838 (archived at https://perma.cc/W382-5R57)

3 D Nelken. Interviewed for Alt Marketing School podcast, 2025.

4 Airbnb. Airbnb 2023 summer release: Introducing Airbnb Rooms, an all-new take on the original Airbnb. 3 May 2023. news.airbnb.com/2023-summer-release (archived at https://perma.cc/J2JE-BXPB)

5 Refy Beauty. Instagram post, 21 July 2024. www.instagram.com/p/C9rZ0yIuoi8 (archived at https://perma.cc/DK6F-28Y5)

6 HubSpot. HubSpot signs agreement to acquire The Hustle, adding content to help scaling companies grow better, 3 February 2021. www.hubspot.com/company-news/hubspot-signs-agreement-to-acquire-the-hustle-adding-content-to-help-scaling-companies-grow-better (archived at https://perma.cc/RS8X-JAQX)

7 Lululemon. Ambassador programme, nd. www.lululemon.co.uk/en-gb/c/community/ambassadors

8 F Giovanetti. Spotify Wrapped: What the viral campaign can teach marketers, Alt Marketing School, December 2022. altmarketingschool.com/spotify-wrapped/ (archived at https://perma.cc/JF57-2RTY)

9 J Shepherd. 23 essential Spotify statistics you need to know in 2025, The Social Shepherd, 2025. thesocialshepherd.com/blog/spotify-statistics (archived at https://perma.cc/3M7G-Q6VG)

01

The evolution
of marketing strategies

REMINDER

The essence of marketing – capturing attention and communicating effectively –
has been a part of human culture for centuries

I've always been interested in the history of things. At university, I studied foreign languages and cultures, fascinated by literature and stories – a passion that, as it turns out, has come in handy as a marketer more than once. I've always been drawn to understanding the reasons behind events, the shifts in culture and the ways the world evolves. Just as literature is deeply tied to history and world events, marketing is linked to societal changes, patterns in behaviour and how we grow collectively.

Ask any marketer to name one universal truth about marketing and they'll probably tell you that change is constant. It's a good philosophy for life in general, but for marketing it's the bread-and-butter of what we do.

The truth is, marketing didn't really start out as *marketing* – and that's what makes it so interesting to look at. It gives us perspective on how long we've associated the idea of marketing with buying, selling and transactions. Even when we dive into the origin of the word, it's clear that for many centuries, marketing has been associated with bustling markets, haggling, negotiations and transactions.

As a linguist at heart, I find the origins of words fascinating – and the history behind marketing is no exception. It sheds light on the misconceptions we still hold about what marketing truly is and what it's meant to be.

According to the Online Etymology Dictionary, the term dates to the 1560s and meant 'buying and selling, act of transacting business in a market', derived from the verb *market*.

By 1701, it had evolved to include 'produce bought or sold at a market'. It wasn't until 1897 that marketing took on the business sense we know today – 'the process of moving goods from producer to consumer with an emphasis on advertising and sales'.[1]

So, the evolution of modern marketing reflects the ways people have continually adapted the process of buying and selling, weaving in persuasion, communication, branding and association.

Strategies adapt, evolve and shift all the time – especially in today's fast-paced world. This got me thinking, as any curious investigator would: is this just how marketing is right now, with algorithms changing, technology advancing and new platforms springing up? Or has marketing always been this way?

Thanks to my imaginary DeLorean, I am going to hop back and forward in time with this chapter, taking a retrospective look at the evolution of marketing strategies, not only to give you insight into how the field has changed, but also to reveal the constants that remain.

By understanding marketing's journey and its cultural connections, we can uncover the timeless principles that still hold power today, allowing us to adapt with greater confidence and clarity.

The origin of marketing

Let's travel back to 35 BCE, to the bustling streets of Pompeii. Among the many traders thriving in this ancient society was a fish sauce producer named Umbricius Scauras. Scauras was a merchant, but little did he know he was also about to become a pioneer in branding.

He had this wild idea: to place mosaics depicting amphorae, each one adorned with his brand and quality claims, strategically around the city for everyone to see. These mosaics became a powerful form of advertising, spreading the word across Pompeii – and, soon enough, throughout the entire Mediterranean – about the quality of his prized fish sauce.[2]

It's fascinating to see how, even in ancient times, the power of branding and the importance of association were already in play. So, when people tell me there's nothing to learn from the past about marketing, or that so many of the things we do now are new, I can't help but bring out my inner marketing geek.

Because even back then, merchants like Scauras were embedding their brands into the fabric of daily life in Pompeii to build reputation and trust, even across borders. It's proof that the fundamentals of marketing are as old as time itself. Thousands of years ago, the idea of creating a narrative around a product to elevate its value was already a strategy. So, when we talk about the evolution of marketing and how far we've come, it's worth remembering that the roots of branding run much deeper than we might think.

Even 40,000 years ago, people were creating specialized goods like jewellery and figurines, which some historians believe were the earliest signs of marketing in action. The first recorded evidence? That takes us all the way back to ancient Mesopotamia around 1750 BCE, even before our friend Scauras, where clay tablets with cuneiform script were used to advertise and communicate with customers.[3]

Interestingly, during this early stage in marketing history, it was perceived quite differently than we know it today. Back then, marketing was about facilitating simple transactions and announcing the availability of goods and services. It was more like speaking *at* people – broadcasting messages to inform them about what was happening and what was available. In fact, outdoor advertising was also common in many ancient civilizations. Sellers in Egypt, Greece and Rome would paint or carve advertisements onto the sides of buildings or large rocks positioned along busy paths. In places where literacy levels were low or linguistic diversity was high, merchants used image-based signs to depict their primary goods or services.

At its core, marketing in those times revolved around communication and persuasion, which is still a significant part of how marketing is perceived today. And while there's nothing inherently wrong with persuasion, I see customer-driven marketing as being more about guiding and engaging with direction. You'll hear it a lot in this book.

But what's fascinating is that early marketing wasn't just limited to tablets and mosaics. There were some incredible examples of creativity even in those times.

The earliest known printed advertisement comes from China's Song dynasty (960–1279 CE). It promoted high-quality needles and read, 'We buy high quality steel rods and make fine quality needles that are ready for use at home in no time.' The wording might sound surprisingly modern, but that's because consumer needs are timeless.[4]

People have always wanted quality and convenience. This ancient ad even featured a rabbit holding a needle as a logo – an early example of brand identity that made the product memorable and distinctive.

OTHER EXAMPLES FROM AROUND THE WORLD[5]

- Ancient Egyptians used hieroglyphics to advertise goods and services, carving their promotional messages into temple walls and public spaces to capture the attention of potential customers.

- In China, candy makers played bamboo flutes to attract customers – an early form of audio marketing, not too dissimilar to the cheerful chimes of today's ice cream vans.

- Just as modern brands use celebrities for endorsements, Roman gladiators and Greek Olympians were hired to promote products both in and out of the arena. Just imagine Maximus in *Gladiator* endorsing a particular wine merchant – it might have felt jarring to today's audiences, but it would have been historically accurate.

The essence of marketing – capturing attention and communicating effectively – has been a part of human culture for centuries. At this stage, marketing would resemble sales and advertising, over the modern funnel-driven approach we may see these days.

The dawn of advertising in the 15th century

We are back on the street, this time strolling through a European market in the late 15th century, where artists, craftsmen and merchants are all vying for attention. Among the buzz, one name begins to stand out: Albrecht Dürer, a German painter whose works are sought after by nobles and art lovers alike.

In 1498, he introduced a monogram, 'AD', a signature that becomes synonymous with his work and quality. Little does anyone know, this simple act would become one of the earliest examples of strategic branding, setting a precedent for artists and merchants for centuries to come.[6]

But Dürer didn't stop there. He was also ahead of his time in building a distribution network that spread his art across Europe, ensuring that his name – and his brand – was known far and wide. And, in true pioneering spirit, he even took legal action to protect his intellectual property, fighting against those who created unauthorized copies of his work, setting the stage for modern-day trademark and copyright battles!

It's fascinating to see that even centuries ago, the importance of attribution, protecting one's work and creating strategic distribution networks, was already being practised. When people say that the principles of marketing are a modern invention, stories like Dürer's remind us that the roots of marketing go back much further than we often realize.

Not long after Herr Dürer's days, the Industrial Revolution began shaping marketing into something more than just basic communication and persuasion. By the 1600s, merchants were already in the game of vying for people's attention, laying the groundwork for what would become modern advertising.

These early ads were simple and often repetitive, with the same line repeated several times – essentially, the ancestors of ads such as Nike's. It's wild to think that these straightforward messages were laying the foundation for the creative, engaging copy we now consider standard.

With the first ads appearing in England as early as 1625 (with the Americans following suit in 1704 in the *Boston Newsletter*), it was only a matter of time before the first advertising agencies started popping up.[7] William Taylor established the first advertising agency in 1786 in London. We are not talking about advertising agencies as you may know them, but Taylor was among the first to explore marketing beyond the paper format.

Back then, newspaper readership wasn't exactly booming, so merchants got creative with how they reached potential customers. With the British Empire expanding, tactics like banners, people wearing placards and even umbrellas sporting ads became popular advertising media.

A few centuries after Dürer and his paintings, trademarks became a standard practice in the 1700s as governments saw the need for regulations to promote growth in science, technology and the arts. This led to the introduction of patent, trademark and copyright laws, setting the stage for marketing strategies that would become more structured and strategic in the years to come, with the Industrial Revolution paving the way for modern marketing to make its way in.

From the Industrial Revolution to modern marketing

Ads as we know them started to make their way in the 1600s; but what about actual marketing campaigns?

We are back to the UK, with British actress Lillie Langtry, who in 1893 became the world's first modern celebrity endorser when her image graced packages of Pears Soap. Known for her 'ivory complexion', Langtry's endorsement met the new consumer demand for aspirational products and launched a career in advertising that was as lucrative as her life on the stage.

Behind this move (a first of its kind, at least since the Gladiators of Rome) was none other than Thomas James Barratt, who is often called the 'father of modern advertising'. Barratt understood that marketing wasn't just about telling people what a product could do – it was about making them *want* it. 'Any fool can make soap,' Barratt famously said. 'It takes a clever man to sell it.'[8] And sell it he did – turning Pears Soap into the most iconic brand of the nineteenth century.

Still, even with stories like this one, it's hard to pinpoint the exact moment when modern marketing was born. So, naturally, as your trusty researcher and resident marketing geek, I dived into countless resources to try and figure out when we could see a tangible shift in how marketing was perceived.

We can start to see this shift as early as the Industrial Revolution, an era that hints at a shift towards more organized and strategic thinking. Still, throughout the 18th and 19th centuries marketing was still very much about selling.

What stands out during this era is that marketing started shifting from just exposure, persuasion and basic communication to a more strategic approach. Merchants and businesses began to think more carefully about how to present their goods and differentiate themselves from competitors. This is truly where segmentation, competition and branding began to take hold.

The birth of the first advertising agencies during this time laid the groundwork for how marketing would be perceived and practised in future iterations.

These three distinct eras – the **production orientation era, sales orientation era** and **marketing orientation era** – were first outlined in an insightful piece from Full Scale.[9] Understanding these stages helps us see just how marketing grew from basic selling strategies into the more nuanced, customer-centric approach we know today.

Production orientation era (1800s–1920s)

This period was all about mass production and cutting costs. Companies like Ford Motor Company were trailblazers, focusing on maximizing output and making products more affordable and accessible to everyone. But while production was booming, advertising was evolving in its own way.

Take London's iconic Oxford Street, for instance. By 1839, it had become an early adopter of advertising with its storefronts plastered with stationary posters. The sheer volume of these ads got under the skin of politicians, who felt it distracted from a proper shopping experience.

Cue the birth of the 'sandwich men' – human billboards who wore large advertising boards on their front and back while handing out flyers to passers-by. It is said that Charles Dickens coined the term by describing them as 'a piece of human flesh between two slices of paste board'. Harsh, but accurate.[10]

Sandwich men (and women) are still used today, mostly by local shops in tourist towns. They made the news in recent times thanks to David Rowe. A history graduate struggling to find work, Rowe took inspiration from the past in 2012 when, after making countless job applications with no success, he donned a sandwich board that read, 'Hire Me, Please!' and walked around London's financial district.[11]

His bold approach caught the eye of the media, bringing attention not only to the challenges job seekers face but also to how effective a bit of ingenuity and self-marketing can be. It's proof that, even in a modern world full of digital campaigns, sometimes the simplest ideas still catch people's attention.

Sales orientation era (1920s–40s)

From mass production to better resources, in the 1920s competition increased and businesses realized that simply producing goods wasn't enough. The focus shifted to aggressive selling techniques and strategies that could persuade consumers to buy.[12]

This was the era when marketing tactics became more forceful and direct, paving the way for bold, attention-grabbing campaigns.

It's important to emphasize this because it aligns with the idea that, even as marketing evolved, its main goal was to move products into the hands of consumers. And, honestly, as a modern marketer I can't help but smile at this very familiar feeling – ROI and moving units are still big ways to measure success. While there's nothing wrong with focusing sales as a by-product of marketing, it's also interesting to explore where that concept first took root.

As direct selling became the norm, ads started moving into other media, including radio. On 28 August 1922, WEAF radio station in New York aired the first-ever paid radio ad. The host, H M Blackwell, delivered a 10-minute talk (because direct ads were still prohibited) about some apartments at Hawthorne Court in Jackson Heights, Queens.[13]

The cost? Just $50 – but in today's money that would roughly amount to $950.

This event marked a seemingly tiny yet impactful shift, as new media platforms were being harnessed for marketing. It was an early indicator that marketers were willing to push boundaries and explore new channels to reach their audiences – an approach that would only grow stronger as the century progressed.

Marketing orientation era (1940s–70s)

This era marked a real turning point as companies began to realize that understanding customer needs was no longer optional. The 'marketing concept' came to life, with businesses shifting their focus to customer satisfaction and aligning their strategies to what consumers truly wanted. This shift brought about some of the most memorable campaigns that had a clear, compelling message at their heart.

This is something that is still applied today, with examples like M&M's 'Melts in your mouth, not in your hand' slogan[14] or Domino's Pizza's promise of 'Delivery within 30 minutes or it's free'.[15]

These campaigns have been built on what in the 1960s emerged as a new concept, the unique selling proposition (USP). And for that we have Rosser Reeves to thank. He officially coined the term USP in his 1961 book *Reality in Advertising* and outlined what made a campaign stand out from the rest – and potentially started marketers' obsessions with acronyms, but do not quote me on that![16]

According to Reeves, a USP has three essential parts:

1 **A clear proposition:** Each advert needs to make a specific promise to the consumer, offering a distinct benefit that compelled them to act.

2 **Uniqueness:** This promise has to be unique to the brand or a claim that competitors can't or won't make.

3 **Strong appeal:** The proposition has to be powerful enough to draw in new customers and resonate with large audiences.

Reeves' approach focused on identifying a single, standout benefit of a product and hammering it home until it was ingrained in consumers' minds. It was all about making your message so clear and so consistent that it would stick – no matter how many other options were out there.

In this era of marketing, we are witnessing a shift from simply trying to sell to really honing in on what makes a product different and valuable. The USP set the stage for more customer-focused campaigns, proving that successful marketing wasn't just about highlighting features, but also showcasing unique advantages that spoke to consumers' needs.

Even today, the idea of a clear, unique and compelling message remains a cornerstone of great marketing.

The role of academia in modern marketing

Now, we've zoomed all the way to the 1960s, talking about the introduction of the USP and the marketer's best friends – acronyms. But let's hop into my time-travelling DeLorean again and jump back to 1902, the year when the first-ever academic marketing course was introduced at the University of Michigan.[17]

Why does this matter? Well, it's not just me indulging my role as a head teacher and founder of a school, but because it shows that marketing had begun to be recognized as something worth studying, dissecting and understanding at an academic level. It signified that there was something more to explore, a deeper recognition of the impact it could have.

Other universities quickly followed, with the University of Pennsylvania offering a course in 'The Marketing of Products' in 1905. However, back then, the marketing taught in universities still leaned heavily into the *sales orientation* lens. These courses focused on the marketing of goods, branding and the ins-and-outs of wholesale and retail trade. They missed the more nuanced aspects we now value in modern marketing – like the connection between marketing and psychology.[18]

This shift wouldn't truly come until the mid-20th century, especially after World War II, when the focus on aggressive selling reached its peak.

Many of the early 1900s marketing tactics were based on deception and tricks aimed at persuading customers, which only reinforced the idea that marketing was all about persuasion. But marketing, as we now know, is so much more than that.

And all it took was an advertiser to show us that.

Walter Dill Scott: The man who brought psychology into advertising

Walter Dill Scott was one of the first to blend psychology with advertising, changing how consumer behaviour was understood and shaping marketing strategies that were way ahead of their time. His work moved advertising from basic persuasion to something deeper and more impactful.

Scott's journey into this unique blend kicked off in 1902 with his first study, *The Psychology of Advertising in Theory and Practice*. It was a bold move that set the stage for applying psychological insights to marketing.[19]

Scott's big idea was that consumers could be influenced by advertising using emotional and psychological appeals more than logical arguments. He believed advertising had almost a hypnotic effect, playing on suggestibility and reaching beyond rational thought.

- Scott pointed out that emotion, sympathy and sentimentality were far more effective than logical reasoning in swaying consumer behaviour. This laid the groundwork for what we now take for granted – ads that speak to the heart rather than just the head.

- Scott's work turned advertising into more than just an art – it became a science. He believed that to create truly effective ads, marketers needed to understand what made people tick, what drew them in and what pushed them away. This thinking moved advertising from simple guesswork to more strategic, psychology-based planning.

His influence stretched far, helping shape models like Attention, Interest, Desire, Action (AIDA), yet another acronym that has fast become every copywriter's favourite, by outlining the stages consumers go through when engaging with ads.

- **Attention:** Scott's emphasis on capturing consumer attention with suggestive, compelling messaging was right on the money for the first stage of AIDA. He believed that grabbing attention was the make-or-break moment for any ad, ensuring that people stopped and took notice.

- **Interest and desire:** The focus on emotional appeals fits perfectly with building interest and desire – the middle stages of AIDA. By tapping into emotions like sympathy and sentimentality, he showed that ads could create genuine intrigue and a longing for what was being offered. As it stepped away from logic, it was about making people *feel* something that pulled them in and made them want more.

> • **Action:** The final piece of AIDA is action, and this is where Scott's direct
> command approach shone. He believed in being bold and clear – telling
> consumers exactly what to do, whether it was 'Buy now' or 'Try this today'.
> His take was that, if you've done the work to capture attention, spark interest
> and build desire, you need to seal the deal with a strong, actionable prompt.

Even though some of his ideas have evolved, the core belief that psychology enhances advertising still stands strong in today's marketing world.

Scott's approach marked a big shift toward more thoughtful, strategic and effective advertising. After Scott's first dent into a more customer-driven approach, we had to wait until the 1960s to see new perspectives, with pioneering works that changed the way marketing was viewed.

Robert J Keith's 'The marketing revolution' (1960)

If Scott brought psychology into the chat, Robert J. Keith's 1960 article, 'The marketing revolution', was a real turning point for how marketing was perceived and practised.[20]

Keith highlighted the shift from a production-focused approach to one centred around the customer. It showed that successful marketing is all about understanding and meeting customer needs, not just making products. It set the foundation for the customer-first mindset we talk about so much today.

Keith's article also pulled back the curtain on how companies moved from focusing purely on production efficiency to seeing marketing as a strategic tool for growth. This shift was huge because it meant that marketing was no longer just an afterthought – it was becoming a core part of business strategy, and that changed everything.

Philip Kotler's Marketing Management (1967)

If we're talking about the scholars recognized as the fathers of modern marketing, we have to mention Philip Kotler. His book *Marketing Management* is one of the most influential textbooks in marketing. It has been a staple in business schools worldwide and is now in its 15th edition.[21]

His work set the stage for building genuine relationships with their audience and shaped how modern marketing prioritizes customer connection over simple transactions. Kotler introduced refreshing concepts like societal marketing, broadening the scope to include marketing beyond traditional business contexts and considering non-profits and government organizations.

The introduction of societal marketing in particular pushed marketing beyond just meeting customer needs. For the first time, businesses were challenged to go beyond traditional profit-driven motives and think about how their practices could integrate ethical, social and environmental concerns. It was about balancing doing good with doing well.

The concept was built on three key pillars: customer orientation, societal focus and profitability. Kotler's approach builds brand loyalty, boosts reputation and promotes long-term sustainability. As nowadays this kind of marketing has taken many names (ethical, sustainable and beyond), it's intriguing to see how its origin can be pinpointed all the way back to the 1970s.

Kotler introduced many concepts that truly changed marketing and brought it closer to the form in which we know it today:

- He brought the concept of the marketing mix to the forefront, introducing the now-famous four Ps: Product, Price, Place and Promotion. This framework gave businesses a clear and practical way to plan how they bring their products to market.

- Kotler was a strong advocate for marketing that's customer-defined and customer-driven. Yes, we are getting somewhere, dear reader. He believed the key to successful marketing was focusing on meeting customer needs better than the competition. This shift pushed businesses to think beyond just making a sale.

- His book brought together economic insights, organizational thinking and psychological perspectives to create a full picture of effective marketing. This perspective helped marketers appreciate the bigger picture and design strategies that were practical, empathetic and grounded in reality – and helping us consolidate the fact that marketing was never meant to exist on its own.

Robert Bartels' The History of Marketing Thought (1976)

One final honorary mention in this academic hall of fame goes to Robert Bartels and *The History of Marketing Thought*. This book took a deep dive into the evolution of marketing ideas and why it all matters.[22]

- Bartels mapped out the progression of marketing theories from their early days to more modern practices, highlighting key shifts along the way. I may sound like a broken record, but understanding the journey helps marketers see how past lessons have shaped what we do now. It's a reminder that the field is constantly evolving, but the roots run deep.

- Bartels' work laid the groundwork for marketing to be seen as a serious academic discipline. This was a big deal because it moved marketing beyond being just a practical business tool – it became an area for study, debate and continuous learning. It gave marketers and scholars a framework to better understand the ideas that have influenced the field and continue to do so.

So, here we are – at the point where we can really see how marketing has shifted from being solely about persuasion and sales to something much deeper. We're embracing the idea that marketing is about direction. It's about knowing who our customers are, communicating clearly what we offer and being honest about whether we're the right fit for them or not. It's about giving them the choice and letting them take the lead in deciding to commit or walk away.

This all started with understanding how powerful psychology is in shaping our decisions. The realization that our choices aren't just rational, but deeply irrational and influenced by our subconscious, changed the game. It set the stage for marketing to become a discipline that wasn't just about pushing products but about connecting, guiding and empowering consumers to make choices that felt right to them.

And this understanding laid the groundwork as we moved into the 1970s and beyond, where marketing would continue to evolve – ultimately setting the scene for the era of digital marketing that would redefine everything once more.

The journey to digital marketing: 1970s and beyond

It's London and director Ridley Scott – famous for *Blade Runner* and *Alien* – is on set with 200 extras. They're filming what would become one of the most iconic ads of all time: Apple's '1984' Macintosh commercial.

This isn't your average ad. It's bold, risky and costs about $500,000 to produce, facing serious resistance from Apple's board.[23]

The ad, inspired by George Orwell's book *1984* and the classic film *Metropolis*, portrays a cold, conformist society controlled by a Big Brother-like figure. Enter the heroine, played by English athlete Anya Major, who bursts onto the scene and smashes a giant screen with a sledgehammer, symbolizing freedom from conformity. It was a moment of liberation that resonated deeply with audiences.

On 22 January 1984, the ad aired during the Super Bowl to an audience of 96 million. It changed the game, setting a new standard for Super Bowl commercials by focusing on storytelling and emotional impact instead of just product details.[24]

The buzz was incredible. The ad played a significant role in the Macintosh's successful launch, with sales surpassing expectations. It was a landmark moment that showcased how marketing had evolved from straightforward promotion to a sophisticated blend of storytelling, emotion and brand identity.

But only a few years earlier, in the 1970s, marketing was still very different.

Unsuspecting householders received relentless phone calls from strangers trying to sell them things they did not need, and the callers would often not take no for an answer – I have seen my far share of these, usually involving my parents huffing when the landline phone rang for the 100th time. If anything, it's probably a good thing that you can't empathize with that, but trust me, I'm part of the generation that saw the tail end of that era and is relieved this is no longer what marketing stands for.

As outdated as it sounds now, businesses using telemarketing to attract new customers by calling them directly was a hallmark of the 1970s.[25] Today, we'd probably call it an *icky* tactic, but back then, it was a milestone that showed how marketing was shifting. This was the time when Kotler's societal marketing concept was taking shape, technology was advancing at an incredible pace and public interest and customer satisfaction were becoming more important than ever. Marketing was evolving and it was getting more complex.

By the 1980s, with the rise of computers – IBM's and then Apple's first-ever Macintosh in 1984 – marketing as we knew it shifted dramatically.

But beyond the technological leaps of the 1980s and 1990s, there was a quieter but important change happening: a growing focus on customer retention and long-term relationships. While today that's a core part of marketing strategy, back then it was relatively uncharted territory.

Marketers were starting to understand what customer loyalty meant and explore new tools like customer relations management (CRM) systems to personalize their outreach and put a tangible value on their customer relationships – something we now call lifetime value.

And while we're about groundbreaking changes in the 1990s, it's impossible not to mention search engine optimization (SEO) and the rise of blogging. Though SEO feels like a modern must-have, it started back in 1995, with the first recorded use of the term appearing that year. Just like today, search algorithms depended on meta data, keyword density and other on-page elements from webmasters, all aimed at one thing: giving searchers the best experience possible.[26]

Then came 1998, which changed everything with the arrival of Google and MSN.[27]

And if you were part of *my* generation, you'll remember MSN as the best way to keep in touch with your friends, update your statuses with far too many emojis and spend hours crafting the perfect 'away' message.[28] To me and many others, it was a digital hangout spot and it marked a turning point in how we interacted online.

Around the same time, in 1999, blogging platforms like Blogger.com launched, opening a whole new world of content creation. By 2006, there were 50 million blogs out there! But most early blogs weren't the polished, beautifully designed sites we see today.

I remember creating my very first website in the early 2000s on a platform called Altervista. And yes, I coded it myself using the simplest HTML you can imagine. It was a fun fan site dedicated to *Malcolm in the Middle* and I still smile when I think about those early days of the internet when everything felt new and full of possibilities.[29]

In just a few decades, marketing changed so much – and it changed fast. But if that felt like a lot, what came next in the digital era was an absolute whirlwind.

As pay-per-click advertising first came onto the scene in the year 2000, it brought the birth of platforms that became household names. It still surprises many to learn that LinkedIn was one of the oldest social platforms out there, as it began in co-founder Reid Hoffman's living room in 2002 and was officially launched on 5 May 2003.[30]

Then came Myspace, with its iconic invitation from Tom (if you know, you know) and Facebook, YouTube and later Instagram – all platforms that changed how we connected and marketed forever.

It's fascinating to think that just as social platforms were finding their footing so much else started to change. Mobile phones became mainstream, and with them came mobile marketing and a push for mobile-friendly content. Data analytics grew into a massive industry, giving marketers access to insights and consumer behaviours like never before. This explosion of digital experiences brought us knowledge and tools that marketers a decade prior could only have dreamed of.

And if I had to pinpoint the most game-changing shifts in recent years, it would have to be the rise of AI in marketing and the adoption of omnichannel strategies that define the 2020s.

These trends highlight just how far we've come, but at the same time they remind us that when marketing first began it was all about clarity, communication, branding and positioning – even from those early days.

As our trusty DeLorean brings us back to the present day, we cannot deny the significant shifts marketing has been through, with emotional connection and psychology only stepping into the spotlight in the 1900s (a bit late to the party, if I'm honest).

What's beautiful about looking at marketing through the ages is that it reminds us just how much we've shifted our perspective on what marketing was and what it should be. These shifts didn't happen by accident – they came from trial, error and a growing understanding of how to resonate with people. Marketing has evolved into a practice that's not only strategic and impactful for businesses but also one that enriches the lives of customers.

This leads us to dig deeper into the real 'why' behind it all: relationship-building as the foundation of successful marketing. And that, truly, is all about creating genuine connections with customers that last.

KEY POINTS

- Marketing's evolution spans thousands of years, from ancient civilizations to modern digital strategies.
- The dawn of advertising in the 15th century marked key developments in branding and intellectual property protection.
- The Industrial Revolution era can be divided into three distinct periods: production orientation (1800s–1920s), sales orientation (1920s–40s) and marketing orientation (1940s–70s).
- The concept of the unique selling proposition emerged in the 1960s, revolutionizing how brands differentiated themselves.
- Early marketing strategies included creative solutions like 'sandwich men' and strategic placement of adverts in public spaces.
- Academic research and scholarly work in marketing began in the early 1900s, with universities establishing dedicated marketing departments and developing formal theories.
- The rise of digital marketing in the late 20th century revolutionized how businesses reach and engage with customers, introducing data-driven strategies and personalization.

Notes

1   Etymonline. Marketing, nd. www.etymonline.com/word/marketing (archived at https://perma.cc/T22D-SUE9)

2   Z S Demirdjian. Rise and fall of marketing in Mesopotamia: A conundrum in the cradle of civilization, in L Neilson (ed.) (2025) *The Future of Marketing's Past: Proceedings of the 12th annual conference on historical analysis and research in marketing*, Longman, Association for Analysis and Research in Marketing, Harlow

3   Marketing History. Milestones in marketing history, nd. marketing.museum/marketing-history (archived at https://perma.cc/K7RL-4VJS)

4   C LaFleur. The ancient origins and history of modern marketing and advertising, 26 July 2016. lafleur.marketing/blog/ancient-origins-history-modern-marketing-advertising/ (archived at https://perma.cc/7P42-TTQG)

5   Q Schwartz. The history of influencers and why they matter in 2025, Grin, 2025. grin.co/blog/the-history-of-influencer-marketing (archived at https://perma.cc/AME4-ESJN)

6   Marketing History. Milestones in marketing history, nd. marketing.museum/marketing-history (archived at https://perma.cc/4HWU-Q3HM)

7   E O'Neill. History of branding, LCCA, 17 December 2015. www.lcca.org.uk/blog/education/history-of-branding (archived at https://perma.cc/P2KB-XQCZ)

8   Studied Monuments. Thomas James Barratt: The father of modern advertising, 29 April 2025. studiedmonuments.wordpress.com/2015/04/29/thomas-james-barratt-the-father-of-modern-advertising/ (archived at https://perma.cc/7T7H-YL4G)

9   Full Scale. The evolution of marketing, Full Scale, nd. fullscale.io/blog/the-evolution-of-marketing/ (archived at https://perma.cc/XQ7B-MVBK)

10 Urban75. London placard carriers and 'sandwich men', 1820–1840, 31 January 2010. www.urban75.org/london/billboards.html (archived at https://perma.cc/4PA2-89N3)

11 Campaign Live. 'Job wanted' sandwich board grad hired by JCDecaux, 9 October 2009. www.campaignlive.co.uk/article/job-wanted-sandwich-board-grad-hired-jcdecaux/944651 (archived at https://perma.cc/VF33-L6YQ)

12 BBC Bitesize. The 'Roaring Twenties' – CCEA, BBC Bitesize, nd. www.bbc.co.uk/bitesize/articles/zhg9mbk#znc86rd (archived at https://perma.cc/YTV9-DTNP)

13 S Mikhail. The history of radio advertisements, Jungle Communications, 30 October 2023. www.junglecommunications.com/the-history-of-radio-advertisements/?t (archived at https://perma.cc/DNR8-ZJSG)

14 J Kosinski. M&M's: Melts in your mouth, not in your hands, *Journal of Antiques*, nd. journalofantiques.com/columns/antiques-peek/mms-melts-in-your-mouth-not-in-your-hands/ (archived at https://perma.cc/GGR3-5ZFY)

15   M Dent. The failure of the Domino's 30-minute delivery guarantee, The Hustle, 19 April 2024. thehustle.co/originals/the-failure-of-the-dominos-30-minute-delivery-guarantee (archived at https://perma.cc/8YAT-F9EJ)

16   R Reeves (1961) *Reality in Advertising*, Alfred A. Knopf: New York

17   E Applegate (2008) *The Development of Advertising and Marketing Education: The first 75 years*, Middle Tennessee State University, Murfreesboro, TN. files.eric.ed.gov/fulltext/ED502731.pdf (archived at https://perma.cc/TPU9-ENKM)

18   E Applegate (2008) *The Development of Advertising and Marketing Education: The first 75 years*, Middle Tennessee State University, Murfreesboro, TN. files.eric.ed.gov/fulltext/ED502731.pdf (archived at https://perma.cc/KP55-WY7W)

19   W D Scott (1902) *The Psychology of Advertising in Theory and Practice: A simple exposition of the principles of psychology in their relation to successful advertising*, Small, Maynard & Company, Boston

20   R J Keith. The marketing revolution, *Journal of Marketing*, 1960, 24 (3), 35–38

21   P Kotler (2015) *Marketing Management*, 15th edn, Pearson Education, New York

22   R Bartels (1976) *The History of Marketing Thought*, 2nd edn, Grid Inc, Columbus, OH

23   InsideHook. How Apple's '1984' Macintosh ad changed advertising forever, InsideHook, nd. www.insidehook.com/television/apple-1984-macintosh-advertising (archived at https://perma.cc/HY28-CRQ9)

24   InsideHook. How Apple's '1984' Macintosh ad changed advertising forever, InsideHook, nd. www.insidehook.com/television/apple-1984-macintosh-advertising (archived at https://perma.cc/A8MT-KSTE)

25   J A Gallegos. 1970s vs 2020s: History and evolution of advertising, Tint Blog, December 2019. www.tintup.com/blog/advertising-in-1970-vs-advertising-in-2020/ (archived at https://perma.cc/H59F-MXGC)

26   SWW Marketing. A timeline of marketing, SWW Marketing, nd. www.swwmarketing.com/marketing-insights-blog/a-timeline-of-marketing (archived at https://perma.cc/7DZ4-QQ5F)

27   Google. Our story: From the garage to the Googleplex, Google, nd. about.google/company-info/our-story/ (archived at https://perma.cc/UP92-GFHK)

28   Zippia. MSN history, Zippia, nd. www.zippia.com/msn-careers-32079/history/ (archived at https://perma.cc/QMV6-UHNR)

29   SWW Marketing. A timeline of marketing, SWW Marketing, nd. www.swwmarketing.com/marketing-insights-blog/a-timeline-of-marketing (archived at https://perma.cc/P65B-YUP7)

30   LinkedIn. About LinkedIn, LinkedIn, nd. about.linkedin.com (archived at https://perma.cc/44UU-WKFP)

02

Building relationships

The core of marketing

> **REMINDER**
>
> Great marketing is about direction, not persuasion.

I've always been fascinated by how people come up with quotes that stick. You know, those taglines or sayings that become part of their identity and their personal brand. I often wondered, how does that happen?

The moment I learned it for myself wasn't during a brainstorming session or a brand positioning workshop – it happened while recording a podcast. As marketers, the more we share our thoughts about how we perceive marketing, what we love and what frustrates us, the more we understand what kind of marketers we are.

That's how I landed on one of the quotes I use constantly these days: *great marketing is about direction, not persuasion.*

It came naturally, but what made it stick was how many times people repeated it back to me after hearing it on a podcast or in conversation. I say it often because, when I'm asked about the biggest mistakes marketers make or the misconceptions that still linger, persuasion is usually at the top of the list.

It's all about how we view persuasion. Too often, it's tied to transactions, to pushing people to act. That, to me, leans more towards sales than marketing. And while I absolutely see how marketing and sales overlap, they're different in this exact way: marketing done right is about creating a journey, building an experience and fostering a relationship that guides the right people towards you.

Yes, there are moments and touch points where we encourage them to act, but it's when they're ready – not because we've forced them there.

I can accept persuasion as part of the process, but not as the primary approach. Not as a tool to push people when they're not ready, or to present what we do in a way that pressures a *yes* when the answer should really be *no*.

So, what are we going to explore in this chapter? We'll take a deeper look at the importance of relationship building in marketing and how trust has become such a crucial cornerstone – even if it's not an official metric. This ties into one of the marketing superpowers that doesn't get nearly enough attention: empathy.

Whether you see it as a practical, cut-and-dry strategy or a more meaningful, people-focused practice, building relationships that tap into the irrational and the subconscious, and being upfront about the good and the bad makes marketing not just more efficient and effective but also more human.

The importance of putting people first

I don't know about you, but I love a good dinner party. There was a time when supper clubs were really in vogue in the UK and I was lucky enough to be part of a few. Supper clubs had a twist: they felt like a dinner party where you barely knew anyone there.

Sure, you came for the food, but you were also there, whether you realized it or not, for the connections and the people.

The funny thing is, you don't truly understand how important people are, even at a dinner party where the food is meant to be the star, until you have a very bad experience. So, picture yourself at your favourite themed dinner party. You're not hosting, just enjoying it as a guest, mingling and soaking in the atmosphere. Whether you're more of an introvert or an extrovert, you find yourself people-watching, getting a feel for the crowd.

There's one guest who spends the entire evening talking about themselves, dropping stories to impress and making sure everyone knows their accomplishments. They might throw out the occasional question, but only as a springboard to talk about themselves. They're charming, they tell some funny stories, but they dominate the conversation. They might get a few laughs and fleeting moments of attention, but you don't feel invested in them.

Then there's another guest. This one is different. They're more focused on listening than talking. They ask thoughtful questions and show genuine interest in what you're saying. They pick up on little details, relate to your stories and dive deeper into shared experiences. By the end of the night, who would you be more excited to see at the next dinner party?

If you're like me, it's probably the second guest.

See, relationship-driven marketing – or, in my humble opinion, marketing in general – should work in a similar way.

And, thankfully, results, again and again, have shown the same. Brands that spend all their time broadcasting their own greatness may grab a moment of attention. But it's the brands that take the time to engage, listen and connect that build lasting loyalty.

It all sounds well and groovy, but you might be wondering, *how do I get there?* How can I build better connections with my audience? Well, the truth is, all the tactics, touch points and experiences that lead to loyalty and advocacy stem from the efforts we put into building trust. And before we can even start building trust, we need to understand our audience and our customers.

This is an important shift we need to make, because before we dive into funnels or worry about how we retain customers or keep them engaged, we need to be honest with ourselves and ask the age-old question: *how well do I know my customers?* How well do I know my people?

Being a marketer also means being humble enough to recognize that sometimes, whether it's because we didn't know better, or maybe we're working with a new client, or we've just joined a team that skipped doing their homework the first time around, we have to take a step back and really get to know our customers before we can start building relationships with them.

One of the most eye-opening experiences during our Positive Impact Marketing certification came during a hot seat session, where one of our students presented their findings on building an audience persona and a branded entity deck for their business. Their business was aimed at middle-aged women who were ready to reinvent themselves and step into a new stage of life, pursuing their passions or even a new career after years of prioritizing their families and others.

As they shared their journey, something interesting happened. The discussion took off, with other students chiming in, asking questions and sharing reflections. What can I say? Our marketing rebels are the best people.

In the middle of this conversation, the student had an 'Aha!' moment. Our student had been struggling to craft a clear, concise message that would resonate deeply with their audience. To gain clarity, they reached out to some of their past clients and asked insightful questions to better understand what these women were seeking when they first connected with them.

Their initial assumption was that these clients were primarily looking for the confidence to step back into their identity and take the first steps towards reinvention.

But what emerged was surprising: it wasn't confidence that was holding them back – it was guilt. They felt guilty for wanting to invest time in themselves after years of putting others first. What these women truly needed was the guidance to choose the right path and the reassurance that it was okay to do so without feeling selfish. This shift in understanding completely reframed how the student positioned themselves and their services.

The aspirations, fears and blocks their clients faced were different than initially thought and acknowledging that made all the difference in how they approached their marketing strategy.

This story serves as a powerful reminder that, sometimes, the gap between the audience we think we're attracting and the audience we're actually attracting can be wider than we expect. But with the right questions and a willingness to listen, we can bridge that gap and make our marketing more aligned and impactful.

REFLECTION TIME

How well do you know your customers?

There's nothing to be ashamed of and no reason to feel like a failure if, when taking a step back, you realize that you might not know your customers as well as you thought. This is a common discovery and it happens because we often overlook a key truth: there's an intersection between the people we *want* to attract and the people we *are* attracting. And, often, this intersection reveals a gap.

From working with many clients and teaching countless students, I've learned that a huge reason marketing strategies can fall short is due to this exact realization. The people we think we're attracting and the people we draw in are sometimes not the same.

Once we identify how far off we are from this expectation, we can then make an informed choice: do we adapt to the audience we currently have and make sure we're serving them in the best way possible, or do we adjust our strategy, positioning and messaging to start attracting the audience we really want?

To guide you through this reflection, here's a simple yet powerful exercise.

Ask yourself three core questions to help bridge this gap. You can gather these insights through a customer survey if you already have an established customer base, or by posting these questions on social media over three consecutive weeks to engage your audience. These questions should help you understand *why* people are coming to you and *what* they're coming to you for.

Examples I have used with students before include:

1   What hesitations or concerns did you have before deciding to act on the specific problem we solve?

2   How would you describe your ideal outcome or transformation after using our product/service?

3   What's the biggest obstacle preventing you from achieving your goals right now?

4   What solutions have you tried before to solve this problem?

5   What would success look like for you in the next three–six months?

Questions like these complement the existing set you have for current customers while helping you understand the barriers and decision-making process of potential customers.

Here's my challenge for you: Choose three questions that can illuminate your audience's motivations and expectations. Use this as an opportunity to listen and learn.

Yes, this may stretch you, but it's time to lay some solid groundwork. So, dear reader, I believe you're ready for this step. Get your questions ready and let's discover how well you really know your customers.

The role of trust and empathy in marketing

One of the shared loves my husband and I have is food – specifically, trying different dishes and exploring new restaurants and cuisines, whether we're at home or travelling. But over the years, I've discovered that as much as I'm an adventurer when it comes to food, I'm also a creature of habit. I might explore new places, but I have a soft spot for a few favourite restaurants that I return to time and time again. One of them is a dumpling place in Cambridge, not far from where we live. Dumplings are one of my love languages and I'm a bit obsessed.

The reason we first tried that place was simple: a trusted recommendation from a friend. And I'm sure I'm not alone in that experience – following a friend's suggestion to check out a spot they swear by. The outcome of that recommendation shapes whether we'll trust their future suggestions.

Thankfully, this dumpling place was everything they promised and more, so now it's our go-to whenever we're craving comfort without the mental gymnastics of choosing a new place. When we're on the lookout for more food spots in Cambridge, guess who we ask? That friend. Their taste has proven reliable and we trust them.

Now, a food analogy might seem a bit far-fetched but hear me out: trust in marketing works in a very similar way.

A huge part of marketing today is built on creating word-of-mouth, social proof and that sense of reliability that turns casual customers into loyal advocates. But going deeper, the core of trust, in my opinion, lies in a simple premise: when a brand consistently delivers on its promises, customers will come back and engage with them again.

And yes, let's address the elephant in the room – negative experiences do happen and we worry they might damage the trust we've built because trust takes time to earn and can be lost in an instant. It's during these moments that brands who have invested in relationship-building truly stand out. Strong customer service, reliable support and clear communication become the backbone of your customer journey and every step of your marketing funnel.

When we're talking about trust, I can't think of any quick fixes or shortcuts that can get us there. But there *is* a way for us to use some superpowers that can help build trust faster than most brands do these days: empathy.

If you're wondering what empathy really means, it's simply the ability to share someone else's experiences or feelings by imagining what it would be like to be in their situation.

And the beauty of empathy in marketing? It's not just about putting a whole lot of heart into what we do – it circles back to the crucial question we touched on earlier: *how well do I know my customers?*

- How deeply do you understand what they're going through?
- What are their biggest challenges, fears, aspirations and goals?

Empathy allows us to connect with people on a truly human level, but it doesn't come without effort. It requires prioritizing compassion and sincerity in the way we operate.

Empathy-driven marketing often means understanding and listening to the stories our customers are living. It's about creating a practice of collecting and valuing their experiences, something that's incredibly important when it comes to building trust. Empathetic communication resonates because it feels authentic – it feels like we're speaking their language. And, well, that's because we are.

But make no mistake, this kind of work takes effort. It might sound counterintuitive, but it ties right back into having strong systems and processes in place (yes, I did talk about this in the introduction!).

Building a system to collect and learn from customer stories and experiences is key. It's about answering the questions that reveal what's most important to your customers:

- What do they think you stand for?
- Where do they feel you're missing the mark?

When you start using your customer's voice and asking questions like, *What do they say? What do they see? What do they hear? What do they need to do to make a change in their lives?* you unlock something powerful.

You create marketing that highlights conversations and touches on topics that many brands shy away from, things that others aren't bold or brave enough to spotlight.

REAL-WORLD EXAMPLE
Valerie's Perimenopause campaign

Talking about empathy, what happens when a brand dares to break the silence on a topic most people avoid?

Valerie, a supplement and health company, aimed to support perimenopausal changes. They ran a billboard campaign on the often-ignored topic of perimenopause, aiming to break the silence and stigma surrounding this natural phase of life.

Candid and humorous billboards that feature quotes like 'Can you stop breathing near me?' highlighted symptoms of perimenopause such as vaginal dryness and irritability. The campaign spotlighted the rollercoaster of perimenopausal symptoms in a way that's both relatable and refreshingly human.[1]

Online, this approach resonated deeply with the 90 per cent of women and individuals who experience perimenopause, making them feel seen, heard and less isolated.

Valerie positioned itself not just as a brand, but as an advocate for women's health. By acknowledging the gender data gap in healthcare and calling for more research and medication options, Valerie emphasized the need for better resources and support for women and individuals going through perimenopause.

The campaign extended to social media, particularly Instagram, where Valerie engaged its audience through live sessions with nurses, therapists and other women's health experts. This strategy created a safe space for women and individuals to share their experiences and access the tools they need to take control of this stage of life.

What makes this campaign so powerful is how it tackles the shame and secrecy often surrounding perimenopause. By normalizing the conversation, Valerie encouraged women and individuals to stop suffering in silence and start sharing their stories. It's an approach that speaks directly to the importance of empathy in marketing – listening, understanding and addressing what really matters to your audience.

Valerie's effort to use humour and real stories added a layer of trust and relatability. They met their audience where they were, offering both education and a community to lean on. This kind of trust-building strategy highlights how brands that are willing to take risks and put their audience's needs first can transform a campaign from just another advertisement into a movement.

Valerie's campaign is a prime example of how empathetic communication, bold messaging and community support can come together to create not just a memorable campaign, but one that leaves a lasting impact on its audience.

Hopefully, this is the first example of many provided in this book that demonstrates simple ways we can truly integrate empathy and trust into a strategy. At the end of the day, customer-driven strategies shouldn't feel misaligned with what we stand for, what we want to do and how we aim to transform the lives of our customers. That's the biggest mindset shift we need to make when thinking about what *customer-driven* really means.

When you humanize your brand voice, you make interactions with your audience more personable because you speak their language. To me, the most powerful thing you can do is create small moments of empathy through storytelling. If you're still struggling or just getting started with this approach, revisit the questions above and ask yourself: *how well do I understand how my customers think?*

Before we move on, I want to remind you of a few key insights that can help you avoid some of the common pitfalls when building trust and empathy.

One of the most important lessons that comes up repeatedly in our courses is: don't underestimate your customers. I often tell our students that in today's world, people can instantly tell when a brand's tone or storytelling feels forced. If you're ever in doubt, take a step back and invest time in gathering real stories and customer experiences that you can weave into your messaging. It's far better to build a system for collecting customer stories than to try to fabricate authenticity just to check off an empathy box.

Another common pitfall is maintaining one-way communication in your marketing. This is one of the biggest issues brands face when they broadcast their messages without genuinely engaging with feedback, comments, questions or polls. Using these channels actively is about making your customers feel heard and using their insights to tailor your approach.

Ignoring customer pain points, particularly those related to your own brand, is another major trap to avoid. Understanding the issues your customers face with your products or services is crucial, as these pain points could disconnect them from their goals and needs.

The role of feedback in your strategy cannot be understated. Taking feedback seriously, especially when it highlights problems, not only helps improve your products and services but also rekindles trust, even after negative experiences.

On that note, one simple yet powerful practice you can adopt is *active listening*. This can be done in various ways, from straightforward social media questions to more structured feedback channels.

A great example of active listening comes from Heartbeat, a community-building platform that we use and know well. They have a page dedicated to upcoming features based on user requests, which is common for digital products.[2] What sets them apart is their weekly email update, which highlights significant changes and acknowledges pressing user feedback. Even if the update isn't always about immediate fixes, just knowing that an issue is on their radar reassures users that their voices are being heard.

Whether you do this privately or publicly, using platforms like social media to ask *'How can we make things even better for you?'* can be a game changer for fostering trust and improving your brand.

REAL-WORLD EXAMPLE
Bodyform's Never Just a Period campaign

Talking about storytelling and empathy, Bodyform truly shows what it means to connect with your audience. When it comes to addressing the unspoken challenges of women's health, Bodyform has always stood out as a fearless advocate. Their period campaign is no exception.

Drawing on their experience from past initiatives, Bodyform used real stories to confront taboos with genuine honesty.[3]

This video campaign paints an accurate and vivid picture of how menstruation can disrupt daily life, challenging the notion that these experiences are minor or exaggerated by showing how they are perceived by real women and individuals Bodyform aims to support. It demonstrates that Bodyform has done its homework, listening to the frustrations and experiences of their audience to create a campaign that doesn't just market a product but validates lived experiences.

Why consistency and trust go hand-in-hand

I know I often say that you can't really cheat in marketing (or you shouldn't cheat in marketing) because you can learn so much more by making the mistakes and experimenting. However, there is one cheat that I love, because it's not really a cheat, but it kind of feels like it.

It is tied to the misconception that in marketing we have to constantly reinvent the wheel, constantly refresh what we say and what we focus on, what we stand for and what we are about. And, hopefully, you already have seen in this chapter that there are good reasons and times for you to do so when your customer shifts their needs and their perceptions and maybe your customer changes altogether.

But also there are other times when you want to do this that are more tied to your brand – when your product changes, when your brand shifts. But the truth is that unless you need to make these shifts, the best, most under-rated marketing cheat is that in marketing, what you really want to learn to do well is the exact same message a hundred thousand different ways, again and again and again.

And, funnily enough, this cheat, this nugget, is probably one of the hardest ones for a lot of marketers to master.

This way of marketing really goes back to what is the core message that you're trying to bring into the space, and it's what your strategy is rooted in. This will build familiarity. And when you show up and you're consistently reiterating that message and reinforcing your values, your mission and how you support people, you build a very important – not even skill – a very important block in your relationship: reliability.

As well as that, repetition helps customers associate specific values or ideas with your brand. This is why things like taglines, key phrases and even quotes help when communicating with an audience.

The truth is that this kind of consistency doesn't always come easy.

REFLECTION TIME
Are you the go-to brand?

My husband comes from a family of sandwich lovers – they are versatile and deliver as a speedy lunch. Now, as an Italian, I would pick pasta over a sandwich any day. For us, pasta is a given for a quick and easy meal. However, my husband's love for sandwiches goes so deep that in the past he owned all sorts of gizmos and gadgets to make every kind of toasty imaginable.

Recently, as I was scrolling online (as you do), I came across an ad for a company that specializes in one thing: crimping wraps and sandwiches. They create accessories that crimp the edges of wraps and toasties to turn them into sealed pockets of joy, like calzones or pasties. That's their niche and they own it. In fact, their crimping device even went viral on TikTok.

When I showed it to my husband and asked if he'd like it added to our Christmas wish list, he wholeheartedly said, 'Yes!'

This shows not only that my husband is a marketer's dream for kitchen gadgets, but also the power of being the go-to in your space. This company is known for one thing and for doing it well. By doing that (using repetition and trust by delivering on their promise of crimped lunch goodies) they became the go-to for this specific kitchen tool.

Think about what that means for you and your brand. Becoming the go-to doesn't mean being the only brand in your industry. It means positioning yourself in a way that when someone thinks of a specific solution, need or experience, they think of you first.

This might come more naturally for personal brands – you're the go-to expert in your niche. But even for larger brands, being the go-to means mastering one specific job that your product or service fulfils for your audience, like our crimping device example.

Different ways to position yourself as the go-to include:

- owning your industry
- specializing in a unique task your product or service solves
- focusing on a niche that you can serve better than anyone else

There isn't one right way to zero in. Your audience can be broad while your message or offering is specific.

For example, I had the pleasure of interviewing Charlie Terry from CEEK, an agency known for its omnichannel strategies across a wide variety of sectors.[4] Despite serving different industries, CEEK's strength lies in their unique process and their fresh approach to omnichannel marketing. He fully owned on his unique expertise and built his agency around it.

So, what about you and your brand? Can you be the go-to? And if so, how would you make it happen?

Measuring long-term relationship results

One of my favourite quotes that doesn't come from me but from good old Benjamin Franklin is about the importance of planning. It's the very famous, very well-known, 'Fail to plan, plan to fail.' Goodness knows if I haven't told this to hundreds of students during my teaching years – and with good reason. Because, like any other effort we put into our marketing, building relationships, especially ones that prove to be long-term, should not be left to chance. We should be able to see this happening, track it and respond accordingly.

So, one of the things I want you to consider is how to integrate specific metrics and valuable insights that, together, can give you a better understanding of the impact of the relationships you are building in your marketing.

Here are some practical ways to do that by measuring the lifetime impact of your customer relationships, also known as lifetime value.

First and foremost, we have **customer retention rate**. This is the percentage of customers who continue to do business with your brand over a given period. The beauty of this metric is that it's something you can already track using Excel or even some AI tools if you're not particularly skilled with formulas. This percentage gives you an idea of how many people you retain and may also be referred to as 'customer churn' in some contexts. Remember, higher retention rates show that your relationship-building efforts are working and that your trust-building strategies are getting customers to come back.

Another key metric is the **repeat purchase rate**. This measures the percentage of customers who have made more than one purchase from your business. While there are manual ways to track individual user behaviour, this metric can be a bit harder to monitor if done without automation. What's interesting is that understanding this rate can reveal which products or services resonate the most with your audience and encourage them to return.

Then there's the **net promoter score (NPS)**, which often sparks love-or-hate reactions from marketers. Regardless of where you stand, it's worth mentioning because you may measure NPS without even realizing!

Essentially, NPS measures how likely your customers are to recommend your business to others. You can use official NPS tools, but at the school we keep it simple by surveying our students and asking them to rate their likelihood of recommending our courses on a scale of 1 to 10. Whether you use a traditional NPS calculation or a simpler version, this can be incredibly insightful. It can tell you when it's time to practise the active listening we discussed in this chapter and go back to ask questions, improving trust and addressing any negative experiences head-on.

And, speaking of feedback, **customer feedback and reviews** play an essential role in any customer-driven strategy. I can't stress enough how crucial this is in helping you understand the lifetime value of your customers. Collecting reviews, testimonials and feedback forms is something I'm known for being relentless about at the school.

You might wonder, *'Fab, why so intense?'* – and you'd be correct, I am. But by doing this, I can create a message that's more empathetically driven and speaks directly to my audience. I'm not guessing why people love our courses or why they choose us over others – I know. And this feedback helps us improve our product offerings, customer service and overall marketing strategy.

Lastly, you might be wondering about **engagement metrics** – things like average session duration on your website, social interactions and email click-through rates. These metrics are still important and have their place, especially when bringing new audiences into your world. But I want you to use these more for content and brand awareness, building successful touch points that lead to creating superfans, rather than making these the sole way you gauge how engaged your audience is.

REFLECTION TIME
Understanding lifetime value

When it comes to shifting the focus from short-term gains to long-term relationships, there are plenty of practical steps we can take. But the first thing to consolidate and fully understand is an essential piece of the puzzle: the lifetime value of a customer.

Lifetime value, or, because marketers love acronyms, **LTV**, is the estimated revenue a customer will generate over their entire relationship with your brand. The beauty of this metric is that it can often be calculated automatically using various tools. But even if you don't calculate it to the penny, simply tracking each customer's transactions and interactions can help you start acknowledging that not all customers are created equal.

This understanding opens your eyes to the fact that every customer relationship is unique and it allows you to identify patterns. Some customers may make one or two purchases and move on, while others return time and again, engage with your brand and even recommend it to others.

Recognizing LTV changes how we approach our strategies. The goal becomes finding ways to enhance and increase the lifetime value of each customer. This shift naturally pushes us toward prioritizing strategies focused on retention, loyalty and advocacy. When we truly understand what a customer is worth to our business over time, we're more likely to invest in meaningful experiences, thoughtful touch points and quality customer care that make them feel valued and encourage them to stay.

In a world where it's more cost-effective to retain an existing customer than to acquire a new one, understanding LTV not only leads to better business decisions but also makes your marketing more sustainable and human centric.

Here are a few questions to help you reflect on LTV:

1 How well do you currently understand the LTV of your customers?

2 What practical steps can you take to start calculating or estimating LTV for your business?

3 How can this insight guide your strategy for customer engagement and retention?

Building relationships that last

TIP

People want to feel seen, valued and understood. The brands that succeed in the long run manage to deliver that sense of connection.

If there's one thing to take away from this chapter, it's that relationships – true, meaningful and empathetic connections – are at the very heart of great marketing. It's easy to get caught up in metrics, funnels and the constant churn of campaigns, but at the core of all this activity are people. People who want to feel seen, valued and understood. And the brands that succeed in the long run are the ones that manage to deliver that sense of connection.

Building relationships in marketing is about saying, *'We're here, we care and we've got you'*, even when things don't go perfectly.

It's also about balance. Yes, relationships take time, effort and invest-ment. But the payoff? Loyal customers who stick around for years, advocate for your brand and bring others along with them. And if we're thinking about marketing sustainability – which, let's be honest, we all should be – then focusing on relationships is one of the smartest strategies out there.

So, as you close this chapter and start thinking about how to apply these lessons, ask yourself: *what steps can I take today to build stronger connec-tions with my audience? How can I show them that I'm listening, that I care and that I want to be the brand they trust? And, most importantly, how can I ensure that my marketing reflects not just what my audience needs now, but also how I can support them for the long haul?*

The best marketing isn't about persuasion, but direction. And, like all great relationships, it's built on trust, care and the kind of authenticity that can't be faked. So, here's to building marketing strategies that don't just sell but connect – and that leave your customers feeling like they're truly part of something bigger.

KEY POINTS

- Building relationships is the foundation of successful marketing – it's about direction, not persuasion.
- Marketing should focus on creating journeys and experiences rather than pushing for immediate transactions.
- Understanding your actual audience vs your intended audience is crucial for marketing success.
- Trust is built through consistent delivery of promises and genuine customer engagement.
- Empathy is a marketing superpower that helps create authentic connections with customers.
- Customer feedback and stories should drive marketing strategy and messaging.
- Two-way communication is essential – avoid broadcasting without engaging.
- Addressing customer pain points openly builds credibility and strengthens relationships.

Notes

1   weare.valerie. Instagram post, Instagram, nd. www.instagram.com/p/
DA3fJiUtaa8 (archived at https://perma.cc/93AB-6U23)

2   Heartbeat.chat. Feedback, Heartbeat, nd. feedback.heartbeat.chat (archived at
https://perma.cc/76PX-QE9N)

3   Bodyform. Never Just a Period, Bodyform, nd. shop.bodyform.co.uk/collections/
never-just-a-period (archived at https://perma.cc/3SWD-49H6)

4   Alt Marketing School. Behind the campaign: Charlie Terry, Alt Marketing
School, nd. altmarketingschool.com/behind-the-campaign-charlie-terry/
(archived at https://perma.cc/N9F3-FN2D)

03

Trust

The currency of modern marketing

> **REMINDER**
>
> Trust isn't about perfection, but accountability, transparency and showing up, even when things go sideways.

You're lacing up your trusty running shoes for your morning jog when you notice the sole starting to peel off. Yes, this has happened to me before. Let's be honest – your running shoes have seen better days.

After your run, you hop online to order a replacement and, to your surprise, your favourite brand is running an incredible deal. Premium running shoes are 75 per cent off. At first, you're ecstatic. But then doubt creeps in. You ask yourself, *why are they so cheap? Are they faulty?* You're almost tempted not to pursue your purchase any further.

But then you scroll and the answer becomes clear. The brand is discontinuing this style to make room for new designs. This is literally the last chance to buy those shoes. You check that your size is available and buy them without hesitation.

Why did knowing the reason behind the sale make you trust the offer more? Because, as humans, inherently we don't want to feel like we're being sold to – *until* we know that we're being sold to.

Psychology is a funny thing, I know. But it's a great reminder that often, all we need to know is *what* we're being sold and *why* we're being sold it. And that really shows how a lot of marketing stems from making expectations as clear as possible and being as transparent as possible when it comes to how you show up.

Without trust – one that encompasses so many different elements of a great customer-driven strategy – you can't really build a strategy in the first place.

Building trust: A framework for success

Building trust isn't a one-and-done exercise – it's a series of deliberate actions over time. To me, this really speaks to the fact that trust becomes an integral part of our strategy, not just a foundational step we tick off.

Every brand might take a slightly different approach, but there are three key pillars that, to me, signify trust in marketing: **reliability, authenticity** and **transparency**. Together, these create a framework that allows you to consistently show up for your audience in a way that feels honest, dependable and human.

Reliability: Being consistent and dependable

Reliability is about being consistent and dependable – it's one of the core foundations of trust. It's about being there for your customers when they need you and consistently delivering on your promises.

One of the easiest ways to start building this is by re-evaluating, re-identifying and strengthening your brand values. This is often seen as part of a branding exercise, but it's just as important for marketing.

If you haven't done this yet, it's a good time to explore your values now.

First, identifying your values helps you set clear expectations. It lets your customers know what they can expect from you and helps you identify tangible actions to reinforce that. Values are a way for you to:

- direct yourself and lead from a place of clarity
- steer your team to get collective buy-in
- deeply connect with the exact people you're aiming to serve

Values also help break silos within your business. As a marketing team, you're not working in isolation. In fact, you are part of a bigger ecosystem that connects with customer service, sales and the entire customer journey. When your values are clear and consistently applied, they guide every step of the customer journey – a journey we've already touched on as the centre of your marketing strategy.

If you're struggling to identify your values or reinforce them, here are prompts I often share with students at our marketing school:

- Make them actionable.

- Make them memorable.
- Make them unique to your brand.
- Make them specific.
- Make them accessible.

For us at Alt Marketing School, our values are summarized as **making marketing impactful, human and fun.** Which means everything we do is tinted with those lenses. For example, impactful stands for marketing that is inclusive and accessible. Having helped hundreds of students, I have seen the power of carrying out a simple yet powerful exercise like the one below.

So, how do you want your brand to be perceived? Here are a few ways to start identifying definitions that clearly represent your values.

1 What's important about the way the business is run?

2 How do you want customers to feel when they work with you?

3 And what keeps you working, even when things are tough?

From your values, you can identify what expectations you want to set for your customers, whether it's delivery times, product quality or customer service.

These expectations become clearer because they reflect your values. And they add that delicious flair of turning values into action – something I do not see enough brands doing these days.

We often underestimate how much our actions (how we show up) play a role in building reliability. As a marketer, it's your job to communicate in the clearest way possible and translate your brand's values into tangible behaviours and choices. And yes, it spans into the world of operations, customer service and potentially other areas that have nothing to do with marketing but can still help reinforce your values.

Think of values as the 'how you think' – they guide your principles, aspirations and beliefs. But unless those values transform into visible actions – or 'how you show up' – they remain abstract and fail to build trust.

Internally, values must shape team dynamics, decision-making and daily operations. This means embedding them into:

- aligning values with company culture, customer relationships and internal policies
- creating procedures that actively reflect these values
- ensuring your team understands and embodies these principles, fostering a cohesive and value-driven culture

For example, if sustainability is a core value, how does it reflect in your packaging, waste management or supplier partnerships?

Externally, your values should guide how you interact with your audience, partners and the broader community in a variety of areas.

- **Marketing and communication:** Crafting messages that are aligned with your values and showing up consistently across platforms.

- **Social responsibility:** Taking tangible steps that reflect your ethical stance – such as supporting causes or adopting sustainable practices.

- **Partnerships and collaborations:** Choosing to work with others who share your values, which strengthens the authenticity of your actions.

- **Transparency and accountability:** Being open about your challenges and celebrating your progress in living your values.

Let me share a real example of how we turn values into action at Alt Marketing School. One of our core values is the belief that marketing should speak to hearts by focusing on building relationships. Now, you might be wondering – how do we make that happen?

Well, it starts from within. Every time a new student joins our school we create a personalized welcome video just for them. And because we believe in those magical moments that make relationships special, we keep track of our community members' birthdays to surprise them with personalized e-cards. It's these little touches that make all the difference.

But it doesn't stop there. We practise what we preach in our external communications too. Our content strategy isn't just about teaching – we specifically focus on educating our audience about the importance of retention alongside acquisition. This reinforces our belief that marketing should speak to hearts by focusing on building relationships – and by doing that, shows our value in action.

One final word to the wise: the best way to turn values into actions is under-promising in a realistic way and then finding opportunities to over-deliver, exceeding customer expectations. These little magical moments are the ones that truly leave a lasting impression. They show that you're not just reliable but memorable.

Looking at the bridge between reliability and authenticity, your journey starts with operationalizing your values and ensuring every touchpoint reinforces them. The added benefit is that showing up regularly also reinforces reliability. When you know exactly which values you want to represent and uphold, your communication and actions will be consistent. Over time, this builds association and reputation while giving customers that subconscious sense of trust and dependability they're looking for.

REFLECTION TIME
Living your values

Let's turn those values we've been discussing into tangible actions. After all, values without action are just pretty words on a page. Think of this exercise as your practical roadmap to making your values come alive in your day-to-day operations.

It truly goes back to consistently showing up in a way that aligns with what you say you stand for. This exercise will help you bridge the gap between stating your values and living them.

Take a moment to reflect:

- What specific actions can you take to better integrate your values into your team, decision-making and company culture?
- How can you more authentically express your values in your marketing, customer service and daily interactions?
- What accountability mechanisms can you put in place to ensure your brand continuously lives out these values?

Reliability can be a lot of things – but when looking at a customer-driven approach, it roots onto demonstrating that your values guide both your intentions and your actions. When customers can see, feel and experience your values in every interaction, that's when trust is truly earned.

Authenticity: Be real, not perfect

In a world where perfection is often the goal, it's counterintuitive to think that showing imperfections can build trust. But that's exactly what the **Pratfall Effect** teaches us.[1] This psychological principle suggests that people are more likely to trust and relate to brands – or individuals – that display minor imperfections. Why? Because it makes them feel more *human*.

Imagine you're at a party and someone walks in looking flawless – perfect hair, impeccable outfit and unshakable confidence. At first, you're impressed, maybe even in awe. But as the evening goes on, they feel… distant, maybe even a little intimidating or too good to be true.

Now, imagine that same person spills a bit of wine on their sleeve. They laugh it off, brushing it aside with a self-deprecating joke. Suddenly, everything shifts. They're real, relatable and, dare I say, more likable.

The same principle applies to marketing. In a world overflowing with polished campaigns and meticulously curated Instagram grids, it's easy for brands to come across as distant or inauthentic. But when they let their guard down – showcasing small, genuine imperfections – something magical happens. They feel human. They feel real.

This is where the Pratfall Effect comes into play when it comes to authenticity and trust. The idea is simple yet powerful: when a brand already has credibility and is perceived as competent, showing minor imperfections can make them more relatable and trustworthy.

The key, of course, is balance. It's about small, human moments – the kind that make you think, *'Ah, they're just like me.'* But it's worth noting that this effect only works when the foundation of competence is already there.

Minor missteps can add authenticity, but too big of a swing? It can erode trust faster than you can say 'Oops!'

The lesson here? Perfection might seem appealing, but relatability – and a touch of vulnerability – is what truly builds connections. So, let your brand spill a little wine now and then. Just make sure you're still the kind of guest everyone wants at the party.

For example:

- A restaurant might share a behind-the-scenes blooper of a chef dropping a tray (as long as it's not during service!).
- A tech company could poke fun at its own longstanding quirks.

The Pratfall Effect is more than pointing out your mistakes or making intentional blunders. It's about showing the human side of your brand. Think of campaigns like Domino's admitting that their pizza recipe needed improvement in their 2009 marketing campaign.[2] By acknowledging their flaws and taking action, they not only rebuilt trust but also increased their market share dramatically.

This principle also applies in customer interactions. Imagine a customer service email that includes a personal anecdote or a handwritten apology for a minor issue. That kind of response can turn a negative experience into a trust-building moment.

Transparency: Let them see behind the curtain

Not all sales are created equal, and brands like Lululemon know this better than most. In 2023, Lululemon decided to avoid the sneaky questions that often pop into customers' heads by being upfront. In their sales section, they told buyers exactly why certain products were discounted, specifically due to an overstocking issue.[3]

This straightforward explanation tapped into one of the most well-known principles in marketing and psychology: trust waivers when customers are left guessing.

One of the easiest ways to erode trust is by being vague about why something is on sale or why an event is happening. Often, customers start to wonder: *Is the product low quality? Is it outdated?* And the age-old question, *what's the catch?*

When it comes to transparency, the power of answering one simple question – *why* – cannot be overstated. When our brains can't answer that question, we struggle to make sense of things. And this is exactly where trust begins to falter.

By simply acknowledging that they had made too many, Lululemon created a clear, straightforward message that eliminated doubt. Customers no longer wondered if the quality was lacking or if the items were outdated. They knew the truth: it's just extra inventory the brand wants to move. That transparency transformed hesitation into confidence.

By sharing the *why*, Lululemon not only built trust but also showed respect for their customers, making them feel good about their purchase.

Let's take this idea of transparency a step further and look at an example that might feel a bit closer to home – charitable giving through wills.

An experiment conducted by the University of Bristol explored how transparent communication, combined with emotionally engaging prompts, could significantly influence people's willingness to leave money to charity.[4]

- **Baseline group:** No mention of charitable giving was made. Only 5.9 per cent of participants left money to charity.

- **Weak ask group:** Participants were asked, 'Would you like to leave a charitable gift in your will?' This simple prompt nearly doubled the giving rate to 11.3 per cent.

- **Strong ask group:** Participants were asked, 'Many of our customers like to leave a gift to charity in their will. Are there any causes you're passionate about?' This approach tripled the giving rate to 17.5 per cent.[5]

The study involved 2,670 participants who called a legal service to create their wills. They were split into three groups, each approached differently. Let's imagine Sarah, a 62 year old drafting her will. In the baseline scenario, no one mentions charitable giving, so she doesn't even think about it. But in the weak ask scenario, someone gently asks, *'Would you like to leave a gift to charity?'* and Sarah remembers her local animal shelter. She decides to leave them £5,000.

Now, here's where things get interesting. In the strong ask scenario, Sarah hears, *'Many of our customers like to leave a gift to charity in their will. Are there any causes you're passionate about?'* That small addition makes Sarah pause and reflect on her values. She connects the idea of her legacy with the causes she cares about most and decides to leave £10,000 instead.

What's the takeaway? Transparency, combined with a little emotional framing, creates a powerful moment of reflection.

By being upfront and inviting Sarah to connect her decision with her values – without pressure – the conversation builds trust and aligns her choice with something meaningful.

Transparency starts with clarity and it goes much deeper than that when we look to add context. Below are a few ways I encourage our students to think about it:

- **Explain the 'why':** Whether it's a sale, a price change or a product update, sharing the reasoning behind your actions builds confidence in your brand.

- **Be upfront about mistakes:** When something goes wrong, own it. Acknowledging errors and explaining how you're addressing them builds credibility. Plus, you get extra brownie points by tapping into the Pratfall Effect.

- **Share your process:** Take your audience behind the scenes to show them how your products are made or the thought process behind your decisions.

Whether it's activewear or charitable giving, showing your audience the *why* and *how* behind an offer can make all the difference. Transparency invites action that feels aligned, authentic and human – and that's where trust begins.

REFLECTION TIME
What does trust mean to you?

Take a moment to pause and consider this: What does trust mean to you, personally and professionally?

For me, trust is deeply tied to two core values that guide my life and work: making a positive impact in the world and supporting small businesses. Every little decision I make that aligns with these values feels like a win – whether it's choosing eco-friendly options or supporting local brands.

This combination of values often draws me to smaller companies, where I feel a stronger sense of connection and purpose. One standout example is a skincare brand I support annually through their refill scheme. The process is simple yet impactful: I clean and label my empty skincare packaging, send it back and they refill it for me. It's a small act that saves me money, reduces waste and supports a business I believe in – ticking all the right boxes.

As per usual, I sent my empty packages during the chaotic Black Friday period. A week later, a package arrived and I eagerly opened it, expecting my neatly refilled products. Instead, disappointment hit hard. The box was much smaller than what I'd sent, battered from transit and, worst of all, it contained a random selection of items that weren't mine.

Frustrated, I reached out to the company via email but didn't hear back for a few days. A week later – after following up through their live chat – I finally got a response. Being a small business, I understood the delay, but I didn't hold back in expressing my frustrations.

I explained that one of the biggest hurdles to committing to a refill scheme like this is the trust customers place in the company. So much of the process is outside our control – we rely on them to get it right.

The brand's response was a masterclass in how to rebuild trust. They apologized for the delay in communication, acknowledged the mistake and immediately asked for my order details. Without hesitation, they sent me a brand-new set of products with 24-hour delivery. Their swift action and accountability didn't just fix the problem; it reaffirmed why I chose to support them in the first place.

This experience was a powerful reminder that trust is about more than just getting things right the first time. It's about how a brand listens, responds and takes action when things go wrong. As customers, our fear of disappointment often holds us back from trying something new. But when a brand earns our trust, it becomes the bridge that helps us take that leap.

Think about a time when you placed your trust in a brand. What made you feel confident in their promise? Was it their transparency, consistency or the way they aligned with your values? Perhaps it was the simplicity of their message or the authenticity in their actions.

Now, flip the lens. How does your brand or business work to build trust with its audience? Ask yourself:

- Am I clear and transparent in what I promise my customers?
- Do I follow through consistently, even in small, everyday interactions?
- Do my audience and customers feel seen, heard and valued by my brand?

Trust is built step by step, touchpoint by touchpoint. It's the backbone of every meaningful relationship – personal or professional. So, what can you do today to reinforce trust with your audience and make them feel confident in choosing you?

REAL-WORLD EXAMPLE
Pepsi's breach of trust

In April 2017, Pepsi learned the hard way just how fragile trust can be. The company's Live for Now campaign, featuring model and reality TV star Kendall Jenner, was meant to symbolize unity and hope. Instead, it sparked immediate and widespread criticism.[6]

I rarely like to spotlight huge negative faux passes, but I believe we can learn as much from what *not to do* than learning from what we should be doing.

The ad depicted Jenner handing a can of Pepsi to a police officer at a protest, a gesture that supposedly resolved the tension. Critics quickly pointed out how insensitive it was for PepsiCo to use the aesthetic of social justice movements like Black Lives Matter to sell soda.

The internet erupted. Within hours, Twitter was flooded with posts calling out the ad for trivializing the struggle and sacrifices behind such movements.

The ad's failure stemmed from several avoidable pitfalls:

- **Misalignment with values:** By attempting to co-opt social justice movements without a clear or genuine connection, Pepsi sent a message that felt hollow and exploitative.
- **Failure to read the room:** The campaign revealed a disconnect between the brand and its audience, highlighting a lack of understanding of the sensitivity and gravity of the topic.
- **Lack of empathy:** The ad seemed to prioritize style over substance, ignoring the emotions and lived experiences of those it claimed to represent.

Here's where things got messy. PepsiCo scrambled to do damage control with a rushed Twitter apology that, honestly, missed the mark completely. As Abigail R Meister pointed out in her 2019 thesis on the ad's crisis management response, their attempt to 'defuse' the situation only added fuel to the fire.

They tried again by directly apologizing to Bernice King (daughter of Dr Martin Luther King, Jr and an anti-racism activist) and quietly pulled the ad from circulation. But by then the damage was done.

The numbers tell the story better than I can. Meister reported that Pepsi's public sentiment took a major hit after the Kendall Jenner advert aired. Before the ad, the brand had a 2 per cent net positive sentiment on Twitter, but by 8 April it had fallen by 14 percentage points to −12 per cent.[7]

The public outrage about the Pepsi ad showed just how quickly a brand can go from trusted to out of touch when it fails to read the room. This misstep serves as a textbook example of how trust – painstakingly built over years – can be shattered in an instant. It's also a reminder that while brands can recover from mistakes, doing so requires intention, humility and immediate action.

There are three key steps I recommend following when it comes to crisis management:

1 **Act fast:** When trust is broken, time is of the essence. Just like in my personal skincare refill example, delayed responses can compound frustration. Quick action shows you value your customers and take their concerns seriously.

2 **Own the mistake:** Take full responsibility without making excuses. The skincare brand demonstrated this by immediately sending replacement products. In contrast, Pepsi's initial rushed response shows how a half-hearted apology can make things worse.

3 **Engage directly:** Have real, human conversations with your audience. Listen to their concerns and respond personally, just as the skincare brand did by addressing specific customer feedback about their refill scheme. This direct engagement helps rebuild the bridge of trust.

Talking about human marketing, it's also a reminder that rebuilding trust takes time and sustained effort. Here are a few steps brands can take to recover after a trust breach:

• **Double down on listening:** Use the incident as an opportunity to actively listen to your audience and involve them in shaping future campaigns.

• **Reaffirm core values:** Clearly communicate what your brand stands for, ensuring future actions and campaigns align with those values.

• **Deliver on promises:** Show your audience, through consistent action, that you're committed to doing better.

Maintaining trust in an evolving landscape

Trust isn't static – it's an ever-evolving relationship between brands and their audience. As new tech emerges and customer expectations shift, brands need to adapt while staying true to their values. Now, this isn't easy, especially in the digital age, where data privacy concerns, algorithmic biases and even public missteps do their very best to remind us that trust is an invaluable currency.

On the one hand, you have endless tools to connect and engage with your audience. On the other hand, any misstep can snowball into a PR nightmare.

- **Data privacy:** With so much data floating around, customers are hyper-aware of how their information is used. Being transparent about your data policies isn't just a legal requirement – it's a trust-building opportunity.

- **Algorithmic biases:** If you're using AI or algorithms, your audience expects fairness and equity. It's important to acknowledge where biases may exist and actively work to address them. This is part of being accountable as a brand.

- **Listening over defending:** When mistakes happen, the instinct is often to jump into defence mode. But taking the time to listen – really listen – to what people are saying can completely shift the narrative.

By now you'll know trust isn't about perfection, but it is about accountability, transparency and showing up, even when things go sideways. And this is where I think we don't talk enough about the importance of crisis management.

Crisis management is like firefighting – and yes, I'm about to give you another analogy. Just like a fire needs heat, fuel and oxygen to burn, a crisis needs three things: the issue itself (fuel), the public or customer reaction (heat) and your response (the oxygen). The sooner you step in and manage the situation; the sooner you can prevent it from spreading.

One of the best ways to control a crisis is by being prepared before it happens. Yes, it sounds like a lot of extra work, but trust me, it's worth it. Whether it's a public faux pas or a wave of customer complaints, having a plan in place means you're not scrambling to figure out what to do in the heat of the moment.

So, here's a little cheat sheet for managing those tricky situations:

> - **Acknowledge and act quickly.** Most people just want to feel heard. Start by reaching out to individuals who've raised concerns, even if it's just to let them know you're working on a solution. Ignoring people is a sure-fire way to escalate the situation.
>
> - **Have a crisis plan.** Think of this as your safety net. Create a simple document outlining the steps to take during a crisis. Who's responsible for what? What key messages need to be shared? How do you escalate or address serious issues? Even having a few ready-to-go templates can save you a lot of stress.
>
> - **Be transparent about next steps.** If you're going to fix something, let people know how. It doesn't always mean going public, but when appropriate, assign someone to clearly communicate the steps you're taking to resolve the issue.

At the end of the day, it's not about avoiding mistakes altogether (because, spoiler alert, they're going to happen). It's about how you respond to them. When you own up to your mistakes, act swiftly and involve your audience in the solution, you turn a potential trust-breaker into a trust-builder.

The evolving landscape we're navigating as marketers can feel daunting. But in this complexity lies an incredible opportunity to show up authentically, embrace accountability and continually demonstrate that trust isn't just a buzzword for you – but the foundation of your strategy.

Closing the loop: The power of reciprocal altruism

In December 1976, hundreds of Americans received an unexpected Christmas card from a family they'd never heard of. What they didn't know was that they were part of a psychological study.[8]

Sociologists Phillip Kunz and Michael Woolcott from Brigham Young University sent out 578 Christmas cards to random households and tracked how many people responded. Twenty per cent of recipients took the time to send a card back to complete strangers.

Why would so many go to such lengths? Kunz and Woolcott credited this to the cultural norm of reciprocity – the social pressure to return a favour. The study also highlighted how factors like perceived social status and the effort put into the card (e.g. its quality) can influence reciprocal behaviour.[9]

This is a great example of how one of the most underrated yet powerful forces in marketing is **reciprocal altruism** – the idea that giving value before asking for anything in return can create trust, loyalty and lasting relationships.

This experiment has been replicated multiple times with similar findings. Kunz himself repeated the study in 2000 and observed consistent results.

However, by 2014, social norms seemed to have shifted. A replication by researcher Brian Meier found only a 2 per cent response rate, possibly reflecting how unsolicited messages in the digital age are often viewed as suspicious or spam.[10]

Despite the decline in response rates over time, the original study remains a cornerstone in understanding human behaviour, particularly in marketing. Reciprocity – the instinct to return a favour – is still a powerful tool for building relationships and fostering loyalty.

The **Norm of Reciprocity** dates to the 1960s when Alvin Gouldner first explored the benefits of cooperative interaction between two people.[11] As marketers, we now know it thanks to Dr Robert Cialdini's book *Influence: The psychology of persuasion* as he took it a step further and explored how this rule might apply to business and marketing.[12] He noticed a common marketing strategy among business owners that tapped into basic survival mechanisms repeatedly. Simply put, they were all offering a reward to their potential customers before they even made a purchase.

Let's think about this in everyday terms. When someone unexpectedly does something kind for you – like holding the lift when you're rushing or buying you a coffee – it stays with you, doesn't it? You might not repay them directly, but you carry that feeling of goodwill forward. That's the beauty of reciprocal altruism.

Imagine finishing a delicious meal at a restaurant and, as the waiter drops off the bill, they leave you a small gesture of gratitude – a free mint. It's a small token, but it leaves an impression. Now, what if instead of one mint, the waiter offers you two? The gesture feels even more thoughtful, doesn't it? But here's where it gets interesting: imagine the waiter leaves one mint with the bill and then, just as they're about to walk away, they pause, turn back and say, *'You know what? Here's another mint, just for you.'* That simple act of personalizing the gesture leads to a big difference in behaviour. According to a study published in the *Journal of Applied Social Psychology* these subtle changes had a significant impact on tipping:[13]

- When diners were given one mint, tips increased by 3 per cent.
- Offering two mints boosted tips by 14 per cent.
- But when the waiter added that personalized touch – returning with a second mint 'just for you' – tips soared by 23 per cent.

Why does this work? Reciprocity isn't just about the value of the gift; it's about the feeling it creates. The second mint feels personal, deliberate and thoughtful. It shifts the gesture from transactional to relational, leaving the diner with a positive emotional response and a sense of obligation to give back.

This clearly demonstrates the power of an unexpected gift. As customers feel special, the chances they'll do something in return dramatically increase.

Plus, let's face it – we all like free stuff. It's wired into us. When a brand gives you something for free, whether it's a product sample, a discount code or even an e-book, it sparks a sense of appreciation and connection. More importantly, it activates a psychological principle known as the **reciprocity norm** – the natural human tendency to return a favour.

In marketing, this means that when you give shoppers something upfront, they're more likely to return the favour by engaging with your brand, making a purchase or even advocating for you. It doesn't have to be anything huge. A free audit, a guide or a small discount can make all the difference. It's about showing that you're willing to invest in your audience before expecting anything back.

In 2011, Converse stepped up in a way that made waves in the creative world. The brand opened a fully equipped recording studio in Brooklyn, offering emerging artists the chance to record their songs – completely free of charge.[14]

For many musicians, breaking into the industry feels like an impossible dream. Studio time is expensive and high-quality facilities are often out of reach for those just starting out. By providing a professional-grade recording space at no cost, Converse handed over an opportunity for artists to showcase their talent and pursue their dreams.

What makes this move so brilliant is how deeply it aligned with Converse's identity. The brand has always championed creativity, individuality and self-expression – values that resonate with musicians and artists everywhere. Converse's initiative is a perfect example of the power of giving value without asking for anything in return. Converse knew their community valued creativity and individuality, so they created something that spoke directly to those values. Everything about this campaign screamed 'Converse'.

So, how can you bring this into your marketing? No need to open a studio or a pop-up shop, or start sending Christmas cards to all your email list – even if that may be a nice surprise. You can follow any of these principles to help:

- **Educate and empower:** Share free tools, tutorials or resources that solve a problem or inspire your audience. Let them see that your brand genuinely wants to help.

- **Surprise and delight:** Send an unexpected thank-you note, a small product sample or a surprise upgrade. These thoughtful touches can leave a lasting impression.
- **Listen and respond:** Take time to ask your audience what they need, listen deeply and respond in a way that makes them feel heard.

Reciprocal altruism isn't about giving to get. It's about showing up with generosity and humanity. When you lead with kindness, trust naturally follows. People remember how you make them feel and that feeling becomes the cornerstone of loyalty.

So, as you think about your marketing, ask yourself this: *What can I give to my audience today that makes them feel seen and valued?* Because, in the end, the brands that win hearts are the ones that go beyond the sale and into something much more meaningful.

Building trust that lasts

> TIP
>
> Trust is not built by chance. It's intentional, it's earned and it's a process that requires you to show up consistently, with honesty and heart.

Whether it's through transparency, reliability or the simple magic of giving first, the brands that thrive are the ones that make trust their cornerstone – not just of their marketing but of every interaction.

Throughout this chapter, we've explored how trust comes to life: through small, thoughtful gestures, major initiatives and even the way brands handle mistakes.

I'm not expecting for you to get it right every time. It's about how you respond, how you listen and how you move forward with your customers in mind. Those moments are what people remember.

So, here's the big question: how is your brand showing up to build trust? Are you taking the time to demonstrate that you're not just a business, but a partner your audience can rely on? Are you putting your values into action and backing them up with every step of the customer journey?

The answers to these questions are what sets you apart. It's what turns someone who casually interacts with your brand into a loyal advocate. And the best part? Trust isn't about perfection – it's about being human.

Let this chapter be your reminder that trust is the thread weaving everything together. It's the reason behind the campaigns you create, the relationships you nurture and the communities you build. And it's the single most important thing you can offer.

So now it's your turn. How will you show up to earn it?

KEY POINTS

- Trust isn't built by chance – it requires consistent, intentional actions over time.
- The three pillars of trust in marketing are reliability, authenticity and transparency.
- Reliability comes from showing up consistently, delivering on promises and reinforcing your brand's values in everything you do.
- Authenticity is about aligning your actions with your values and showing the human side of your brand.
- Transparency builds trust by being open about the 'why' behind your decisions, whether it's explaining a discount or admitting a mistake.
- Reciprocity fosters loyalty – giving value before asking for anything in return creates meaningful connections.
- Mistakes happen, but how you handle them matters. Acknowledge issues quickly, communicate clearly and take accountability to rebuild trust.
- Trust is about connection over perfection. Show your audience you're human, dependable and aligned with their needs.

Notes

1   E Aronson, B Willerman and J Floyd. The effect of a pratfall on increasing interpersonal appeal, *Psychonomic Science*, 1966, 4 (6), 227–28
2   Ad Age. Domino's talks radical authenticity, Ad Age, 18 November 2010. adage.com/article/special-report-ideaconference/domino-s-talks-radical-authenticity/146782 (archived at https://perma.cc/L3BF-5SM6)
3   Women's Health. 10 best picks from Lululemon's 'we made too much section' this month: Score 50% off now, Women's Health, 3 January 2023. www.womenshealthmag.com/fitness/g42191697/lululemon-we-made-too-much/ (archived at https://perma.cc/82MA-ETJU)

4 M Sanders and S Smith. A warm glow in the after life? The determinants of charitable bequests, Centre for Market and Public Organisation, University of Bristol, June 2014. www.bristol.ac.uk/media-library/sites/cmpo/migrated/documents/wp326.pdf (archived at https://perma.cc/PS6W-EUUK)

5 M Sanders and S Smith. The role of social networks in shaping educational decisions, Centre for Market and Public Organisation, University of Bristol, June 2014. www.bristol.ac.uk/media-library/sites/cmpo/migrated/documents/wp326.pdf (archived at https://perma.cc/PS6W-EUUK)

6 A R Meister. The power of apology: How crisis communication practices impact brand reputation, Senior Theses, Honors College, University of South Carolina, 2019

7 A R Meister. The power of apology: How crisis communication practices impact brand reputation, Senior Theses, Honors College, University of South Carolina, 2019

8 R Cialdini (1993) *Influence: Science and practice*, HarperCollins, New York

9 Discover Magazine. Only 2 per cent of people will return a Christmas card from a stranger, Discover Magazine, 23 December 2015. www.discovermagazine.com/mind/only-2-of-people-will-return-a-christmas-card-from-a-stranger (archived at https://perma.cc/S8TA-HQ8G)

10 Discover Magazine. Only 2 per cent of people will return a Christmas card from a stranger, Discover Magazine, 23 December 2015. www.discovermagazine.com/mind/only-2-of-people-will-return-a-christmas-card-from-a-stranger (archived at https://perma.cc/LZ47-VGA4)

11 A W Gouldner. The norm of reciprocity: A preliminary statement, *American Sociological Review*, 1960, 25 (2), 161–78

12 R Cialdini (1984) *Influence: The psychology of persuasion*, Harper Business, New York

13 D B Strohmetz, B Rind, R Fisher and M Lynn. Sweetening the till: The use of candy to increase restaurant tipping, *Journal of Applied Social Psychology*, 2002, 32, 300–09

14 Billboard. Converse's free recording studio, Rubber Tracks, opens, Billboard, 13 July 2011. www.billboard.com/music/music-news/converses-free-recording-studio-rubber-tracks-opens-1177132/ (archived at https://perma.cc/46NV-ZM46)

04

Building a marketing plan
A practical guide

REMINDER

A strategy isn't built upon a single action, tip or hack. It's built from a plan designed to connect the dots between your goals and the actions you take to achieve them.

It's the middle of Q2 and your team is feeling the pressure. Sales are lagging and if you don't figure out a way to drive more buyers soon, your growth goals are at serious risk. *Cue the tension.*

So, you decide to shake things up and experiment with a new campaign – let's say Google Ads. You've never run one before, but you're a fast learner, right? Rather than outsourcing to a specialist, you dive in yourself. You set aside five hours to learn the ropes, build the campaign and get everything live. That feels like plenty of time… until it isn't. Three days later – after pouring over tutorials, blog posts and endless troubleshooting – you finally hit 'Publish'.

A week passes. You check the results. The conversion rate is dismal and the ads cost way more than you'd budgeted. It's a tough pill to swallow, but you know it's all part of the learning process. Rather than throw in the towel, you regroup. You commit to testing a few more campaigns to find what works. But here's the real question: *knowing how long it took you to get your first campaign live, how much time do you set aside this time?*

Here's where most of us run into trouble. As marketers, we're often guilty of falling into what's known as the **planning fallacy** – the tendency to underestimate how long it will take to finish a project. And without a clear plan, timelines stretch, strategies stall and results fall short.

This is why having a well-thought-out marketing plan is so important. A strong plan will save you time, money and sanity by giving you clarity and focus from the start.

Why mapping out a marketing strategy matters

When it comes to marketing, everyone loves talking about strategy. But many of us confuse a strategy with a tactic.

Posting daily on Instagram? That's not a strategy. Creating a branded hashtag? Not a strategy either. These are all great tactics, but they're not strategies. Think of them as the tools in your marketing toolkit – useful, but not the full plan.

A strategy isn't built upon a single action, tip or hack. It's built from a plan designed to connect the dots between your goals and the actions you take to achieve them. Without it, even the best efforts can feel disjointed, like pieces of a puzzle that don't quite fit together.

Imagine you're planning a trip.

- Your **strategy** is the plan – your destination, the route you'll take and the stops you'll make along the way.
- Your **tactics** are the tools and actions that help you get there – the car you'll drive, the GPS you'll use and the snacks you pack for the road. Both are essential, but without the strategy, your journey lacks direction.

It's the same with marketing. While tactics like posting reels, running ads or launching a hashtag campaign are valuable, they're only effective when they're part of a bigger picture. Your strategy connects these tactics to your goals so that every action serves a purpose.

A marketing plan is a map that outlines how you're going to reach your audience, achieve your goals and make the most of your resources. It's where your strategies, objectives and tactics all meet.

- **Strategy:** The overarching roadmap that ties everything together.
- **Objectives:** Clear, measurable goals.
- **Tactics:** The specific actions you'll take to reach your audience.

And it doesn't stop there. A marketing plan should also analyse your current position in the market, who your audience is and what mix of marketing tools (aka your marketing mix) you're going to use to get the job done. In short, it's the plan that connects the dots between what you want to achieve and how you're going to make it happen.

So, how do we build a strategy through our plan? A true strategy answers big-picture questions like:

- What are we trying to achieve?
- Why are we pursuing these goals?
- When and where will we show up to reach our audience?
- How often should we engage to remain effective?
- Who is our target market and how do we speak their language?
- What does success look like and how will we measure it?

A strong strategy anticipates what might go wrong and what could go surprisingly right. It asks:

- **What if we succeed?** What's our next step to scale or evolve?
- **What if we fall short?** How do we adjust without losing momentum?
- **What if something unexpected happens?** Are we flexible enough to pivot?

For example, imagine your latest campaign completely exceeds expectations. How do you handle the sudden surge of demand? On the flip side, if things fall flat, how do you regroup and make smarter choices for your next move?

These 'what ifs' aren't about predicting the future. They're about being ready for it, whatever it looks like. When your strategy has built-in flexibility, you're planning for success – but also, you're building resilience – and that's what smart marketers do.

In this chapter, we're going to map out exactly how to build your marketing plan step by step. By the end, you'll have a clear strategy to guide your efforts, align your team and deliver results without the guesswork. Because let's face it – marketing success doesn't happen by accident. It happens when you've got a plan.

What makes a customer-driven plan different

Your marketing plan starts by answering the most important question: *Who are we talking to?* Understanding your audience – not just what they buy, but why – sets the foundation for everything.

In the next chapter, we'll dig deeper into identifying customer pain points and creating strategies that resonate on an emotional level. However, your marketing plan is where this work begins.

A customer-driven marketing plan doesn't just focus on quick wins – it's built for the long haul. That means planning for customer journeys that don't stop at conversion but lead to loyalty and advocacy, two key areas we'll explore later in this book.

When your plan accounts for every stage of the customer experience, you're not just selling a product – you're building a relationship. This ties back to the 'what ifs' we talked about earlier – your plan isn't just a guide for what you'll do; it's a safety net for when things don't go as expected.

As we move through this book, you'll see how each element of a marketing plan – understanding pain points, building trust, personalizing experiences and measuring results – works together to create something powerful. But it all starts here, with the plan. Because when your strategy is grounded in customer needs, aligned with your brand's mission and built to adapt, you're creating marketing that makes an impact.

Start with objectives and key results

Every Christmas, my husband's family has a little tradition. Between the chaos of festive meals and unwrapping presents, we sit down to work on a jigsaw puzzle. My sister-in-law is the biggest puzzle enthusiast of us all and she always gets gifted a box with the most intricate designs – think a 2,000-piece puzzle of Minions, which means a lot of yellow.

Now, let me tell you, I've learned something crucial about puzzles over the years: you *need* to keep the picture on the box in sight. Without it, you're left guessing which pieces fit together. Sure, you might stumble across a few matches here and there, but most of the time, you'll be spinning your wheels, frustrated that nothing seems to connect.

Marketing objectives work the same way. They're the picture on the box, showing you what the finished result should look like. Without them, you might be doing all the right things – running campaigns, writing blogs, posting on social – but none of it comes together in a meaningful way.

When you have clear objectives, every piece of your marketing strategy has a purpose. They're the anchor that keeps your efforts aligned and moving toward a common goal. So, before you start snapping pieces together, take a step back and ask yourself: *What's the picture I'm trying to create?*

Because, trust me, whether it's a Christmas puzzle or your next big marketing campaign, it's a lot easier when you know what you're aiming for.

Starting with the why

When it comes to building a marketing plan, before we even dive into tactics, research or filling in any part of the plan, one of the most important steps is figuring out *what* we're trying to do and *why* we're doing it. So, let me introduce our next acronym, **OKRs**, also known as **objectives and key results.**

Because we're marketers, we have a love–hate relationship with acronyms. Honestly, I often ask myself, *why on earth do we need so many acronyms in marketing?* Sure, they make communication faster (or at least more efficient), but sometimes they just feel like more jargon to explain already complex ideas.

Take OKRs, for example. For students new to marketing, they can feel really daunting or just plain confusing. But at their core, OKRs are simple: they're about setting goals and defining how you'll measure success.

If I were to explain OKRs into plain terms, here's how I'd do it: objectives are your big-picture goals – what you want to achieve and why it matters. Think of them as what and *why* in the equation. Example: 'Increase brand awareness in a new market (Australia).' Key results are the measurable outcomes that show how you're making progress toward your objective. Think of them as the *how* – how you'll track success. Example: 'Achieve 50 per cent growth in social media followers in Australia by the end of Q2.'

Here's where we can bring another acronym, **SMART**, into the mix (sorry, not sorry). Just as much as objectives need to be aligned and clear, your key results should always be:

- specific
- measurable
- actionable
- relevant
- time-bound

To me, this is where the magic happens. While objectives set the direction, it's the key results that give you the clarity and accountability to track success. OKRs are really two parts of the same picture. The objectives give you the vision and the key results help you measure how close you are to achieving it.

Common mistakes when setting OKRs for marketing

It's the 1970s and Intel is at a crossroads. The company is shifting from being a memory manufacturer to focusing entirely on microprocessors. It's a bold move that could redefine its future, but one that requires precision and alignment across every level of the organization.

Enter Andy Grove, Intel's visionary CEO, who introduces a simple yet revolutionary framework: OKRs – objectives and key results. Basically, OKRs were designed to do one thing: provide clarity.[1] They gave everyone at Intel a north star, a set of priorities that ensured every team member, from leadership to entry-level employees, was rowing in the same direction.

Grove used OKRs to create transparency. Everyone could see not only their own OKRs but also those of their managers, peers and even Andy Grove himself. It resulted in a culture of accountability and alignment that powered Intel through one of the most critical transitions in its history.

Among those inspired by the system was a young engineer named John Doerr. He kept his OKRs pinned up in his office, writing new ones every quarter and seeing first-hand how this framework could turn bold ideas into actionable steps.

Fast forward to 1999. John Doerr walks into a small, scrappy startup called Google. With just 30 employees and sky-high ambitions, Google needs something to help them focus their energy, align their team and measure success. Doerr pitches OKRs, not as a rigid management tool, but as a way to bring clarity and purpose to the chaos of building a company.[2] At the time, Larry Page and Sergey Brin were hooked. They immediately saw how OKRs could connect their vision to the daily actions of their team. From there, OKRs became part of Google's DNA, shaping everything from its internal culture to its biggest successes, including Search, Chrome and YouTube.[3] And guess what – Larry Page still writes his personal OKRs to this day. Because even when you're running one of the biggest companies in the world, having a clear north star makes all the difference.

Of course, like anything in marketing, OKRs aren't a magic bullet. They only work when they're used correctly. And while the framework is simple, there are a few common pitfalls to keep in mind. Before we dive into questions to help refine your OKRs, let's look at the biggest mistakes people make when setting them.

Setting vague objectives

This is one of the biggest mistakes I see again and again. If we go back to the SMART acronym, you can already see that by following its prompts – specific, measurable, actionable, relevant and time-bound – you should be able to set very clear and actionable objectives. But that doesn't always happen.

Every time students submit their marketing plans for our certification, I see objectives like 'grow brand awareness'. And yes, in theory, that sounds great. But as a marketer, if you were handed an objective like 'grow brand awareness' without any specifics, how would you act on it?

Think about this: if you take that vague objective and use it as the foundation of your marketing plan, you're setting yourself up for misalignment across your team or clients. What you think 'grow brand awareness' looks like could be completely different from what someone else on your team expects.

One way to help out is to go deeper by asking yourself my favourite question, *'Why is that?'* Let me give you an example. If your initial objective is to 'grow brand awareness', ask yourself 'Why is that?'

'Because we want to reach more potential customers.'

Why is that?

'Because we've identified an untapped market in Australia.'

Why is that important?

'Because our product analytics show high engagement from existing Australian customers, suggesting strong market fit.'

Now we can transform that vague 'grow brand awareness' into a specific objective:

'Increase brand visibility and engagement in the Australian market to capitalize on proven product-market fit.'

Finally, as one extra layer of complexity, we encourage students in our school to focus on just two objectives per quarter:

- one objective focused on **growth** (e.g. acquisition or revenue)
- one objective focused on **retention** (e.g. keeping customers happy and engaged)

When you try to focus on everything, you focus on nothing. By narrowing your objectives, especially for quarterly plans, you'll avoid spreading your efforts too thin and ensure meaningful progress.

Overcomplicating key results

Let me be clear here: I just said being specific is important and I stand by that. But when it comes to key results, there's a danger in overcomplicating things.

Your key results are the measurable outcomes, the *how* you're going to achieve your goals. But if they're too complex, they become impossible to track. And if you can't track your progress, how will you celebrate your wins?

Let me give you a real example. Say your objective is to 'Increase brand awareness in the Australian market.' Here's what an overcomplicated key result might look like:

> 'Achieve a 50 per cent increase in Australian social media followers across Instagram, Facebook and LinkedIn, while maintaining a minimum engagement rate of 3.5 per cent per post, ensuring at least 65 per cent of new followers are from our target demographic of female entrepreneurs aged 25–40 in major metropolitan areas, with a cost per acquisition below $2.50, all while achieving a sentiment score above 4.2 out of 5 based on social listening tools.'

Phew! Just reading that is exhausting, right? While all these metrics might be valuable, cramming them into a single key result makes it nearly impossible to track effectively.

Instead, you could break this down into simpler, more manageable key results:

> 'Increase Australian social media followers by 50 per cent across all platforms.'
>
> 'Maintain an average engagement rate of 3.5 per cent per post.'
>
> 'Ensure 65 per cent of new followers match our target demographic.'

If your key results feel overwhelming, they'll only lead to frustration and disappointment. When in doubt, keep them aligned, keep them specific, but also keep them simple.

So, while specificity is important, balance it with simplicity. A good question to keep in your mind is: *How can I make these key results clear and actionable without overcomplicating them?*

Ignoring alignment

This is a big one. If your marketing OKRs aren't connected to your company's overall goals, they're going to feel irrelevant, disjointed or like extra work. And, honestly, that's the last thing you need when you're already balancing a full strategy. Everything in your marketing plan should tie back to the bigger picture. If it doesn't, you'll feel like you're working in a silo and that disconnect will ripple across your team and the rest of the company.

Let me share a real example from one of our students. When discussing goal setting together, we realized their marketing team set a retention objective to 'Increase email newsletter open rates by 50 per cent in Q2.' At first glance, this seems like a solid retention-focused goal. The problem? The company's overall objective that quarter was to reduce customer support tickets and improve product satisfaction scores.

While improving email engagement isn't inherently bad, in this case it wasn't aligned with what the company truly needed. The marketing team was investing time and resources into crafting perfect email subject lines and A/B testing send times when they should have been focusing on creating helpful product education content and proactive customer success communications.

By doing that they achieved their email open rate goal but saw no improvement in customer satisfaction. Their support ticket volume remained high because they weren't addressing the root cause: customers needed better guidance on using the product, not more promotional emails.

Here's my advice: take the time to brainstorm your OKRs as a marketing team first. Then, bring them back to the wider team before you lock them in.

OKRs don't need to be perfect from the start. The key is refining them with the right questions. Honestly, prompts are one of the best tools in a marketer's arsenal (and a shortcut I will always allow). Here are a few questions to help you refine your OKRs and avoid these mistakes:

- Are my objectives clear and specific enough to act on?
- Are my key results simple enough to track progress?
- How do my OKRs connect to the company's wider goals?
- If I achieve this objective, what will success look like?
- What adjustments can I make to align these OKRs with what matters most right now?

REFLECTION TIME
Setting your growth and retention OKRs

Now it's time to put what you've learned into action. You'll start by creating one growth-focused OKR, one retention-focused OKR and one campaign-specific OKR focused on seasonal conversions.

This exercise is structured to guide you step-by-step. First, you'll answer three key questions to define each OKR. Then, you'll choose from three templates to frame your final objective and key results in a way that works best for you.

Focus on increasing website traffic as your growth goal. Use these questions to guide you:

- What is the specific growth area you want to focus on this quarter?
  - *Example: New visitors, organic traffic, referral traffic, etc.*
- Why is this growth area important for your overall strategy?
  - *Example: More visitors mean more opportunities to convert leads into customers.*
- What measurable outcomes will show progress toward this growth goal?
  - *Example: Grow monthly website visits by 20 per cent, increase time spent on site by 15 per cent, etc.*

Shift to your retention goal. These questions will help shape your objective:

- What aspect of customer retention needs attention this quarter?
  - *Example: Renewal rates, subscription extensions, repeat purchases, etc.*
- Why is this specific aspect of retention important for your business right now?
  - *Example: Higher renewal rates increase lifetime value and reduce churn.*
- What measurable outcomes will show progress toward your retention goal?
  - *Example: Improve renewal rates by 10 per cent, increase customer engagement with loyalty emails, etc.*

Once you've answered the questions, you should have a draft for each goal. Choose the template that works best for you – because I told you, templates and prompts are the best kind of cheat.

Template 1: The classic

'Our goal is to [quantifiable objective] *by* [timeframe or deadline]. [Key players or teams] *will accomplish this goal by* [what steps you'll take].'

Example: Our goal is to grow monthly website traffic by 20 per cent by the end of Q2. The marketing team will accomplish this by optimizing blog posts for SEO and publishing one new blog per week.

Template 2: Outcome-focused

'We will achieve [specific objective] *by* [timeframe], *measured by* [key results].'

Example: We will increase subscription renewals by 20 per cent by the end of the quarter, measured by engagement with loyalty emails and a reduction in churn.

Template 3: The simplified bullet approach

Objective: [Big picture goal]

    Key result 1: [Measurable milestone]

    Key result 2: [Measurable milestone]

    Key result 3: [Optional milestone]

Example:

Objective: Boost holiday sales

    Key result 1: Achieve a 15 per cent conversion rate on landing pages.

    Key result 2: Generate $50,000 in revenue from holiday offers.

    Key result 3: Increase email click-through rates by 20 per cent.

Running a SWOT analysis

It's a beautiful spring Saturday morning and you're feeling energized. You've decided to finally tackle the chaotic wardrobe that's been haunting you for months.

As you open the doors, it's a mess – clothes spilling out, forgotten shoes and a box of who-knows-what shoved in the corner. It's overwhelming, but you're ready to get organized.

You grab a notepad and split it into four quadrants.

1. **Strengths:** You start listing what's working. Your favourite jumper? Always looks great and goes with everything. That pair of jeans? Perfect fit every time. These are the items that make you feel fabulous.

2. **Weaknesses:** Then, you confront the reality. The jumper with the mystery stain? Not wearable. The shoes that pinch your toes? Ouch. These are the pieces that hold you back.

> **3 Opportunities:** Next, you dream a little. What's missing? Maybe a classic blazer for smart-casual events or a statement belt to pull outfits together. There's potential to upgrade and enhance.
>
> **4 Threats:** Lastly, you consider what could derail your tidy wardrobe. Those impulse buys that don't suit you? Trendy pieces that will be out of style in a month? Temptations that clutter instead of elevating?

By the time you're done, you have a clear picture – what stays, what goes and what's next. The result? A streamlined wardrobe that reflects your style and gives you confidence every morning.

Now imagine applying this clarity to your business decisions, your marketing or even your personal goals. That's the power of a SWOT analysis.

Here's a little piece of SWOT history to keep in your back pocket for your next trivia night. The origins of SWOT analysis trace back to the 1960s at Stanford University, where Albert Humphrey and his team were working with data from Fortune 500 companies to improve long-term planning and change management processes.[4]

But here's the twist – before it was called SWOT, it was actually known as SOFT analysis!

It wasn't until a seminar in Zurich in 1964 that 'Faults' became 'Weaknesses' and 'Satisfactory' was renamed 'Strengths', giving us the structured framework we know today as SWOT.[5]

SWOT stands for:

- **Strengths:** What are you doing well? What gives your brand a competitive edge?
- **Weaknesses:** Where do you have gaps? What's holding you back?
- **Opportunities:** What trends, shifts or market gaps can you take advantage of?
- **Threats:** What external factors could hinder your progress?

At its core, a SWOT analysis helps you step back, assess where you're at and identify where to focus your energy moving forward. It can also serve as a great way to refine your objectives, as it goes deeper into the day-to-day realities of your brand's position.

Breaking down SWOT: Internal vs external

When conducting a SWOT analysis, one of the most common mistakes I see is people confusing internal and external factors. Understanding the distinction between the two is key to making your analysis actionable.

- **Internal factors** are elements within your control. They're all about what's happening inside your business or marketing team.

- **External factors** are things happening outside your business that you may not control but need to adapt to.

Whenever I tell our students about the importance of doing a SWOT analysis before diving into tactics and individual strategies, I always frame it as a diagnostic tool. Think of it as the check-up your strategy needs before you start running full steam ahead.

A SWOT analysis gives you everything you need to know to understand what's working, what's not and what external factors you need to account for. It's not just about looking forward – it's about reflecting on what's already happened. What has been working? What hasn't? By grounding your plan in this understanding, you're not relying on guesswork to make decisions. You're building your plan on a foundation of clarity and insight.

SWOT IN ACTION: A PRACTICAL EXERCISE

Create your SWOT grid. Draw a simple grid with four quadrants (or download our worksheet to help you out) – one each for strengths, weaknesses, opportunities and threats.

1 **Fill it in:** Take 10–15 minutes to brainstorm as many points as possible for each quadrant. Use the prompts below to help you.

2 **Prioritize and act:** Not everything on your SWOT list will demand equal attention. Prioritize the top two–three points in each quadrant and identify how they'll shape your strategy.

Setting up a SWOT grid might seem straightforward in theory, but without the right prompts it can feel surprisingly challenging to get meaningful ideas on paper. That's why I always recommend using a few targeted questions to guide the process. Here's a quick starting point:

Strengths:

- What do we consistently excel at?
- What makes us stand out from competitors?
- What do our customers rave about?

Weaknesses:

- Where are we falling short?
- What do we consistently struggle with?
- What feedback have we ignored that needs addressing?

Opportunities:

- What trends or shifts in the market can we leverage?
- Are there untapped customer needs we can meet?
- What tools, platforms or partnerships could give us an edge?

Threats:

- Who or what could disrupt our progress?
- Are there industry trends working against us?
- Are there external risks – economic, competitive or technological – we need to prepare for?

A SWOT analysis may look simple, but it's also one of the most effective tools you can have in your marketing toolkit. It forces you to pause, step back and get real about where you're at and where you need to go before you go ahead and start mapping the stages for your customer journey.

Setting up the marketing funnel stages

And here we go, straight into the *pièce de résistance*, the big daddy of our plan. When it comes to building a marketing plan, breaking it down into **funnel stages** is where things really start to come together.

For all the marketers out there scratching their head and asking, *'This is all well and good Fab, but what is a funnel?'* funnels are journeys that as customers we are on all the time – in fact we are either building a funnel or are *in* one at any given time.

Each journey begins with **awareness**. Let's say you have just opened a new coffee shop in town – just like in a classic Hallmark Christmas movie and no one knows about your cosy little spot yet. So, you get the word out. Posters on the community board. Local influencers sipping your signature flat white. A cheeky ad on Instagram showing your barista pouring a perfect heart-shaped latte. People start noticing – *'Oh, that's the new coffee shop near the park!'*

Next comes **consideration**. They've seen your posts, maybe even walked by and peeked inside. They're intrigued by the idea of locally roasted beans and your promise of the best cinnamon rolls in town. Reviews start to pop up online: *'A lovely vibe!'* or *'Looks cosy – planning to visit soon!'* Now they're debating – should they give it a go?

Then, **conversion**. One morning, someone decides, *'Why not?'* They step in, greeted by the smell of freshly brewed coffee and the warm smile of your team. They try your latte – it's creamy, rich, perfection. That's it; they're hooked.

But you don't stop there. Enter **loyalty**. Your customer is back the next day, then the next. They know your barista by name and they don't even have to say their order anymore – it's already being prepared when they walk in. You start a loyalty card and they're counting down to their free drink.

Finally, you've earned their **advocacy**. They're snapping pics of their morning brew for Instagram, tagging your shop in stories. They bring their friends on the weekend, boasting, *'You have to try this place!'* Soon enough, you're the talk of the town, all because of the journey you created for your customers.

But here's the catch: a journey like the one in our funnels is not just about tactics, or actions you'll take to attract and retain customers. To set up the funnel effectively, we need to layer in a few key components at each stage.

---

1 **Define your audience:** Who are you talking to at this stage? Your audience's mindset and behaviours will differ at each funnel stage. Start by identifying exactly who you're speaking to and where they are in their journey.

2 **Identify their needs:** What do they need most right now? At every stage, your audience has specific questions, concerns or desires. Pinpointing these needs ensures your messaging hits home.

3 **Assign a key message:** What's the core message they need to hear? This message acts as a guiding light for your content and campaigns at each stage. It's what connects your audience's needs to the solutions your brand offers.

4 **List tactics:** What actions will you take to move them forward? Now that you've identified the audience, their needs and your message, it's time to plan your tactics. These are the specific activities – ads, social posts, email campaigns, etc. – that will drive results at each stage. This book has lots of tangible ideas for you to explore and add to your arsenal.

We'll walk through each stage of the funnel – **awareness, consideration, conversion, loyalty** and **advocacy** – and for every stage, we'll focus on these four elements:

1 Defining the audience.

2 Identifying their needs.

3 Crafting the key message.

4 Choosing two–three tactics to engage them effectively.

Once we've mapped this out, we'll move on to turning these tactics into a timeline. Because a great plan isn't just about having the right ideas – they're about executing them in the right order.

Understanding your audience: When and where to do research

Here's where I back up, after I got us all excited about building funnels – but with good reason. Aren't we forgetting anything?

Before you even begin to build a marketing plan, there's one step that can't be skipped: truly understanding who your audience is. And while in this chapter we'll talk about how to identify your audience and their needs within the context of the funnel, this kind of deep dive into your audience deserves its own dedicated effort.

For our students, we strongly encourage doing this work as a separate project before even starting to map out a strategy. Here's why: identifying audience pain points and desires – or at the very least, a detailed one-pager – provides you with far more data and nuances than you'll ever need in a single plan. And that's the point.

A well-developed audience goes beyond demographics. Here's what you'll want to include.

- **Demographics and psychographics:** Age, gender, location, income level, lifestyle preferences, values, interests, attitudes and behaviours.
- **Needs and pain points:** What are their biggest challenges or goals?
- **Motivations:** Why would they choose your product or service over others?
- **Preferred communication channels:** Do they prefer email, social media or something else?

How does this fit into the plan?

While your audience personas will provide a treasure trove of insights, your strategy won't use everything. Instead, think of this research as your foundation – it's there to guide you when you need it.

For example:

- When building a funnel, you'll refer to your personas to define the specific audience for each stage.
- When crafting messages, you'll draw on their needs, pain points and motivations to create content that resonates.
- When choosing tactics, you'll focus on the channels they prefer and the behaviours they've shown.

If the thought of creating a full presentation sounds overwhelming, start with a one-pager for each audience segment. Cover the essentials – who they are, what they need and how your brand fits into their lives. For the overachievers, go all in with a full audience persona deck that captures every detail, from their favourite platforms to their morning routines.

The goal isn't to overwhelm yourself but to arm your strategy with the insights that will make it sharper, more targeted and more impactful.

By treating audience research as a separate process, you're giving your marketing plan the strongest possible foundation, which is why it's the sole focus of our next chapter. It's about knowing who you're talking to and truly understanding them before you start building your strategy.

The psychology behind each stage of the marketing funnel

When breaking down the marketing funnel into its stages, there is power in understanding the psychology driving your customers at each point in their journey. Each stage is like a step in a relationship, with different needs, motivations and behaviours shaping how your audience interacts with your brand.

Let's briefly explore the psychology behind each stage of the funnel and how it influences your strategy, as this will also help you understanding what key messages to focus on.

At the **awareness stage**, your audience isn't actively looking for you – they may not even know they have a problem yet. Your role here is to spark curiosity and capture attention by showing them something they didn't realize they needed. What works:

- content that educates, entertains or inspires (think blog posts, videos or social media)
- messaging that taps into the 'Aha!' moment, helping them identify a challenge or desire

Now that your audience knows about you, they're weighing their options through the **consideration stage**. They're asking, *'Why should I choose you?'* This stage is all about trust and credibility. What works:

- case studies, testimonials and in-depth content that shows your expertise
- comparisons and transparent messaging that highlight what makes you different

At the **conversion stage**, your audience is ready to take action – but they might have lingering doubts. Your job is to remove barriers and give them the confidence to commit. What works:

- clear CTAs, limited time offers and seamless user experiences
- addressing common objections and reinforcing the value they'll get

Once someone becomes a customer, the relationship doesn't stop. **Loyalty** is about making them feel valued and turning them into repeat customers. It's the stage where you deepen the connection. What works:

- personalized follow-ups, loyalty rewards and exclusive perks
- showing appreciation and staying engaged through email or social

Finally, **advocacy** is driven by emotion. When people feel genuinely excited about your brand, they naturally want to share it with others. Your role here is to amplify that excitement. What works:

- referral programmes, shareable content and community-building initiatives
- celebrating your advocates and giving them tools to spread the word

The key to mastering the funnel is more than knowing what tactics to use – you want to understand *why* those tactics work by connecting with the psychology behind each stage and here's where channels and key performance indicators (KPIs) come in.

Setting channels and KPIs

> **TIP**
>
> It's not just about having the right ingredients but using the right tools for the job.

As an Italian, food is literally my love language. Cooking dishes that tap into my heritage and origins feels like a way of sharing a piece of myself. But the best part? Actually, sharing that food with others. Preparing a meal – especially something as comforting as lasagne – for a dinner party is one of the most wholesome and meaningful ways I connect with people.

That said, I've learned a thing or two about cooking lasagne in my day. You start with the best ingredients – a rich, slow-cooked ragu, creamy béchamel and perfectly al dente pasta sheets. But even with the finest components, things can go terribly wrong if you don't use the right tools.

Like the time I tried to make lasagne in a dish that was far too small. Halfway through layering, the sauce started spilling over the edges. Or the time I thought a flat sheet pan might work in a pinch – it did not. The layers dried out before they had a chance to meld into that glorious, gooey perfection.

It's not just about having the right ingredients but also using the right tools for the job.

It's the same with marketing. Your message might be amazing, your audience eager, but if you don't align the channel with the goal – if you're trying to cook lasagne in a cookie tray, so to speak – you won't get the results you're hoping for.

The truth is, not every channel will work for every audience or goal. This is why I like to start by identifying two key elements: the key messages I want to communicate and the key audiences I want to reach. From there, I can confirm which channels to focus on, depending on the specific stage of the customer journey.

Understanding the role of each channel

When it comes to choosing the right channels for your marketing strategy, there are some common practices we can lean on – certain channels tend to have strengths that align naturally with specific stages of the customer journey.

I want to give you a starting point with a few ideas to help you see where these channels might fit. But here's the thing: great marketing often comes from daring to step outside the proverbial box.

For example, while events and webinars are often seen as tools for lead generation, they can also be powerful for engaging existing customers and building loyalty. By using a channel in an unexpected way, you can deliver something fresh and exciting that surprises your audience and goes beyond their expectations.

So, consider this list your guiding light – a way to spark ideas, especially if you're just getting started. But if you're a more experienced marketer, I want to challenge you to take it one step further. Think about how you can match channels to the right stages in a way that feels fresh, bold and uniquely suited to your brand. Because let's be honest, these steps of the marketing plan are where your confidence, creativity and willingness to experiment will shine. Don't be afraid to play and see what happens. After all, innovation often comes from pushing yourself just outside your comfort zone.

Here's a breakdown of common marketing channels and how their strengths typically align with different stages of the customer journey. Use this as a starting point, but remember – it's always worth exploring how you can stretch the potential of each channel beyond its traditional strengths.

STRENGTHS OF COMMON MARKETING CHANNELS

Social media

- **Awareness:** Building visibility through engaging content, shareable posts and influencer collaborations.
- **Consideration:** Showcasing testimonials, reviews or product demos via stories, reels or posts.
- **Loyalty:** Fostering community by engaging directly with customers through comments and direct messages (DMs).

Email marketing

- **Consideration:** Nurturing leads with personalized content, drip campaigns and value-packed newsletters.
- **Loyalty:** Keeping customers engaged with exclusive offers, updates and personalized recommendations.
- **Advocacy:** Encouraging happy customers to share reviews, referrals or testimonials.

SEO and content marketing

- **Awareness:** Capturing organic traffic with blog posts, guides and educational content that answer common questions.
- **Consideration:** Building credibility with in-depth case studies, white papers or long-form content.
- **Conversion:** Supporting decision-making with targeted landing pages or product comparison posts.

Paid media (pay-per-click, social ads)

- **Awareness:** Reaching new audiences quickly with targeted campaigns.
- **Consideration:** Retargeting visitors to keep your brand top of mind.
- **Conversion:** Offering time-sensitive discounts or deals to encourage immediate action.

Events and webinars

- **Awareness:** Generating buzz and capturing interest with live experiences or collaborative events.
- **Consideration:** Building trust and showcasing expertise by engaging with attendees directly.
- **Loyalty:** Strengthening connections by offering customers access to VIP experiences or behind-the-scenes content.

Influencers and partnerships

- **Awareness:** Leveraging trusted voices to reach new audiences.
- **Consideration:** Creating authentic content that shows your product or service in action.
- **Advocacy:** Encouraging influencers to share their genuine love for your brand, inspiring their followers to do the same.

When to flip channels on their heads

While this list provides a tried-and-tested foundation, don't stop here. What happens if you flip the script? For example:

- Could email marketing play a role in awareness by sending thought-leadership newsletters to new audiences?
- Could events shift from loyalty-building to lead generation by collaborating with partners in untapped markets?

The best strategies often come from testing boundaries and seeing what works for your unique brand and audience.

KPIs and metrics: What's the difference

Last but not least, how do we know we chose the right channels and that the channels are performing the right way?

In marketing, KPIs and metrics are often used interchangeably, but they're not the same thing. This may actually be among the top questions my students ask me on a weekly basis. Both play an essential role in your strategy, but they serve distinct purposes.

Metrics are the raw data points that measure specific activities or outcomes. They're the individual building blocks of your reporting, giving you insights into what's happening on a granular level. Think website traffic, social media impressions, email open rates and cost per click (CPC).

Key performance indicators are the critical metrics you choose to measure progress toward your primary objectives, as in they are the metrics showing you whether your strategy is delivering results. Conversion rate (tied to increasing purchases) can be measured by looking at website traffic click-throughs and new purchases, for example. KPIs can be made by one or more metrics. If metrics are puzzle pieces, KPIs are the finished puzzle – they align individual data points to your strategy, showing whether you're on track to meet your goals.

Why channels matter in KPI selection

Just when you thought you had it all under control, there's a twist: KPIs aren't just tied to your objectives – they're also tied to the **channels** you use to achieve them.

Different channels play different roles in the funnel and the KPIs you track should reflect those roles. For example:

- **Social media:** KPIs such as engagement rate or reach make sense at the awareness stage, but conversion-focused KPIs (like click-through rates) are more relevant further down the funnel.

- **Paid ads:** KPIs like cost per acquisition (CPA) and return on ad spend (ROAS) are directly tied to conversion objectives, but for early-stage awareness campaigns, impressions or click-through rates might be better indicators.

Choosing the right KPIs means understanding not only your objective but also the channel's strengths and where it fits into the customer journey.

In short, all KPIs are metrics, but not all metrics are KPIs. The right KPIs link your metrics to your overall strategy, giving you actionable insights for each channel and stage of the funnel.

REFLECTION TIME
How to choose the right KPIs for channels

How many KPIs should you be adding to each channel? There is really no right or wrong answer, but I always tend to suggest sticking to two or three KPIs per channel.

Tracking matters, but remember, you will more likely than not have to explain, justify and break down your tracking to team members, clients and stakeholders at any given time. So, the old adage of 'less is more' is really important in this instance.

When defining KPIs, you can reflect deeper into what you are trying to achieve:

1   What's the goal of this stage in the funnel?

(Example: Awareness might focus on reach; conversion might focus on sales.)

2   Which metrics align with this channel's purpose?

(Example: Use engagement metrics for social media; use open rates for email.)

3   Which metrics directly measure progress toward my objective?

(Example: For paid ads, track CPC for cost efficiency; for retention, track repeat purchases.)

Once you add those to your plan and tie them to your funnel stages, you show exactly how you'll be measuring progress at any given time.

Implementation and timeline planning

When I first crafted the strategy plan that we use and recommend to our students, especially those working toward our certification, I thought I had everything covered. We had all the building blocks – the objectives, channels, KPIs and tactics. It felt like a solid foundation.

But, as always, part of my ethos – and the ethos of our school – is to continuously evolve and adapt. And one of the biggest lessons I've learned is that listening to your audience is key. Our students helped us see something important: while the plan had all the right pieces, it lacked something crucial – a way to translate all this goodness into action without feeling overwhelming.

A great plan doesn't just sit in a document. It takes everything – the objectives, channels, KPIs and tactics – and organizes those tactics into a structured timeline. This isn't just about being neat and tidy; it's about creating a system that works in practice.

Here are a few reasons why timeline planning is non-negotiable.

- **Avoid overwhelm:** Marketers are notorious for trying to do too much at once. A timeline helps you focus on the right things at the right time, so you don't burn out or dilute your efforts.

- **Sequence your efforts:** By breaking down your tactics and aligning them with your funnel stages, you can create a logical flow that moves your audience through their journey.

- **Tailor to your brand's needs:** Not every brand will follow the same sequence. If you're an established brand, you might prioritize retention before circling back to brand awareness. A timeline allows you to adapt your strategy to your specific goals.

- **Prevent bottlenecks:** A clear timeline ensures tasks don't pile up at the wrong times, helping your team stay on track and accountable.

- **Encourage experimentation:** With a timeline in place, you can space out your efforts, giving yourself room to test, learn and adapt as you go.

Mapping tactics and setting milestones: Working quarterly

TIP

Your strategy is not the same as your campaign.

This is all well and groovy, but when it came to putting something practical into my plan, I came across a familiar roadblock: *how do I build a timeline? What criteria do I use?*

Fifteen years in marketing and four years running a school gave me some insight into this and here's what I've learned – the best strategies are the ones that have enough time to mature and simmer. For me, that sweet spot is about three months.

If you don't know, I'm from the region of Parmesan cheese, which, let's be honest, is one of the best cheeses in the world. And one of the things I learned early on – thanks to countless school trips to Parmesan factories – is that there's magic in letting things mature and age.

The same applies to strategies. Of course, you'll want to implement, adapt and evolve, but you also need to give things time. Even if you're only testing a few tactics across different channels, you need at least three months to let those tactics run, gather data and show results – or, at the very least, offer some insights.

There's no hard and fast rule, but I've found that **quarterly strategies** work best. I tell my clients this all the time: even if we're building a strategy with a longer lifespan, I still break it down into quarters. Why? Because quarterly reviews force us to pause, assess and refine.

This approach has been my go-to for six years now and it's been far more successful than trying to cram everything into short-term strategies or locking myself into 12-month plans that don't adapt to changes.

Since we are talking about timing, here's another important distinction to make: your strategy is not the same as your campaign.

A campaign – like a holiday promotion or a Black Friday sale – is a time-enclosed series of activities with a specific goal, audience and message. It might last a week, two weeks or even six months, depending on your needs.

Your strategy, on the other hand, is the bigger picture. It's the roadmap that aligns your business goals, audience needs and tactical execution across all your campaigns. While a holiday campaign might dominate your activities for a quarter, your overall strategy should focus on multiple areas, like building awareness, driving conversions and retaining customers.

Creating your timeline

If you're looking to take your tactics and put them into a timeline, my suggestion is to think in three-month increments. Over those three months, I ask myself this question: '*Where can I allocate the different tactics to keep things flowing steadily?*'

As a rule of thumb, remember these best practices:

- Maintain a consistent rhythm throughout the quarter.
- Allow flexibility to adjust tactics as needed.
- Avoid cramming too many tactics into one period.

Think of this as a strategic calendar. It helps you outline what needs to happen throughout the quarter, but it also provides flexibility. You can adapt as needed – reducing your efforts in one area to focus more energy on another.

I've seen how powerful this approach can be for our students. Whether they're crafting plans for their own businesses or taking these strategies back to their companies, this method has proven to be easy to apply and incredibly effective.

From crafting clear OKRs to conducting a meaningful SWOT analysis and from mapping out funnel stages to balancing tactics on a timeline, every step builds on the last to create a plan that works in the real world.

The final piece? Implementation. By breaking your strategy into three-month increments and keeping your efforts balanced, you give yourself the space to test, adapt and refine without losing momentum.

A little help when putting it all together

Now, I wouldn't leave you hanging after all this strategic goodness, would I? As part of this book, I wanted to make sure you had everything you needed to put these concepts into action.

That's why I've created an exclusive marketing plan template that brings together all the elements we've discussed – from OKRs to SWOT analysis, funnel mapping to timeline planning. It's designed to make the process as straightforward as possible while maintaining the flexibility you need to make it your own.

To get your hands on this template, simply head over to altmarketingschool. com/book. Consider it my little gift to help you kickstart your strategic planning journey. Remember, this template isn't meant to be a rigid framework – it's a starting point that you can adapt and modify based on your unique needs and circumstances. Just like your strategy, it's meant to grow with you.

KEY POINTS

- A marketing plan outlines your strategy, objectives and tactics to align your efforts and achieve your goals.
- It starts with defining clear OKRs to give your strategy focus and direction.
- SWOT analysis provides a diagnostic tool to assess your strengths, weaknesses, opportunities and threats, helping you build a grounded strategy.

- Each stage of the marketing funnel requires identifying your audience, understanding their needs, crafting key messages and assigning actionable tactics.

- Metrics and KPIs are different: metrics tell you what's happening, but KPIs show you what matters in relation to your objectives.

- Strategies and campaigns are not the same: campaigns are time-specific bursts, while strategies connect multiple efforts into a cohesive plan.

- Quarterly planning offers enough time for tactics to work while staying agile and adaptable.

Notes

1 BetterWorks. Keys to OKR success: Q&A with John Doerr, BetterWorks Magazine, April 2022. www.betterworks.com/magazine/keys-okr-success-qa-john-doerr (archived at https://perma.cc/2HJU-C7GS)

2 BetterWorks. Keys to OKR success: Q&A with John Doerr, BetterWorks Magazine, April 2022. www.betterworks.com/magazine/keys-okr-success-qa-john-doerr (archived at https://perma.cc/2HJU-C7GS)

3 BetterWorks. Keys to OKR success: Q&A with John Doerr, BetterWorks Magazine, April 2022. www.betterworks.com/magazine/keys-okr-success-qa-john-doerr (archived at https://perma.cc/2HJU-C7GS)

4 T Friesner. History of swot analysis, Marketing Teacher, 2011. www.marketingteacher.com/history-of-swot-analysis (archived at https://perma.cc/7ZXJ-7MY9)

5 T Friesner. History of swot analysis, Marketing Teacher, 2011. www.marketingteacher.com/history-of-swot-analysis (archived at https://perma.cc/7ZXJ-7MY9)

05

Identifying customer pain points

> **REMINDER**
>
> Great (customer-driven) marketing is about directing people to the right solution.

Let's start with a little thought experiment: King Charles and the late Ozzy Osbourne.[1] Both born in 1948, grew up in England, made headlines in the press, are wildly successful, wealthy, spend their winters in the Alps and are dog lovers. You'd think they'd have a lot in common, right?

Except they couldn't be more different. Their interests, values, goals and challenges? Completely worlds apart. And if you were trying to market to both using the same message, you'd fail spectacularly.

Here's why: demographics are just the surface. They might give you the 'what', but they'll never give you the 'why'. To truly connect, to really create something meaningful for your audience, you have to go deeper. And that's where **pain points** come in.

Let me give you one further example: let's say you're planning a party, you social butterfly. Not just any party – the party of the year. You'd need to know who's coming, right? Are they into wild dance floors or intimate acoustic vibes? Would they prefer gourmet sushi or classic pizza? Knowing these details is the difference between your guests leaving raving or regretting.

Now, take that same principle and apply it to your customers. Pain points are windows into what keeps them up at night, what they secretly hope for and what frustrates them so much they're ready to make a change. And if you can tap into that? Magic happens.

The big question is: why should you care? Why spend time digging into your customers' pain points? Because here's the truth: if you're trying to please everyone, you'll resonate with no one. Pain points help you focus your efforts where they matter most – on the people who are waiting for a solution you can provide. They're the guiding light for your campaigns, your messaging and even the way you build your products. Think of it like this: pain points are the map and your brand is the solution. Without them, you're just wandering, hoping something clicks. With them, you're strategic. Intentional. Impactful.

In this chapter, we're diving deep. We'll uncover the most common types of pain points, explore the psychology behind why they exist and give you practical methods to find and address them.

Bridging back to audience research

Remember in the last chapter when we talked about the absolutely must-do step before diving into funnels or crafting strategies? That deep dive into audience research – the one where you really get to know who you're speaking to.

Here's where it gets even better: understanding pain points is only part of the story. To truly elevate your personas, you need to weave in our customer-driven approach, which is directly tied to buyer psychology.

I was having a chat with a friend of mine – a dedicated crafter, as she likes to call herself. She told me about her 'craft dungeon' (her words, not mine), a space filled to the brim with supplies, half-started projects and materials waiting for their moment.

As we talked, she reflected on why her craft dungeon had grown to such epic proportions. She said something that stuck with me: 'You know, I've realized that a lot of these projects weren't started for who I am now. I got them because of who I wanted to be.'

It hit me like a lightning bolt. Her decisions – the things she bought, the projects she began – weren't about her current self. They were about her future self, her imagined self. The creative genius who would one day complete every intricate embroidery kit or build that perfect scrapbook.

This is a perfect example of how we, as humans, make decisions – especially when it comes to buying. We don't always buy for who we are today. We buy for the person we want to become. That's why understanding buyer psychology and the buyer process is so crucial in marketing. When you understand that people are motivated not by their present realities but by their aspirations, you can connect with them on a deeper level.

The fitness app isn't selling to who you are now, binge-watching TV in your pyjamas. It's selling to the version of you that gets up at 6 a.m. for a run. The luxury handbag isn't about practicality. It's about who you want to be when you walk into that big meeting or night out.

As marketers, our job isn't just to meet customers where they are. It's to meet them where they *want* to be, to tap into their dreams, their hopes, their imagined futures.

Because, let's be honest, we're all crafting our own 'dungeons', filled with the tools for the selves we aspire to be. And understanding that? That's where the magic of customer-driven marketing truly begins.

Think about it. Many marketers focus on creating personas that are essentially checklists of shared traits: age, job title, hobbies or even lifestyle quirks like being 'caffeine enthusiasts' or 'minimalist decor fans'. It's useful, sure, but it's surface-level. It tells you what your audience does, but not why they buy.

This is the real magic of customer-driven marketing. It helps you see beyond the labels and into the aspirations of your customers. Your product – whether it's a customizable planner, a wellness retreat, coaching services or an artisanal candle – isn't just a thing. It's a tool that helps your audience become the person they want to be. A more organized version of themselves. A more balanced version. A calmer, more intentional version.

And when you build your strategy with this in mind – when you design your messages to speak to those aspirations – everything clicks. Your marketing becomes magnetic because it's not about selling what you do; it's about selling what your customers dream of.

So, as we dive into identifying and addressing pain points in this chapter, keep this in mind: pain points aren't just problems to solve. They're clues to your customer's desires. Use them to bridge the gap between who your customers are today and who they want to become tomorrow.

Types of pain points: How they evolve through the funnel

> TIP
>
> Pain points are the bridge between your customers' challenges and your brand's solutions.

Your friend won't stop going on about their noise-cancelling headphones. *'Best purchase ever,'* they say, as you nod politely, not fully convinced.

Fast forward to Monday morning. You're on an important Zoom call and just as you're about to make a point that might land you a big opportunity, your neighbour decides it's the perfect time to fire up the lawnmower. And the house works across the road have started full swing, with workers blasting music from their portable radio.

Suddenly, your friend's endless raving makes sense. You're Googling 'best noise-cancelling headphones' before the meeting even ends.

That moment? That's a **trigger event.**

Trigger events are those specific situations that flip the switch in someone's mind – when a need or pain point becomes impossible to ignore. They're the instant when 'nice to have' transforms into 'must have'.

For marketers, understanding trigger events is gold dust. It's the moment you know your audience is primed for action. Whether it's a sudden problem (like a neighbour's mower), an exciting opportunity (like a big presentation) or even a seasonal shift (think running shoes for a New Year's fitness goal), these moments are what spark the decision-making process.

Understanding the decision-making journey purchase can help us better identifying pain points for our customers. But understanding how they shift and change over the buyer journey helps us refining them even more.

Before we dive into the specifics of pain points, let's zoom out and talk about how these pain points shift as your audience moves through the first half of your marketing funnel – what I (and many marketers) like to call the **acquisition stages.**

So, what are the acquisition stages? These are the early phases of your funnel, where your audience moves from simply realizing they have a problem, to actively searching for solutions, to finally deciding on the one that feels right for them – brand awareness, consideration and conversion. It's a journey of clarity, understanding and, ultimately, action. And here's the key: the pain points your audience experiences during these stages don't stay static. They evolve.

Exploring triggers tied to pain points

Every purchase begins with a trigger event. It's the spark that takes your customer from *'Everything's fine'* to *'Something's missing and I need to fix it.'* Smart marketers? They know that if they want to truly connect, they need to start there too.

Let's take a moment to talk about Apple. They've mastered the art of tapping into trigger events. Think about their launches as well as campaigns. They sell the promise of more creative mornings, more connected evenings or capturing the moments that matter most.[2] They understand the trigger – and then they show how their product fits effortlessly into the story.

A trigger event is the moment your customer moves from being oblivious to a problem, to realizing they're in the market for a solution. It's the catalyst that sends them down the path to awareness, research and, ultimately, a decision.[3]

The best part? If you can identify these trigger events, you're stepping in at exactly the right time, with the right message. You're meeting your customers where they are, in a way that feels effortless and intuitive.

Yet not all trigger events have been created equal. Indulge me in this example. It's 3 p.m. and your stomach growls like a bear. The coffee shop sign promising 'freshly baked cookies and a latte special' suddenly becomes irresistible. This type of trigger is biological.

In fact, trigger events come in all shapes and sizes, but they generally fall into four main categories:

---

1 **Biological:** These are the 'can't-ignore-it' moments when our bodies demand action. Hunger. Thirst. Cold. Tiredness. They create immediate needs that customers want solved, fast.

2 **Situational:** Life changes or external circumstances that create new needs. Think milestones, big moves or even tiny shifts that ripple into action.

3 **Emotional:** These triggers are powered by feelings – whether it's inspiration, frustration or the occasional pang of envy.

4 **Social:** These arise from interactions with others. A glowing recommendation from a friend, a not-so-gentle nudge from a spouse or even a competitive spark.

Whatever the reason is, it's this trigger that sparks the journey. It's the moment they realize they may need a new solution.

From this initial realization, the pain points begin to adapt as your audience moves through the funnel, let's look at this more in depth together.

How pain points adapt across the buyer journey

The buyer journey can be summed as a succession of awareness, consideration and decision stage.[4]

At the **awareness stage,** your audience is still trying to make sense of their situation. They've felt the nudge – that trigger event – but they're struggling to articulate exactly what's wrong. Think of it as a foggy morning where they can sense something ahead but haven't yet brought it into focus.

Their questions sound like:

'Why can't I keep track of my tasks anymore?'

'Why do I feel like I'm not progressing in my fitness routine?'

The pain points here are vague and need framing. Your role? Help them give a name to their problem. You're not selling yet – you're educating. You're the guide showing them the foggy shape of what they're experiencing and making it clearer.

In the **consideration stage** the fog has lifted and your audience is crystal clear on what's wrong. They've framed their problem and they've given it a name. They know what they're dealing with and they're ready to explore options.

Their questions shift to:

'What tools are available to help me organize my tasks better?'

'What's the best approach to break through my fitness plateau?'

The pain points at this stage are sharper. Your audience is in research mode, comparing options, looking for insights and starting to picture how a solution might fit into their life. Show them how your product or service aligns with their needs without overwhelming them with options.

The **decision stage** is about choosing the solution. Here's where the real magic happens. Your audience knows their problem and has explored potential solutions. Now they're narrowing it down. They're thinking less about the problem and more about the specifics of their choice.

Their questions now sound like:

'Should I use this app or that app to manage my tasks?'

'Do I invest in a fitness coach, or do I try this online programme instead?'

At this stage, pain points are more about making the right choice:

'Will this work for me?'

'Is this worth the cost?'

'How will this fit into my lifestyle?'

Your role is to remove any barriers to decision-making. Highlight why your solution is the best fit for their needs, reassure them with testimonials or case studies and make it easy to say 'yes'.

Practical methods for identifying pain points

Alright, now that we've covered trigger events and how pain points evolve, it's time to roll up our sleeves and figure out how to spot these pain points like the marketing legends we are. Enter **market research** – the secret sauce behind building customer personas that don't just sit pretty on a slide deck but deliver results.

It's the unsung hero of marketing and, yes, it's time to get geeky. Market research is how we gather, analyse and interpret the data that brings our personas – and their pain points – to life. It's the backbone of understanding your customers.

Simply put, market research is the process of collecting and interpreting information about your audience, competitors and industry. It's the bridge between guesswork and actionable insights and it comes in two flavours:

1 **Primary research:** This is where you roll up your sleeves and gather new data directly from the source. Think surveys, interviews and focus groups – the kind of research that lets you dig deep into your audience's world.

2 **Secondary research:** This involves analysing data that's already out there, like industry reports, competitor reviews or publicly available studies. Another great example is social media, which bridges the gap between primary and secondary.

Surveys: Your starting point

Surveys are like the Swiss Army knife of market research – simple, versatile and incredibly effective when used correctly. I love a good survey, but here's the thing – not all surveys are created equal.

The magic of surveys lies in their ability to scale. Whether you're reaching out to 10 people or 10,000, they give you the ability to tap into your audience's minds and gather a wide range of perspectives. But to make them truly work, you need to think carefully about the design.

- **First, keep it short:** No one wants to spend 20 minutes answering what feels like an endless questionnaire. Attention spans are short, and long surveys will send your audience running for the hills. Aim for clarity and brevity – your customers should know exactly what you're asking and why.

- **Ask specific questions that get straight to the point:** For example, instead of *'What do you think about our product?'* try something like, *'What's the one feature of our product you couldn't live without?'* Clear questions lead to clear answers and clear answers lead to actionable insights.

- **Variety is also your friend:** Mix it up with multiple-choice questions, rating scales and open-ended prompts. This gives you a balanced mix of quantifiable data and qualitative insights, helping you see the big picture while also diving into the details.

We have to take some time to talk about what not to do. Avoid leading questions that push respondents toward a specific answer. For example, *'How much do you love our product?'* isn't going to give you honest feedback – it's just going to stroke your ego. Be neutral and open in your phrasing.

And please, for the love of all things marketing, avoid using jargon that makes you sound like a walking thesaurus.

Use simple, conversational language that feels approachable and keep the survey focused on one or two key objectives. The more streamlined the experience, the better your results will be.

Thanks to tools like SurveyMonkey,[5] creating and distributing surveys has never been easier. These platforms let you design your survey, send it out via email or social media and collect responses all in one place. They even analyse the data for you, so you can focus on what really matters – understanding your audience.

Interviews and focus groups: Your deep dive

If surveys give you a broad snapshot of your audience, interviews are where you zoom in and uncover the essential details. Think of them as the long, unfiltered heart-to-hearts of market research. They're personal, in-depth and incredibly insightful when done right.

- **Interviews:** One-on-one chats that let you dig into the nitty-gritty. Think of it as having coffee with your customer and really listening (without interrupting to talk about yourself).
- **Focus groups:** Small group discussions that reveal trends and give you multiple perspectives in one go.

During an interview, your main job is to listen. Really listen. It's tempting to jump in and offer solutions or steer the conversation, but this is their time to speak and your time to absorb. Ask follow-up questions if something sparks your curiosity but avoid leading them toward a specific answer.

One trick I swear by is leaving a moment of silence after someone finishes speaking. Often, they'll fill that silence with even more detail, giving you deeper insights.

Recording your interviews is also a game-changer. Tools like Otter.ai can transcribe conversations for you, so you can focus on the discussion instead of scribbling notes. Afterward, go through the transcripts and look for recurring themes, surprising insights and the exact words your customers use. Their language is marketing gold.

Social media: Bridging the gap between primary and secondary

If you think social media is just for memes and puppy videos, think again. It's a goldmine of insights about your audience's preferences and behaviours and the best part? It's all there waiting for you.

Dig into who's following you. What's their age range, location or interests? Platforms like Instagram and LinkedIn have built-in analytics tools that make it easy to uncover this info. This data helps you tailor your content and messaging to the right people.

Likes, comments, shares – these aren't just ego boosts. They're your audience voting with their time and attention. High engagement on a specific post? That's your clue that the topic, tone or format resonated.

Look at what's performing best. Are people loving your video content? Engaging most with your Q&A posts? Or is it those quirky memes you threw in for fun? Trends in engagement reveal what your audience values.

Beyond the metrics, pay close attention to the actual conversations happening on your platforms. Comments, replies and direct messages are full of unfiltered customer feedback. They'll tell you what's working, what's not and what they wish you'd do differently.

Even better? Use features like Instagram Stories' polls, quizzes and Q&A stickers to ask direct questions and get real-time responses. It's like running a mini-focus group without ever leaving your desk.

Social media also often bridges the gap between primary and secondary research by allowing you to watch your competitors too. What's working for them? What's falling flat? Beware, though, nobody likes a copycat – use the insights to identify gaps and opportunities that you can make your own.

And don't forget to venture into hashtags and community groups where your ideal customers are hanging out. They're likely to be sharing their pain points and aspirations in plain sight. You just need to be there to listen.

Customer feedback and reviews: Honest, real and pure gold

If you're lucky enough to have customers, listen to them. If not, listen to their reviews of similar products or services. Feedback is the cheat code to understanding your audience.

The beauty of customer feedback is that it doesn't require guesswork. It's your customers handing you their thoughts on a silver platter – the good, the bad and sometimes the downright ugly. The key is knowing how to listen, what to look for and how to turn it into actionable insights.

What to look for:

- **Recurring themes:** If multiple reviews mention the same issue, it's probably worth paying attention to.

- **Customer language:** The way people describe their problems and priorities is marketing copy waiting to happen.

- **Strengths and weaknesses:** Know what people love and what drives them mad, and use that intel to refine your offering.

And if you're not mining competitors' reviews, you're leaving money on the table. Mining simply means analysing competitors' reviews for insights, data and patterns. Tools like Trustpilot help you sift through reviews and find the good stuff. Look for:

- strengths your audience loves (and your competitors are missing)

- weaknesses or frustrations that you can turn into opportunities

- specific keywords and phrases that keep popping up – these are gold for tailoring your product or messaging

Turning research into insights

Whether you're using surveys, interviews or social media sleuthing, the goal is the same – to understand what makes your customers tick, what keeps them up at night and how you can be their hero.

Once you've gathered a treasure trove of feedback, it's time to organize it. Group comments into themes, like product features, customer service or overall satisfaction. Highlight the most common pain points and see how they align with what you already know about your audience.

If you're working with a lot of data, tools like Trustpilot or even a good old spreadsheet can help you categorize and analyse the feedback without losing your mind. Once it's all laid out, the patterns will start to jump off the page.

When implementing market research, there are three key instances where it becomes particularly valuable.

- **New strategy development:** Before launching any new marketing strategy or campaign, conduct thorough research to validate your approach and understand current market conditions. This helps ensure your strategy aligns with actual customer needs and market opportunities.

- **Product development:** When working on new products or services, market research becomes crucial for validating ideas, testing concepts and gathering feedback before full deployment. This reduces risk and increases chances of success.

- **Regular monitoring:** Establish at least one recurring market research activity, such as monthly customer surveys or social media sentiment analysis. This helps you stay connected with evolving customer needs and market trends, allowing for quick adjustments when necessary.

The psychology of pain points: Principles that build association

For weeks, you've been seeing ads for a reusable water bottle on Instagram. You know the one – sleek design, keeps water cold for 24 hours, comes in gorgeous colours. Oh and the ads are pretty good too (as a marketer you appreciate great craft). But you're loyal to your trusty old bottle, complete with its scratched exterior and slightly wobbly lid. *'It's still good,'* you tell yourself.

This morning, the same ad pops up while you scroll your favourite news app. You barely notice it, sipping coffee while scrolling past. Life goes on.

Fast forward to lunch. You're heading to the gym after work, so you pack your bag in a rush. As you grab your water bottle, disaster strikes – the wobbly lid finally gives way and the bottle leaks all over your carefully packed gym kit.

Annoyed and drenched, you jump online to find a replacement. You scroll through endless options, but one catches your eye immediately – the sleek, eco-friendly water bottle from all those ads. Without hesitation, you add it to your cart and check out.

Why that bottle? Why that brand?

This is the power of a very well-known psychology principle called **priming**. By repeatedly exposing you to the product, the brand embedded itself in your subconscious. When the moment of decision came, it wasn't just any water bottle you thought of – it was theirs.[6]

This is just an insight into how our brains work when it comes to decision-making.

The cold hard truth, which I am sure you got the gist of, is that it's not always rational. Humans are wired to respond to certain psychological triggers, even when we think we're making logical choices. Two of the most powerful psychological tools in marketing are **anchoring** and **association,** and when you combine these with your customers' pain points, magic happens.

Anchoring: The power of first impressions

In psychology, anchoring happens when the first piece of information we're given influences how we perceive everything that follows. **Anchoring,** for example, explains why 'sale' tags in shops often list the original price in bold, next to the discounted one.[7]

One of the most famous examples of anchoring, specifically price anchoring, comes from Steve Jobs, as he walks onto the stage, ready to unveil Apple's latest creation. The audience waits in anticipation, wondering how the iPad – a product rumoured to revolutionize tech – will be priced.[8]

Jobs begins by showcasing the iPad's features. Unforgettable design, unmatched performance and an intuitive interface – it's like nothing anyone has seen before. As the crowd hangs on his every word, a price appears on the screen: $999.

It makes sense. Industry experts had speculated the iPad would cost around that much. The room seems to accept it. After all, for such cutting-edge innovation, $999 doesn't feel unreasonable.

But then Jobs pauses, looks at the audience and with a knowing smile says, 'We want to make this accessible to everyone.' And, just like that, the price on the screen changes. The bold $999 flips to $499.

The crowd erupts into applause. Gasps ripple through the room. What just happened?

By first presenting $999, he anchored the audience to a high price point, setting their expectations. When he revealed the $499 price, it didn't just seem reasonable – it felt like a bargain. That wasn't an accident. Jobs understood that humans rely heavily on the first piece of information they receive – the anchor – to evaluate subsequent choices. By carefully setting the $999 anchor, he made $499 look like a deal too good to pass up.[9]

That initial number becomes the mental benchmark, even if it's irrelevant.

There are ways you can use anchoring beyond pricing and apply it to framing your customer's pain points.

- **Start with the pain:** The first message your customers encounter should highlight the pain point they're experiencing. *'Are you spending hours on admin instead of growing your business?'*
- **Position your solution:** Follow up immediately with the solution you offer, anchoring their perception of what's possible. *'With our platform, you can automate your admin in minutes and get back to what you love.'*
- **Create familiar messaging:** Familiarity helps your customers make decisions faster by building know, like and trust factors. Meanwhile, repetition helps your them remember important information.

Association: Building bridges in the mind

Another powerful principle is a very simple one, yet one that can make things stick in our minds due to its effectiveness.

Association is all around us, after all. Think McDonald's, for example. They could've chosen any colours for their iconic arches. Neon green? Electric blue? A chic black and white? The possibilities were endless.[10] Yet, they went with red and yellow – and not just because they look bold together. These colours were chosen because they do something remarkable: they make you *hungry* and make you *act*.

Here's how it works: red is a colour that grabs attention and triggers urgency. It's why stop signs and fire trucks are red – they demand focus. Yellow, on the other hand, is warm and inviting. It evokes happiness and optimism, creating a sense of comfort. Together, they're a perfect recipe for priming your brain to crave food *right now*.

When you see McDonald's glowing red-and-yellow signage as you drive by, it's not just a logo. It's a cue that makes you think, *'Hmm, maybe I'll grab a burger and fries.'* And because you've seen this combination since childhood, it's embedded deep in your subconscious. The moment red and yellow appear together, your brain whispers, *'McDonald's.'*

Two colours, working together, to make millions of people feel hungry and ready to act.

If anchoring helps creating a proverbial first hook, association is all about connecting the dots in your customer's mind. It's the reason why certain brands instantly evoke feelings or ideas without needing to say much, just like McDonald's. Think of Coca-Cola and Christmas cheer.[11] Brands like these built them intentionally.

When it comes to pain points, association works like this: you position your brand as the solution that's already tied to the outcome your customer desires. For example:

- A wellness app might associate itself with calm evenings and better sleep.
- A project management tool could evoke images of organized desks and stress-free mornings.

When your messaging taps into these associations, your customers start linking your brand with the outcome they're chasing – often without even realizing it. The example of Gymshark below is a well-known and common one.

REAL-WORLD EXAMPLE
Gymshark's We Do Gym campaign

Gymshark's **We Do Gym** campaign is a masterclass in understanding and embracing the unfiltered truths of its audience. Launched as a platform to anchor the brand's marketing efforts for 2024, the campaign dives headfirst into the raw, often unspoken realities of gym culture.[12]

From the jitters before a heavy lift to the unmistakable clanging of plates and the classic chicken-rice-broccoli meal prep routine, Gymshark captures the essence of what it means to 'do gym'.

It's a nod to the powerlifters with calloused hands, the cardio enthusiasts who live for a runner's high and the gym-goers in oversized tees or, let's be real, the infamous butt-scrunch shorts. This is 'If you know, you know' marketing at its finest.

Gymshark also teaches us another lesson in audience mapping: the brand isn't trying to cater to everyone. In a market flooded with athleisure brands vying for a piece of the pie, they've planted their flag firmly in their roots. Their messaging says it all: **'We're not good at everything. We're great at one thing.'** That one thing? Gym culture. The real, gritty, no-frills version that resonates with their community.

By anchoring their identity to these shared experiences, Gymshark set themselves apart in a crowded market. They're selling a sense of belonging, a shared language and a culture that gym-goers can see themselves in.

This authenticity builds a bridge between the brand and its audience, creating not just loyalty but advocacy – oh my, are we spanning across multiple funnel stages?

And finally, going back to pain points, Gymshark don't just speak to their audience, they speak like their audience. They understand the inside jokes, the struggles and the triumphs that make up the gym-goer's world. From pre-workout memes to the pride of chalk-covered hands, the campaign taps into a collective identity.

Addressing pain points with empathy

Addressing your customers' pain points with empathy means going beyond the surface-level fixes and showing them that you truly understand what they feel, see and hear in their day-to-day lives.

It's about speaking to their reality in a way that feels personal, human and real. When you use your customers' own language and reflect their experiences back to them, you're building trust.

One of the most popular classes we run is our audience persona one. In fact, I tell this to our students all the time: when you mirror that language in your messaging, you're meeting them exactly where they are.

For example, if customers describe feeling 'overwhelmed' by managing their to-do lists, you don't talk about 'increased productivity' – you talk about helping them 'stop feeling buried under tasks'. If they say they're looking for 'something that fits my budget but still feels premium', you lean into messaging like 'luxury that doesn't break the bank'.

Ask yourself why

Empathy means digging into the emotions behind the pain points. It's not just about knowing they're frustrated or stuck – it's about understanding what that frustration feels like. Is it anxiety over a looming deadline? The helplessness of not knowing where to start? Or maybe the small joy of discovering a product that finally works in the way they hoped?

When you understand their emotional state, you can create messaging that not only solves the problem but also reassures and inspires. Words like 'relief', 'confidence' and 'freedom' tap into the emotional transformation your product or service offers.

When it comes to understanding your customers, there's always more beneath the surface. Sure, they might tell you they're choosing a product because it's cheaper, faster or easier, but the real magic lies in uncovering the deeper, often subconscious beliefs that drive their decisions.

This is where brand laddering comes in. It's a technique that helps you go beyond the obvious and dig into the underlying motivations, values and emotions that shape your customers' choices – or, in some cases, their inaction.[13]

The breakdown below is slightly adapted from traditional brand laddering and it's what we teach at the school. In its simplest form, all it asks us to do is to answer the question 'why'. It works incredibly well when tied to a trigger event you identified for your audience.

Brand laddering helps you uncover three critical levels of insight:

- **Functional reasons:** The practical, surface-level reasons customers make decisions. Example: *'I need a faster way to manage my tasks.'*
- **Emotional benefits:** The feelings your customers associate with achieving their goals or solving their pain points. Example: *'If I manage my tasks better, I'll feel less stressed and more in control.'*
- **Subconscious beliefs:** This is where the gold lies. These deeper motivations often reflect what your customers value most in life. Example: *'Being in control of my time lets me feel like I'm a better parent, partner or professional.'*

These deeper beliefs often operate on autopilot, influencing decisions without customers even realizing it. Brand laddering helps you bring them to the surface.

When you understand the deeper motivations behind your customers' decisions, you can create messaging and solutions that resonate on a meaningful level.

- **Address subconscious beliefs:** If your customers fear failure, reassure them with stories of people like them who've succeeded. If they value freedom, highlight how your product gives them more of it.
- **Connect functional and emotional benefits:** Don't just sell the 'what' – sell the 'why'. Show how your product or service doesn't just solve a problem but also delivers the feelings your customers are chasing.
- **Speak to their values:** Whether it's family, achievement or self-expression, tie your messaging to the core values that matter most to your audience.

The best way to try this method is to have real conversations with customers, or potential customers, and go down the rabbit hole of 'why'. It may feel odd at first, but it does work!

Hear what your customers hear

Your customers are constantly bombarded with messages – from friends, family, colleagues and, yes, other brands. Understanding the noise they're surrounded by helps you stand out.

- What advice or opinions are they hearing from their inner circle?

- What conflicting messages might they be absorbing from other brands?
- How can you cut through that noise with a voice that's clear, supportive and authentic?

When you understand their soundscape, you can position yourself as the voice of reason. Instead of adding to the noise, you become the voice that simplifies, reassures and empowers.

When you use your customers' language, step into their world and reflect their emotions, you're not just solving their pain points – you're building trust. They'll see your brand as one that truly understands them, one that's on their side.

And here's the beauty of empathy-driven marketing: when you connect with your audience on a human level, you don't just create customers – you create advocates.

So, take the time to understand what your customers feel, see and hear. Speak their language. Feel their world. That's where the magic happens.

REAL-WORLD EXAMPLE
Girlfriend Collective opt-out strategy

Girlfriend Collective, a sustainable clothing brand with a loyal following, is known for its thoughtful and human approach to marketing. While the brand regularly uses email to share new products, upcoming launches and personalized recommendations, one email stood out as a masterclass in empathetic marketing.

Before Mother's Day in 2018, Girlfriend Collective sent an email offering customers the choice to opt out of receiving Mother's Day-related promotions.[14] The message was simple, clear and deeply empathetic, acknowledging that this holiday can be emotionally complex for some people. Instead of assuming their entire audience would be excited about Mother's Day gift ideas, the brand created space for those who might find it challenging.

Holidays like Mother's Day or Father's Day often evoke strong emotions – both joyful and difficult. For customers who may have lost a parent, struggled with infertility or experienced strained relationships, these promotions can feel like salt in a wound.

Instead of ignoring the emotional complexities tied to the holiday, Girlfriend Collective leaned into them. They recognized that their audience is diverse and that not every message is universally well-received.

This campaign created trust by showing that Girlfriend Collective listens and cares about the nuances of its audience's experiences. When customers feel understood, they're more likely to remain loyal to a brand.

Here's what you can learn from Girlfriend Collective's empathetic approach:

- **Acknowledge emotional complexity:** Not every occasion or campaign will land the same way with every customer. Recognizing this diversity of experience sets your brand apart.

- **Give customers a choice:** Offering opt-outs or alternatives shows that you respect your customers' boundaries and autonomy, deepening your connection with them.

- **See your customers as humans:** Empathy in marketing more than a feel-good strategy – it's a competitive advantage. When you make your audience feel seen and understood, you build trust and loyalty that goes far beyond the sales cycle.

REFLECTION TIME
Spot the pain points

Now it's time to put everything we've discussed into action, my all-time favourite part.

Use the prompts below to organize your notes into language your audience would actually use. These prompts will help you identify common patterns at different stages of the customer journey, from awareness to decision-making.

Do what you can to get the right data: run interviews, surveys or social media polls to get clearer on how your customers think and talk about their challenges. Focus on capturing their natural voice – the way they describe their frustrations, dreams and barriers to action.

1 *'I've always struggled with...'* What challenges do your customers repeatedly face? Listen for frustration or resignation in their tone – this often points to deeply ingrained pain points.

2 *'I'm tired of feeling...'* Emotional pain points often come out here. Pay attention to feelings like frustration, anxiety or overwhelm.

3 *'I wish I knew how to...'* This reveals where they feel stuck and where your product or service can step in to help.

As you dig deeper into your data, explore the emotions and aspirations behind their words for the consideration stage. Don't just settle for surface-level insights – look for what drives them or holds them back. Use these prompts to uncover deeper motivations:

1 *'I've been searching for...'* What is the missing piece they hope your solution will provide?

2 *'What if there was a better way to...'* This tells you what they're tired of dealing with and what change they're ready to embrace.

3 *'I want to stop...'* Listen for what they're trying to escape or avoid – this is a key part of their decision-making process.

Finally, reflect on the barriers that prevent customers from taking action from our decision stage. These often manifest as objections and your job is to address them head-on. Use these phrases to identify and overcome their doubts:

1 *'I don't have enough time.'* How can your solution save them time or make their life easier?

2 *'I don't have enough money.'* What value or cost-saving benefits can you highlight to justify the investment?

3 *'Imagine if I could finally...'* What goals or dreams do they associate with your solution?

Once you've gathered insights using these prompts, the next step is to weave them into your messaging. When your copy reflects the way your customers talk and think, it builds trust, because they feel seen and understood.

Pain points as opportunities

Remember – who gets closer to the customer wins, and that is a fact.

Throughout this chapter, we've explored how pain points evolve through the funnel, how to identify them with tools like surveys, interviews and social media, and how to address them with empathy. We've looked at the deeper 'why' behind customer decisions using brand laddering and how to connect with their subconscious beliefs. And we've seen how leading brands like Girlfriend Collective and Gymshark leverage these insights to create marketing that truly resonates.

But here's the most important takeaway: your customers don't just want to be sold to. They want to be seen, heard and understood. When you take the time to listen – to use their words, understand their emotions and reflect their experiences – you're doing more than solving their problems. You're creating a relationship built on trust and empathy.

Pain points are the bridge between your customers' challenges and your brand's solutions. They're the threads that tie their needs to your offering. And when you address them with intention and care, you're opening the door to loyalty, advocacy and long-term success.

So, as you move forward, remember great (customer-driven) marketing isn't about persuasion. It's about directing people to the right solution. Once you know that, you can build a better strategy and a plan to tap into your customers' hearts.

KEY POINTS

- Pain points are more than problems – they're windows into your customers' challenges, aspirations and emotions, offering opportunities to connect and build trust.

- Pain points shift across the funnel: from framing their problem (awareness) to exploring solutions (consideration) to overcoming objections (decision).

- Understand what your customers feel, see and hear and reflect their language back to them to create relatable, human messaging.

- Use surveys, interviews, social media and feedback to uncover what truly drives your audience's decisions, focusing on recurring themes and emotional triggers.

- Dig deeper with brand laddering by repeatedly asking 'why' to identify subconscious beliefs and emotional motivators behind customer decisions.

Notes

1 Biography Editors. King Charles III, Biography, nd. www.biography.com/royalty/prince-charles (archived at https://perma.cc/4Y2Q-E34K); Encyclopædia Britannica. Ozzy Osbourne, Britannica, nd. www.britannica.com/biography/Ozzy-Osbourne (archived at https://perma.cc/T9E4-R7GY)

2 M Lakhiani. Apple's product launch strategy: The art of building anticipation, Beehiiv, 2023. marishalakhiani.beehiiv.com/p/apples-product-launch-strategy-art-building-anticipation (archived at https://perma.cc/6TQL-G2CY)

3 Dealfront. What are trigger events? Dealfront, December 2024. www.dealfront.com/blog/what-are-trigger-events (archived at https://perma.cc/5FGK-GAYP)

 4 J Thompson. What is the buyer's journey? HubSpot, 14 June 2016. blog.hubspot.com/sales/what-is-the-buyers-journey (archived at https://perma.cc/274U-EA2P)

 5 SurveyMonkey. Create online surveys and forms that mean business, SurveyMonkey, nd. www.surveymonkey.com (archived at https://perma.cc/P6QF-44G9)

 6 C Loersch and B K Payne. The situated inference model: An integrative account of the effects of primes on perception, behavior and motivation, *Current Opinion in Psychology*, 2016, 12, 5–10. pubmed.ncbi.nlm.nih.gov/26168515 (archived at https://perma.cc/A4B8-FCQF)

 7 C Notaras. The power of anchoring effect, PCMA, 28 August 2019. www.pcma.org/the-power-of-anchoring-effect (archived at https://perma.cc/BJ52-LUV6)

 8 Q Wang. Anchoring effect and people's behaviour decision making: A case study, *Highlights in Business Economics and Management*, 2023, 11, 206–10. doi: 10.54097/hbem.v11i.8099 (archived at https://perma.cc/92GG-GVYX)

 9 C Notaras. The power of anchoring effect, PCMA, 28 August 2019. www.pcma.org/the-power-of-anchoring-effect (archived at https://perma.cc/UAP2-KJJP)

10 L Hawken. I'm a psychologist and here's why the McDonald's logo is red and yellow – it has a *very* specific purpose, *Daily Mail*, 10 July 2023. www.dailymail.co.uk/femail/food/article-12020955/Im-psychologist-heres-McDonalds-logo-red-yellow-specific-purpose.html (archived at https://perma.cc/YN7U-8EA8)

11 E Ferraro. The story of Santa and Coca-Cola, CITMA, December 2020. www.citma.org.uk/resources/the-story-of-santa-and-coca-cola-blog.html (archived at https://perma.cc/BY9V-TYPQ)

12 Gymshark. We do gym, Gymshark, nd. uk.gymshark.com/pages/we-do-gym (archived at https://perma.cc/EPE9-FPZJ)

13 M Veludo-de-Oliveira, A A Ikeda and M C Campomar. Laddering in the practice of marketing research: Barriers and solutions, *Qualitative Market Research: An international journal*, 2006, 9(3), 297–306. doi.org/10.1108/13522750610671707 (archived at https://perma.cc/3PY2-XCDX)

14 Girlfriend. girlfriend.com (archived at https://perma.cc/XLA9-YU43)

06

Creating brand awareness
through belonging

REMINDER

Creating a sense of belonging drives brand awareness and encourages
customers to engage in ways that transcend traditional marketing.

Let's say you love to get the right playlist so much so that you have a playlist
for any occasion – this may or may be not based on real-life events. In fact,
you've spent hours curating the perfect Spotify playlist.

Every track has been meticulously chosen to create the ultimate vibe –
upbeat but not too chaotic, with a couple of deep cuts to show off your
excellent taste. Proud of your creation, you send it to your friends, confident
they'll be blown away.

But instead of praise, you get a stream of critiques.

'Why is this song here?'

'Did you seriously add a Nickelback track?'

'This doesn't flow at all!'

Defensive, you fire back. Sure, it might not be *their* perfect playlist, but it's
yours. You spent time piecing it together, making choices, swapping songs in
and out. That effort makes it feel personal – a reflection of you.

This is the **IKEA Effect** in action.[1]

I remember the last time I assembled a piece of IKEA furniture. I dropped
the same screw twice, and halfway through I realized I'd attached a panel
backwards. But when it was done? I stood back and marvelled at my work.
It was *my* bookshelf, even if the left side tilted ever so slightly.

The IKEA Effect explains why we value things more when we've put effort into them. Whether it's a Spotify playlist, a bookshelf or customizing a product online, that investment of time and energy makes the end result feel special.

Brands like Spotify, IKEA and Nike know this well. By involving customers in the creation process, they tap into that emotional connection. The more effort people put in, the more they value what they get out – and the stronger their sense of belonging to the brand.

Originally published as a working paper in 2011 and later in the *Journal of Consumer Psychology* in 2012, the original IKEA Effect study revealed something fascinating: people place a higher value on products they've built themselves compared to identical pre-assembled ones.[2]

In one of their early experiments, participants were handed flat-pack IKEA boxes – the kind with cryptic instructions and too many screws. Half were tasked with assembling the boxes themselves, while the others received pre-assembled versions. When asked to assign value to the boxes, the DIYers consistently rated theirs higher than the ready-made ones. It was a revelation. The sweat equity – the time, energy and mild frustration of putting something together – transformed a standard product into something special.

This simple yet profound insight reminds us of a universal truth: effort creates emotional attachment. The act of building transforms something ordinary into something *yours*. When people feel like they've played a role in creating something – whether it's assembling a shelf, designing a product or contributing to a community – their connection to it strengthens.

For us as marketers, this is a reminder that fostering belonging isn't just something to focus on at the end of the customer journey. In fact, it's the foundation of building relationships rooted in shared ownership and mutual respect.

And here's the magic – when we invite our audiences to become co-creators early in their journey, we shift the dynamic. A one-way interaction transforms into a two-way relationship, and with it something powerful happens: our customers are the ones who help us amplify our message.

This approach doesn't just build awareness. It simultaneously creates belonging, loyalty and advocacy. It's a three-for-one win. And honestly, who doesn't love a three-for-one?

The psychology of belonging

Did you know that as much as 50 per cent of Walt Disney World visitors don't have kids? That's right – a growing trend of child-free 'Disney adults' is reshaping the way Disney approaches its theme parks. With Disney pouring $60 billion into its parks division, nostalgia is at the heart of this transformation.[3]

For Millennials and Gen Z, Disney is a portal to their childhoods. These visitors, who grew up with Disney's films and characters, are seeking more than just rides and attractions. They're chasing the feelings those stories once gave them – comfort, joy and a sense of wonder. The parks offer not just escapism, but a tangible connection to cherished memories, a break from the weight of adult responsibilities.

This desire to connect with something bigger – whether it's childhood memories, a shared love of magic or a sense of belonging within the Disney community – reflects a deeper truth about human nature. We've been wired to seek connection – to feel seen, understood and valued within a group. It's why we gravitate toward communities and brands that share our interests, values or goals.

At the heart of belonging lies self-identity. People want to see their values and aspirations reflected in the communities they join and the brands they support. When a brand speaks to who we are – or even better, who we aspire to be – the connection goes deeper. This is where personalization becomes a powerful tool. By tailoring experiences, products or messages, brands can make their audiences feel seen and understood on a deeply personal level.

When these elements come together, something magical happens. Belonging transforms from a fleeting emotion into a lasting bond. It's no longer about buying a product or participating in a campaign – it's about being part of something that feels like home.

Tapping into shared memories

Do you remember when Pokémon GO sent Millennials running through parks, reliving the magic of their Game Boy days?[4]

I have a similar feeling every time I see Clippy in the wild – yes, that adorable yet mildly annoying paperclip from Microsoft Word that became a trusty companion for many Millennials (sorry, Gen Zers). Suddenly, I'm transported back to the early 2000s, sitting at the family desktop, wrestling with homework while Clippy cheerfully (and uselessly) offered help.

For a brief moment, I'm not in my 30s juggling work and life – I'm a teenager again, stressing over an essay and sneaking MSN chats with my friends. That warm, fuzzy feeling? That's the **Nostalgia Effect** and it's a powerful tool for marketers looking to build belonging early on in the customer journey.

Researcher Jannine Lasaleta and her team explored this phenomenon by helping people revisit fond memories of the past.[5] The findings showed that nostalgia fills us with a sense of connection and belonging, satisfying some of our most basic emotional needs. When those needs are fulfilled, something fascinating happens. People view money as less important and desirable. In other words, when we feel nostalgic, we're more willing to part with our cash. That's why smart marketers are infusing their campaigns with nostalgic elements, knowing full well the emotional pull it creates.

Think about fashion brands reviving Y2K trends for Gen Z. We already know emotions drive buying decisions. Nostalgia is the hyper-specific version of that, wrapping people in the warm, fuzzy feelings of belonging and social connection. By helping our audience revisit cherished memories, we're building belonging at the early stages of our customers' journeys.

There are plenty of ways to tap into the warm, fuzzy feeling of belonging through nostalgia – and it doesn't always require a time machine. It could be as simple as creating special editions of products or experiences featuring retro designs or packaging. Nostalgia-powered collaborations are particularly effective. Few things evoke a sense of belonging quite like revisiting memorable moments, trends or experiences – especially when wrapped in a heartwarming story.

Walmart's 2024 Christmas ad, Get the Gift that Shows You Get Them, is a perfect example of nostalgic storytelling done right.[6] Set in the cosy, small-town charm of Luke's iconic diner from *Gilmore Girls*, the ad takes viewers straight back to Stars Hollow. Revisiting Lorelai's famous coffee obsession, Luke gifts her a coffee machine, quipping, 'You're drinking me out of business'. Even 17 years after the show's finale, the dynamic between these two remains as charming as ever. It's a warm, humorous and utterly relatable scene for Millennials, waiting to be tugged at the heartstrings.

Here's why this ad works so well:

- Revisiting *Gilmore Girls*, a series cherished for its warmth and wit, creates an instant emotional connection. Walmart captures the essence of winter evenings spent binge-watching the show, evoking feelings of comfort and familiarity.

- Luke's gift of a coffee machine is a thoughtful nod to his and Lorelai's relationship, while his sarcastic remark keeps the humour intact.

- Pairing the sentimentality of gift-giving with *Gilmore Girls*' iconic scenes makes this ad feel personal, heartwarming and true to the holiday spirit.

This use of nostalgic storytelling strengthens the emotional connection between Walmart and its audience.

REAL-WORLD EXAMPLE
Memes marketing

In 1976, around the time Steve Jobs introduced the first Apple computer, evolutionary biologist Richard Dawkins coined the term 'meme'.[7]

He described it as a unit of cultural transmission – an idea, belief or behaviour passed from one person to another, shaping the fabric of culture over time. Little did he know that memes would become a cultural sensation 50 years later.

Fast forward to today and memes have become the internet's universal language. From the iconic 'Distracted boyfriend' to the ever-evolving Drake 'Hotline bling' format, memes now go far beyond entertainment. With the rise of social media, they've evolved into powerful tools for communication, connection and, yes, marketing. Did I hear the word nostalgia, by any chance?

For brands that hop on the bandwagon, memes aren't *just* for laughs anymore. Memes can be educational, entertaining and relatable – showing your customers you *get* them.

For example, fast food giant Wendy's have carved out an unforgettable online persona, thanks to a bold and hilariously sassy approach to social media. Their Twitter (now X) presence is a masterclass in roasting, memes and witty comebacks that walk the fine line between cheeky and downright savage.

What makes this strategy work so well? Wendy's know how to stay relevant and playful while tying everything back to their brand. In 2018, they officially jumped on the 'I don't feel so good' meme trend – a nod to Iron Man's emotional scene in *Avengers: Infinity War*.[8] But in true Wendy's style, they used the meme to take a jab at rival McDonald's, quipping that the golden arches might not be feeling so good, but Wendy's certainly was.

How can you take a leaf out of Wendy's book and start using memes strategically to build connection and awareness?

Memes can be a clever way to call out the challenges your ideal customers face – the same pain points we explored in Chapter 5. But instead of framing these pain points through traditional storytelling, memes let you approach them with humour and relatability. For example, a productivity app might use the 'This is fine' meme to poke fun at the chaos of juggling tasks, subtly positioning their tool as the antidote.

Combining trending news with memes is a popular form of what we know as **news-jacking**. It can be an effective way to tap into pop culture moments.[9] When done right, it shows your brand is culturally aware and quick to engage with current events. For example, during major sporting events or award shows, brands can create relevant memes that connect their message to the moment, sparking conversations and increasing visibility.

Memes can simplify complex ideas and make them more relatable. Whether you're a financial advisor explaining budgeting or a fitness coach promoting healthy habits, memes break down barriers and deliver education in a way that's easy to understand and remember. It's a way to sell what your audience *wants* while giving them what they *need*.

When used strategically, memes are cultural tools that can build awareness in an incredibly relatable way. After all, nothing says 'I see you' quite like the perfect meme. Meme marketing is an art – yet timing and tone are crucial. The key is to:

- react quickly while the moment is still fresh
- ensure the connection to your brand feels natural, not forced
- add value to the conversation rather than just jumping on trends

---

Building awareness through belonging

In 2024, ASOS took their iconic ASOS Insiders programme to a new level. Originally an influencer initiative, it was expanded to include employees with distinctive styles and fashion senses.[10]

This is part of a growing trend where employees are stepping in front of the camera to become the new faces of their companies. Employees are fast becoming the new influencers – and not just on LinkedIn. Brands are increasingly empowering their teams to step in front of the camera, becoming the faces of their companies and actively connecting with audiences in authentic, relatable ways. This shift toward employee-generated content (EGC) is transforming how businesses build community and drive awareness.

Take SheerLuxe, for example. Their TikTok is a behind-the-scenes look at their workplace culture, celebrating their team and attracting top talent.[11] An all-time favourite is The Perfume Shop, as they even turned in-store staff into TikTok stars, with one employee's catchphrase going viral last year, proving that frontline staff can create connections that corporate ads simply can't replicate.[12]

This trend highlights a key insight: building awareness can start from within in more than one way.

Historically, belonging has often been viewed as something that begins once people are part of a wider community – usually in the consideration or loyalty stages of their journey. But when we shift our perspective and see belonging as something we can nurture across every stage of the funnel, the entire journey becomes far more customer-driven.

At the end of the day, it's the members of your community – whether public or private – who drive the conversations and connections that matter most. This makes belonging not just an outcome but a powerful strategy for building awareness and engagement from the start.

When thinking about belonging, there are two approaches to consider:

1 **Start internally:** Build strong customer communities first and expand their influence outward. By showcasing the stories, successes and connections within your existing customer base, you can amplify their impact to attract broader audiences. Or you can go the SheerLuxe route and empower your employees by fostering belonging internally while extending that sense of connection outward to attract new audiences.

2 **Focus publicly:** Create public-facing communities or nurture a community of superfans who aren't yet committed to purchasing your products. This approach is about fostering belonging early on and turning potential customers into advocates before they even buy in.

Each strategy has its merits, but the choice depends on your brand's goals and how you want to shape your community's role in driving awareness.

REFLECTION TIME
Building brand communities

To determine whether to focus on nurturing existing customer communities or building broader public-facing communities, consider these elements:

- Define your **target audience** by identifying whether you want to focus on engaging existing customers or attracting new potential customers to your brand.

  o How do your customers currently interact with your brand?

  o Are they forming natural connections with one another, or is there an opportunity to foster these relationships?

- Your **primary goal** should define whether you want to deepen loyalty and advocacy among your existing community or focus on raising brand awareness to grow your audience.

  o How does belonging fit into your overall funnel strategy?

  o Do you need to drive conversions, engagement or trust?

- You need to assess whether you have adequate **tools and resources** for building and maintaining a thriving private customer community.

  o Do you have the tools and resources to build and maintain a thriving private customer community?

  o Would a public-facing strategy (e.g. social media groups, campaigns or events) be more accessible and impactful for your brand right now?

- Take a moment to reflect on **your brand's personality**. Does it naturally lend itself to private, exclusive communities or more open, public spaces? Write down which approach feels more authentic to your brand and why.

  o Would your customers respond better to an exclusive, member-focused experience or a more inclusive, outward-facing community?

  o Are there opportunities to incorporate elements of both strategies, depending on your audience segments?

By reflecting on these questions, you can better align your approach with your brand's needs and goals. Whether you build belonging internally with loyal customers or outwardly to attract new ones, the key is to make every stage of the journey feel intentional and human.

Turning friction into engagement for user-generated content

Talking about building community, we have to address the elephant in the room. Because when you put your community in the spotlight, nothing happens unless someone is willing to get under those bright lights.

If your product requires some assembly or is customizable, chances are your customers would love to show off their handiwork. The key is making it easy – and rewarding – for them to share.

Take HelloFresh, for example. Their meal kits naturally lend themselves to Instagram-worthy posts and the brand encourages sharing in clever ways. They remind customers to tag the brand in their posts, often offering incentives like special discounts or affiliate opportunities.

It's a win–win: customers get recognized for their creations and HelloFresh benefits from authentic user-generated content. The results speak for themselves – to date, there are over 260,000 Instagram posts tagged with #hellofreshpics.[13]

A quarter of a million customers sharing their experience is the dream for many marketers, but how can we overcome common barriers to sharing? Whether it's effort, privacy concerns or perceived relevance, reducing friction is essential for encouraging your audience to amplify your brand.

Simplify the process and offer clear benefits

Make sharing as effortless as possible by providing tools like pre-written captions, branded hashtags or shareable templates. When customers don't have to overthink their posts, they're more likely to hit 'share'.

Seeing others share often inspires action. Highlight posts from your community or celebrate user-generated milestones. Peloton excels at this, showcasing users' workouts and achievements to motivate others.[14]

Customization boosts the likelihood of sharing. Personalized experiences or campaigns, like Peloton plans, invite customers to share their journey in a way that feels authentic and meaningful, which helped them achieve an almost unheard-of 95 per cent retention rate, which they call Connected Fitness Subscribers, while maintaining a monthly churn rate of 0.65 per cent.[15]

Create moments worth sharing

Sometimes friction isn't about effort – it's about relevance. Focus on creating memorable experiences that people *want* to share, like Spotify's personalized Wrapped playlists or the ALS Ice Bucket Challenge.[16] The key is to make participation irresistible.

Give your audience an actual reason to share. Rewards like discounts, exclusive content or chances to be featured on your platform can tip the scale. For example, Starbucks' Red Cup Contest invited users to share photos of their festive drinks for a chance to be highlighted on the brand's social channels.[17]

As you do that, do not forget to reassure your audience about how their content will be used. Transparency builds trust, making them more comfortable sharing. By reducing barriers and creating opportunities for seamless sharing, you can turn your audience into advocates who are excited to amplify your message. Just like HelloFresh, the right mix of incentives and community spirit can transform everyday actions into awareness for your brand.

REAL-WORLD EXAMPLE
LEGO's customer community approach

It's the late 1990s and LEGO, the beloved toy of countless childhoods, is struggling. The once-iconic brand is facing financial challenges, grappling with a world of video games and digital distractions pulling kids away from building bricks.

LEGO needs a way to reconnect – not just with kids, but with their most passionate fans. Enter LEGO Mindstorms, a robotics kit launched in 1998. It was meant for kids, a bold move into tech-savvy play.[18] But something unexpected happened: adults loved it. And something even more unexpected happened. A flock of engineers and tinkering enthusiasts started hacking the kit, pushing its capabilities far beyond what LEGO had envisioned (oh hello, IKEA Effect call-back).

LEGO could have fought back, tightening control over their product. Instead, they leaned in. They saw the passion of these Adult Fans of LEGO (AFOLs) and recognized an opportunity by also riding on the nostalgia.

It's no wonder, then, that LEGO has become a masterclass in building customer communities. From inspiring young builders to fostering a passionate global network of Adult Fans of LEGO (AFOLs), the brand has perfected the art of turning customers into co-creators.

In the original IKEA Effect study, participants didn't just assemble IKEA boxes – they also built LEGO sets, further confirming the increased valuation of self-assembled items.[19] So, it's no surprise that LEGO's community is one of the most beloved and studied examples of customer-driven engagement. It's an example we often use in our certification and courses to illustrate the power of fostering belonging through co-creation and collaboration.[20]

Here are some elements that make the LEGO community so impactful:

- **LEGO empowers its fans to become co-creators** through initiatives like *LEGO Ideas*. This platform allows enthusiasts to submit their own designs, which the community can vote on. Winning ideas are turned into official LEGO sets, giving fans the unique opportunity to see their creations come to life. This not only fuels creativity but also deepens emotional investment in the brand.

- **LEGO actively showcases the creations of its community members**, whether through social media campaigns, exhibitions or dedicated spaces on their website. By celebrating fan projects, LEGO reinforces the idea that their customers are contributors to their movement.

- **LEGO understands the power of storytelling** and amplifies the voices of its fans. Whether it's a child's imaginative play session or an AFOL's intricate build, LEGO turns these stories into campaigns that inspire and unite the community. By doing so, they position their customers as the heroes of their brand story.

By embracing their community's creativity and passion, LEGO created a model for customer-driven growth that continues to inspire brands today. Their success shows that when brands trust their community and give them space to create, share and connect, to create lasting relationships that naturally amplify their message.

Ways to foster belonging beyond community

You're sitting at a new restaurant, flipping through the menu. Everything sounds incredible and you're stuck in a classic dilemma – steak or pasta? Risotto or scallops? Your dining partner orders confidently, but you're still lost in the choices.

Just as you're about to blurt out a random pick, the waiter leans in and says with a smile, *'The truffle pasta is our most popular dish. Almost everyone orders it.'*

That's it. Decision made. You close the menu and say, *'I'll have the truffle pasta too.'*

Why? Because if it's the most popular dish, it *must* be the best, right? Surely all those people can't be wrong. Even if you'd never considered truffle pasta before, the crowd's choice convinces you it's the right one.

This is the **Bandwagon Effect** in action – the psychological phenomenon where we're drawn to something simply because others like it. The popularity of the dish gives it an allure, making it feel like the safest (and tastiest) option.[21] When your plate arrives, you dive in, savouring every bite – partly because it's good and partly because it feels like you're in on the crowd's secret.

For marketers, the Bandwagon Effect is a powerful tool. Whether it's highlighting 'best sellers' or showcasing glowing reviews, it's about creating that moment of trust through popularity. Because, let's face it, who doesn't want to be part of what everyone's loving?

Building belonging and driving awareness often go hand-in-hand – as people are more likely to engage with something when they see others doing the same, creating a ripple of connection and shared experience.

The truth is, we experience the Bandwagon Effect all the time.

For example, during my daily meditation with the Headspace app, I once noticed something new – I was not, well, 'alone'. A small feature in the app showed how many people were meditating at the same time as me. It was a simple addition, but it completely changed how I felt about the experience. Meditation, which often feels like a solitary practice, suddenly became a shared moment.

Headspace integrates the Bandwagon Effect seamlessly, reminding users that they're part of something bigger – a global movement toward mindfulness and well-being. This feature not only improves the user experience but also mitigates feelings of isolation, creating a subtle yet impactful sense of community.

Other examples of the Bandwagon Effect:

- Leaderboards showing users how they rank against others in real-time during workouts can motivate them to push harder, as well as showing up for a specific class, even online.

- Platforms like GoFundMe or Kickstarter use social proof to drive engagement by showing how many people have donated or backed a project to create momentum.

- Apps like Duolingo motivate users to maintain their learning streaks and compete with others in their league. Seeing thousands of people actively engaging in language learning fosters a 'we're all in this together' mentality, encouraging users to stay consistent and keep learning.

Now, the Bandwagon Effect is powerful and has a huge impact on our behaviour. It can even sway elections. One study found that seeing polls increased votes for majority options by 7 per cent, regardless of electoral systems or political attitudes.[22]

Beyond products, in the context of social media and online platforms, the Bandwagon Effect is particularly evident as posts with higher engagement (likes, comments, shares) are more likely to receive additional interaction, as users are influenced by these popularity cues. Even more so, user-generated content (UGC) is a great example of leveraging the bandwagon effect by providing social proof, which encourages others to follow suit. When consumers see real people enjoying a product or service (may them be creators, fellow customers or employees), it taps into the Bandwagon Effect, making others more inclined to believe in the product's quality and value.

But for UGC to truly stand out and really embody the customer-driven approach, I encourage you (as I often do in this book) to take a bolder swing – embrace the willingness to lean into meaningful, sometimes under-represented, conversations.

Take Currys, for example. In a standout campaign, the brand collaborated with disabled influencers to highlight the accessibility features of their stores and products. In 2024, Currys partnered with disability marketing agency Purple Goat to launch two innovative campaigns: Currys No Worries and Currys Tech Hacks.[23]

Through social media, they showcased disabled influencers demonstrating store accessibility features and product capabilities. The campaign not only generated positive community feedback but also established Currys as a leader in inclusive tech retail.

By showcasing authentic experiences from members of the disabled community, it validated its commitment to inclusivity. This approach resonated with both disabled and non-disabled audiences alike, proving that UGC can create a powerful sense of trust and belonging while championing important conversations.

This social validation reassures potential customers and gives them confidence in the brand – which in turn builds trust, our old friend.

Ways to get customers to jump on the bandwagon

You are walking across the busy streets of your city and you come across a stunning sunset photo on a billboard. It's not from a professional photographer or a high-end camera – you almost double-take as this picture is yours and it was shot on your iPhone. Yet the picture is now out there, for millions of busy city dwellers to admire every day.

This is exactly what Apple achieved with their #ShotoniPhone campaign, originally launched in 2015.[24]

By inviting users to share their iPhone photography, Apple transformed everyday customers into brand ambassadors while highlighting the broader community's artistic potential. The genius wasn't just in showcasing the iPhone's camera capabilities – it was in making everyone feel like they could be part of something bigger.

The campaign perfectly illustrates how putting your community in the spotlight can create powerful ripples of engagement and awareness. When brands give their users a platform to shine, magic happens.

Here are several effective ways to amplify your community's voice:

- **Customer advisory boards (CAB):** Create an exclusive group of power users who provide regular feedback and shape product direction. Highlight their involvement in marketing materials to demonstrate your commitment to customer-driven development.
- **Social proof popups:** Use tools like Proof to show real-time user activity ('Sarah from London just signed up', '50 people viewing this course'). These micro-moments of social proof build trust through visibility.

- **Waitlist management:** Transform fear of missing out (FOMO) into engagement by showcasing waitlist numbers ('Join 5,000+ others waiting for access') and offering priority access for referrals. Tools like Viral Loops can gamify this process.

- **Customer success stories:** Create dedicated spaces for users to share their achievements and implementation stories. Consider a Wall of Love using tools like Senja.

- **Ambassador programmes:** Develop structured programmes for loyal customers to become brand ambassadors, complete with special badges, early access to features and opportunities to contribute to product education.

- **Co-creation workshops:** Host regular virtual or in-person sessions where customers can collaborate on new features or improvements, then highlight these sessions in your marketing.

- **User badges and recognition:** Implement a system of badges or titles that recognize different types of community contributions – from helpful forum responses to feature suggestions that get implemented.

The key is to make these visible and accessible, creating multiple touchpoints where both existing and potential customers can see the community around your product.

REFLECTION TIME
Expand your circle

You didn't think we were going to finish this chapter without exploring ways you can make belonging work for you and your brand, as part of a customer-driven strategy? Let's pause for a moment and reflect on how your brand can foster belonging and grow your circle.

First things first:

- How does your brand already create belonging?

- Is it through a buzzing customer community, a killer campaign or personalized moments that make people feel seen?

- Whatever it is, take a moment to celebrate what's working. You're already doing something right – how can you amplify it?

Your community is more than your audience – it's your biggest advocate. Think about:

- Are you telling their stories? Sharing their wins?

- How can you turn testimonials, UGC or loyalty milestones into social proof that attracts new fans?
- What does your community have to say that could spark connections with new audiences?

Here's your challenge: Write down one way your brand creates belonging today. List three ways to highlight your community and make it the star of your outward messaging.

Belonging as a tool for awareness and trust

TIP

Do not shy away from the conversations that matter. When done thoughtfully, they build trust and awareness in ways that resonate far beyond the product.

As this chapter has explored, belonging can be a powerful strategy at every stage of the customer journey. Whether you're co-creating with your audience, leveraging nostalgia or amplifying community stories, the key is authenticity. When people feel like they're part of something bigger – something meaningful – they're more likely to engage, advocate and stay loyal.

Once you start exploring belonging, you may be surprised by how it can be so much more than connection – for example, it can be about embracing the complexities of human relationships and using those moments to build something meaningful.

In times of divisiveness, brands that use belonging to boldly create spaces for understanding and connection can make a lasting impact. Heineken's Worlds Apart campaign is a great example of this approach.[25]

Heineken went beyond the surface to explore human differences, openness and resolution. Partnering with The Human Library, an organization that challenges prejudice through personal stories, they facilitated honest conversations between individuals with opposing worldviews – from transgender rights to climate change. The campaign acted as a case study in human behaviour, showing how connection can overcome division.

What made this campaign resonate so deeply was its commitment to doing the work. Heineken consulted experts, conducted research and approached sensitive topics with care and authenticity. By prioritizing openness and real resolutions, the brand showcased the power of belonging in bringing people together.

I am ending this chapter by extending an invitation for you, one about not shying away from the conversations that matter. If you're stepping into sensitive territory, do the research, consult experts and partner with organizations that align with your mission. When done thoughtfully, these efforts build trust and awareness in ways that resonate far beyond the product.

The challenge for marketers is to consistently nurture belonging in ways that feel genuine, inclusive and human. The reward is a community that doesn't just support your brand but believes in it.

KEY POINTS

- Belonging taps into the universal human need for connection, making it a powerful driver of brand awareness and loyalty.
- Nostalgia strengthens emotional connections, fostering belonging by evoking cherished memories and shared cultural experiences.
- Building community can begin internally with loyal customers or outwardly with broader audiences, leveraging user-generated content and social proof.
- The IKEA Effect shows that people value what they've helped create, highlighting the importance of inviting customers to co-create or feel ownership in your brand.
- People are more likely to engage with something when they see others doing it, creating a ripple effect of connection and shared experiences.
- Memes, storytelling and inclusive campaigns like Heineken's Worlds Apart demonstrate how brands can spark meaningful connections and tackle important conversations.
- Authenticity is key – fostering belonging requires thoughtful, genuine engagement that resonates with your audience's values and experiences.

TOOLS

- Feature request tools: Canny – canny.io
- Product management: ProductBoard – www.productboard.com
- Social proof tool: Proof – useproof.com
- Waitlist management: Viral Loops – viral-loops.com
- Customer testimonials: Senja – www.senja.io

Notes

1 M I Norton, D Mochon and D Ariely. The IKEA effect: When labour leads to love, *Journal of Consumer Psychology*, 2012, 22 (3), 453–60

2 M I Norton, D Mochon and D Ariely. The IKEA effect: When labour leads to love, *Journal of Consumer Psychology*, 2012, 22 (3), 453–60

3 R Alexander. How child-free 'Disney adults' are transforming the company's theme parks as Disney pours $60 billion into the division, Business Insider, September 2023. www.businessinsider.com/why-disney-parks-top-destinations-millennials-gen-z-2023-9 (archived at https://perma.cc/S56C-KR3M)

4 Bain Insights. The digital marketing lesson of 'Pokémon GO', Forbes, 6 September 2016. www.forbes.com/sites/baininsights/2016/09/06/the-digital-marketing-lesson-of-pokemon-go/ (archived at https://perma.cc/7BEV-JZX3)

5 J Lasaleta, C Sedikides and K Vohs. Nostalgia weakens the desire for money, *Journal of Consumer Research*, 2014, 41, 713–29. doi.org/10.1086/677227 (archived at https://perma.cc/Y9HW-AZUY)

6 Independent. *Gilmore Girls* fan favorite couple reunites for Walmart holiday ad: 'Full circle moment', *Independent*, 2024. www.independent.co.uk/arts-entertainment/tv/news/gilmore-girls-walmart-commercial-2024-b2658247.html (archived at https://perma.cc/XA35-8SRJ)

7 A Benveniste. The meaning and history of memes. *The New York Times*, 14 February 2022. www.nytimes.com/2022/01/26/crosswords/what-is-a-meme.html (archived at https://perma.cc/FVK5-QMUM)

8 Wendy's. TFW yo beef's still frozen, Twitter, 8 May 2018. x.com/Wendys/status/993898832156078080 (archived at https://perma.cc/3KHQ-8UEP)

9 J Jonker. Newsjacking: the Guide. Definitions, examples and all you need to know, PRLab, 13 November 2024. prlab.co/blog/guide-newsjacking-with-examples/ (archived at https://perma.cc/ZV49-PZB6)

10   Fashion United. ASOS relaunches influencer programme with employees, Fashion United, 1 March 2024. fashionunited.uk/news/business/asos-relaunches-influencer-programme-with-employees/2024030174378 (archived at https://perma.cc/KCR3-YU9G)

11   SheerLuxe. Profile, TikTok, nd. www.tiktok.com/@sheerluxe (archived at https://perma.cc/PB6Z-ZX32)

12   The Perfume Shop. Profile, TikTok, nd. www.tiktok.com/@theperfumeshop (archived at https://perma.cc/G6PW-CVR8)

13   R Leach. User-generated content examples, Stellar Content, 20 March 2024. www.stellarcontent.com/blog/content-marketing/user-generated-content-examples (archived at https://perma.cc/XS25-ZHEP)

14   Tactic One. Peloton: A masterclass in personalization, community and growth, Tactic One, 20 December 2024. www.tacticone.co/blog/peloton-personalization-community-and-growth (archived at https://perma.cc/4GD8-CSFY)

15   S Farrell. Peloton marketing strategy: Uncovering key lessons for rapid growth, NoGood Blog, 14 January 2022. nogood.io/2022/01/14/peloton-marketing-strategy (archived at https://perma.cc/2V3G-WKUJ)

16   W Davis. The Ice Bucket Challenge wasn't just for social media. It helped fund a new ALS drug, NPR, 1 October 2022. www.npr.org/2022/10/01/1126397565/the-ice-bucket-challenge-wasnt-just-for-social-media-it-helped-fund-a-new-als-dr (archived at https://perma.cc/D6WA-DKBF)

17   J Hostetter. How Starbucks' red cup became a holiday marketing icon, Neon Supply, 8 November 2024. blog.neonsupply.com/how-starbucks-red-cup-became-holiday-marketing-icon (archived at https://perma.cc/7Z42-B6PH)

18   J V Knudstorp. LEGO CEO Jørgen Vig Knudstorp on leading through survival and growth, *Harvard Business Review*, January 2009. hbr.org/2009/01/lego-ceo-jorgen-vig-knudstorp-on-leading-through-survival-and-growth (archived at https://perma.cc/4RNV-Y8AG)

19   M I Norton, D Mochon and D Ariely. The IKEA effect: When labor leads to love, Harvard Business School, 2012. https://www.hbs.edu/ris/Publication%20Files/11-091.pdf (archived at https://perma.cc/A82R-FBZH)

20   Harvard Business Review. Turn your customers into your community, *Harvard Business Review*, January 2020. hbr.org/2020/01/turn-your-customers-into-your-community (archived at https://perma.cc/7A4L-J9GW)

21   S Bindra, D Sharma, N Parameswar, S Dhir and J Paul. Bandwagon effect revisited: A systematic review to develop future research agenda, *Journal of Business Research*, 2022, 143, 305–17. www.sciencedirect.com/science/article/pii/S0148296322000972 (archived at https://perma.cc/HQ6Q-5BT7)

22   M Farjam. The bandwagon effect in an online voting experiment with real political organizations, *International Journal of Public Opinion Research*, 2021, 33 (2), 412–21. academic.oup.com/ijpor/article/33/2/412/5857291 (archived at https://perma.cc/KR5E-REMG)

23 Purple Goat Agency. Currys, Purple Goat Agency, 2024. www.purplegoatagency. com/case-studies/currys-marketing-campaign/ (archived at https://perma.cc/ 4PCM-B4VP)

24 The Brand Hopper. A case study on Apple's 'Shot on iPhone' brand campaign, The Brand Hopper, 7 January 2024. thebrandhopper.com/2024/01/07/a-case-study-on-apples-shot-on-iphone-brand-campaign/ (archived at https:// perma.cc/A3FY-DFRC)

25 Edelman. Heineken: Worlds apart, Edelman, 2017. Edelman. www.edelman. com/work/heineken-worlds-apart (archived at https://perma.cc/J94B-97QQ)

07

Building emotional connections through personalization

> **REMINDER**
>
> The beauty of personalization lies in its intention. It's about showing your customers that you're listening, that you care and that you're here to make their lives better, one interaction at a time.

It's a busy Monday morning at your local Starbucks. The aroma of fresh coffee fills the air and the sound of steaming milk punctuates the hum of conversation. You shuffle forward in line, groggy but determined, rehearsing your order in your head: *'Grande caramel macchiato.'* When you finally reach the counter, the barista greets you with a warm smile and asks for your name. A quick scribble on your cup later, your name is announced and you grab your drink.

We are so used to see this that we almost take it for granted, but the seemingly simple act of writing names on cups wasn't always a Starbucks staple. It started in 2012, but its roots trace back to one single moment behind the counter, one that would forever change how we experience our morning brew.

Starbucks was already a global coffee giant by the early 2010s, known for its consistent quality and cosy cafe atmosphere. But, as the company expanded, it faced a challenge: maintaining a personal touch in an increasingly transactional environment.

Enter the humble name on the cup.

The idea began in 2012 with a single barista who scribbled a customer's name on a cup to ensure accuracy and speed up the process.[1]

Recognizing the potential of this simple act, Starbucks officially rolled out the practice globally that same year. The decision to personalize coffee cups tapped into deeper psychological motivations.

When customers see their name on a cup, it subconsciously feels like their own mug.[2] But here's where things get even more interesting: the names weren't always correct.

Baristas, juggling long lines and endless orders, occasionally misheard or misspelled names. A 'Sarah' might leave with a cup that said 'Cera', or a 'Mark' might find himself mysteriously transformed into 'Shark'.

What started as a simple way to personalize your morning coffee has transformed into a bit of a Russian roulette of sorts, connecting customers with countless others through shared laughter and the simple question: *'I wonder what my name will be today?'*[3]

The humour added an unexpected layer to the campaign. In fact, customers began sharing photos of their 'creative' names on social media, turning Starbucks cups into viral sensations and starting to create relatable moments of belonging. Not only did personalization work, but it also added a whole new layer of personality to the brand.

Sometimes, the smallest gestures have the biggest impact. In a world that's often impersonal, adding a name to a cup can remind someone that they matter.

The psychology behind personalization

Have you ever noticed that you value something more because it's yours?

If you peeked into my wardrobe, you'd find an entire shelf dedicated to one thing: T-shirts. Not just any T-shirts, mind you – band T-shirts. I've got over 30 of them, a mix of concert souvenirs, limited-edition designs and free swag from events. Some are faded, some don't fit quite right anymore and some I haven't worn in a while.

But here's the thing – I cannot part with one.

Each T-shirt holds a story. That AC/DC tee? It's from the first concert my husband and I went to together; the night I screamed every lyric until my voice gave out. Every time I try to declutter, I hold one up, remember the moment and think, *'How could I ever let this go?'*

Turns out, my inability to part with these tees is tied with (surprise, surprise) behavioural science. It's called the **Endowment Effect** and it's a phenomenon discovered by Daniel Kahneman and his research team.[4] They found that once we own something, we value it far more than its objective worth simply because it's ours.

In one famous study, undergraduates at Cornell University were given a simple mug. They were then offered the chance to trade it for something of equal value. But ownership changed everything. Once the students had the mug in their hands, the price they'd demand to give it up doubled.[5]

Ownership transforms value. It's why I hold onto T-shirts that, to anyone else, might look like nothing special. Marketers know this too. Once something feels uniquely yours, it becomes harder to let go.

The Endowment Effect: Why we value what feels personal

Personalization works because it taps into something deeply human – our desire to feel seen, understood and valued. But what makes it so powerful? The answer lies in psychology. When done well, personalization connects with our emotions, rewires how we perceive value and strengthens our ties to a brand. The Endowment Effect explains why people place higher value on things they perceive as 'theirs'.[6]

The classic example? Customizing a product. Think about the excitement of designing your own pair of sneakers or, like we mentioned at the beginning of the chapter, seeing your name on a Starbucks cup. That sense of ownership creates a deeper emotional bond, making the experience more memorable – and the brand more meaningful.

Personalization leverages this by allowing customers to feel like active participants in their journey with a brand and when done prior to the ownership stage, it allows audiences to feel better seen and catered for by a brand – think content segmentation and beyond.

But it goes deeper than that.

The role of dopamine in personalization

Have you ever had a craving for a scoop of creamy, velvety ice cream – maybe your favourite pistachio or a classic stracciatella? You can almost taste it, imagine the chill on your tongue and feel the satisfaction of that first bite. That anticipation is the dopamine kicking in, driving your motivation.

Now imagine heading to the freezer, only to find the ice cream tub empty. The disappointment would be sharp – not just because you're out of ice cream, but because your brain's dopamine cycle has been interrupted.

Instead of reaching the satisfaction phase, your craving intensifies and you're now more motivated than ever to find a way to indulge in that ice cream – perhaps even planning a trip to your favourite gelateria.

This is the **Dopamine Effect** in action and it plays a huge role in human decision-making, even marketing.[7]

Dopamine is the brain's 'feel-good' neurotransmitter, released whenever we anticipate or experience something rewarding. Whether it's indulging in your favourite dessert, receiving a surprise gift or snagging a deal on an item you love, dopamine fuels the cycle of motivation, satisfaction and reinforcement.

In marketing, this cycle is a powerful tool. When a personalized experience – like an offer on a product you've been eyeing or an email greeting you by name with tailored recommendations – meets your expectations, dopamine creates what we call 'purchase pleasure'. It forges a positive emotional bond with the brand, reinforcing loyalty and increasing the likelihood of repeat interactions.

But the reverse is also true. If a personalized experience falls short – say the product isn't available or the personalization feels insincere – it can lead to disappointment, dampening your mood and negatively impacting your perception of the brand.

Research published in *Frontiers of Psychology* shows that customers who make purchases aligning with their personal goals experience higher rates of pleasure.[8] Whether it's through exclusive discounts, tailored recommendations or even simply using a customer's name authentically, the key lies in meeting – and exceeding – their expectations.

Now, let's talk chocolate – and not just any chocolate, but Cadbury, the iconic chocolatier beloved across the globe. In 2014, Cadbury used personalization to transform a simple indulgence into a tailored experience that left customers craving more.[9] The campaign, launched in Australia, invited users to connect their Facebook profiles to a custom video generator. By analysing their age, interests and location – and even incorporating their personal photos – Cadbury crafted unique videos that matched each user with their perfect Dairy Milk flavour.

The result was a 65 per cent click-through rate and an impressive 33.6 per cent conversion rate.

The genius of this campaign wasn't just in using personal data to create a custom experience, but in tapping into the joy of discovery. By personalizing something as simple as a chocolate bar, Cadbury amplified the anticipation, satisfaction and reinforcement that keep customers coming back for more – with a nice boost of dopamine to sweeten the deal.

This is the magic of pairing dopamine with personalization. Whether it's a tailored offer, a well-timed recommendation or a fun, interactive experience like Cadbury's, the combination creates an emotional connection that elevates the brand and deepens customer loyalty.

By understanding the psychology behind personalization – from the dopamine-driven joy of tailored experiences to the deep emotional connections forged through reflective identity – we see why it goes far beyond a name in an email.

From a simple *'Hi [name]'* to dynamic, real-time interactions, the levels of personalization range from the basic to the hyper-advanced. Each approach has its place in the customer journey and knowing when (and how) to use them is where the real strategy lies.

The levels of personalization

What does personalization feel like in our day-to-day, anyway? Look no further than on your streaming habits for an answer.

Take Billie, for example. They sign up for a new streaming service, excited to dive into a world of movies and shows. Within minutes, an email lands in their inbox:

'Hi Billie, welcome! Check out our trending movies.'

It's a nice touch – a simple yet personal way to kick things off. Billie feels noticed and that's always a good start. A few days later, another email arrives. This time, it's more specific:

'Hi Billie, as a fan of action films, you'll love *Mission: Impossible*. Check it out tonight!'

Billie grins. Action films are their thing and this recommendation feels tailored to them. Fast forward to the weekend. Billie logs into the streaming service and the homepage greets them with even more personalized picks:

'Since you watched *Mission: Impossible*, you might enjoy these spy thrillers…'.

The list is spot-on. It's like the platform gets them. Billie dives into a movie marathon, but (wait for it) the real magic happens a week later. It's Saturday evening and Billie is craving a cosy night in. As they open the app, a curated playlist greets them:

'Billie, ready for your Saturday night in? Start with *Skyfall*, followed by *The Bourne Identity*. Don't forget the popcorn!'

The list feels like a gift – perfectly timed, perfectly tailored and perfectly Billie. It even includes options that fit their usual Saturday viewing window and films they've rated highly in the past.

These are the different ways personalization can shape a customer's experience with a brand.

In today's digitally world, customers expect brands to truly know them – their preferences, needs and aspirations. Anything less than that can feel generic and out of touch. So, yeah, personalized email tags (once all the rage of personalization) are now simply not enough to wow your audience.

And here's why it matters: research shows that 71 per cent of consumers expect personalized experiences when engaging with companies, and nearly half of them say they're more likely to stay loyal to a brand when those expectations are met.[10] In fact, brands that prioritize personalization can see a 40 per cent boost in revenue compared to competitors who fall short.[11] Yet achieving effective personalization is easier said than done. While 70 per cent of companies claim it's a top priority, only a fraction are implementing it in ways that truly resonate.[12]

This is why we need to move beyond the basics and explore the full spectrum of personalization. As we'll see in this chapter, when layered effectively, personalization can evolve into something transformative. We'll follow Billie's journey, demonstrating how each level builds on the last to create a truly immersive streaming experience.

Basic personalization

Basic personalization is the foundation of any personalized marketing strategy. It involves simple yet effective touches like addressing a customer by their name in an email, tailoring content to general preferences or acknowledging basic interactions like sign-ups or first purchases.

When Billie signed up for the streaming service, the platform sent a welcome email:

'Hi Billie, welcome! Check out our trending movies.'

This is a classic example of basic personalization. While it doesn't dive into Billie's specific preferences, it acknowledges their presence and extends a friendly introduction to the platform.

It's a solid start – approachable, easy to execute and sets the tone for more personalized interactions down the line. Although Billie isn't yet blown away, they feel noticed, which lays the foundation for a richer personalized experience.

You may recognize some of these examples:

- Adding the customer's name to email subject lines or greetings: *'Hi Billie, welcome to our platform!'*
- Sending welcome emails or introductory offers after sign-ups.
- Highlighting trending products, movies or services to encourage initial engagement.

This level of personalization has its advantages. It's approachable and easy to implement, requiring minimal tools or data. For brands just starting their personalization journey, it's a perfect entry point to show customers they're noticed and appreciated. Even something as simple as using someone's name in an email or sending them a friendly welcome message can help build that initial connection. While it might not be mind-blowing, it's like saying 'hello' when someone walks into your shop – it sets the tone for everything that follows.

However, there are some things to watch out for. Basic personalization can feel generic if it doesn't go beyond surface-level details. While it might have been impressive a decade ago, customers today expect more meaningful interactions.

And getting things wrong (like misspelling someone's name or sending them irrelevant suggestions) can do more harm than good. Think of basic personalization as your starting point, not your end game – it's about building up to those deeper, more meaningful connections over time.

Segmented personalization

Segmented personalization takes things a step further by grouping customers into categories based on shared traits, behaviours or interests. It's a strategic way to deliver more targeted experiences without trying to personalize for everyone from the start.

This is where, a few days after signing up, Billie receives an email, this time tailored to their love of action films:

> 'Hi Billie, as a fan of action films, you'll love *Mission: Impossible*. Check it out tonight!'

By tapping into Billie's interest in action movies, the platform makes its messaging more engaging and relevant.

This step illustrates the power of segmentation done right – specific enough to resonate without being overly complicated. Billie feels a stronger connection to the platform, as it begins to reflect their preferences.

Effective segmentation often starts with a focus on key areas like customer purchase behaviour, defined roles or personal interests. In essence, it starts with looking at the key things that make your customers tick – what they buy, who they are and what they're into. When you get these groups right, your messages just make more sense to people.

Common segments to get started with include:

- **Purchase behaviour:** Identifying frequent buyers or specific product categories.

- **Defined roles:** Creating campaigns for different customer profiles (e.g. new users, returning subscribers).

- **Interests:** Catering to preferences like film genres, hobbies or lifestyle choices.

The beauty of segmentation lies in its versatility. But, at the same time, it presents a Goldilocks conundrum: you don't want to go overboard and slice your audience into tiny pieces (that just gets messy), but you also don't want to be too basic about it. It's kind of like finding that sweet spot – not too hot, not too cold, just right.

When you nail it, everything flows together nicely and your campaigns feel like they're speaking to real people. A well-segmented strategy layers customer insights thoughtfully, creating campaigns that feel cohesive rather than fragmented.

Dynamic personalization

Dynamic personalization takes the concept of tailoring customer experiences to the next level by adapting in real-time. It's no longer just about understanding past behaviours or broad preferences – it's about being responsive to what the customer is doing right now.

From adjusting website content to sending triggered emails or predictive recommendations, dynamic personalization ensures that every interaction feels timely and relevant. This is the moment in which Billie decides to log back into the streaming platform. As soon as they open the homepage, they're greeted with a curated list of personalized recommendations:

'Since you watched *Mission: Impossible*, you might enjoy these spy thrillers...'

The platform highlights titles like *Skyfall* and *The Bourne Identity*, alongside a mix of similar films. This really shows what dynamic personalization can do – it feels natural, responds to what you want and keeps Billie coming back for more.

Common examples:

- Adjusting homepage content based on the user's browsing history or location
- Sending follow-ups or abandoned cart reminders based on a customer's actions (or inaction).
- Suggesting products, services or content based on behavioural patterns.

This approach has a lot going for it. By responding to a customer's immediate context, brands can create moments of delight that feel thoughtful and engaging. When brands can respond to what customers are doing right now, they can create these special moments that just feel right.

Think about it – you open an app and here they are, recommendations that totally match what you're into. And with all the fancy tech behind it (we're talking advanced analytics and machine learning here), brands can refine their messaging and deliver more precise recommendations over time.

However, dynamic personalization isn't without its challenges. Timing is everything – a poorly timed recommendation or irrelevant adjustment can feel intrusive and counterproductive. And there's a sweet spot between being helpful and being that overeager friend who won't stop sending suggestions.

Plus, this kind of personalization needs the right tech tools. We're talking machine learning, predictive analytics, the whole nine yards. That can be expensive and complicated, especially for smaller businesses. But here's the good news: as technology keeps getting better, these tools are becoming more affordable and easier to use. So, more and more brands can start giving their customers that personalized touch.

Hyper-personalization

Hyper-personalization represents the pinnacle of tailored customer experiences. It goes beyond traditional segmentation or dynamic adjustments, using advanced AI and machine learning to deliver interactions that feel uniquely crafted for each individual. At this level, personalization becomes almost intuitive, creating an experience so seamless it feels like magic.

Common examples:

- Platforms like Netflix's Because You Watched feature, using vast data points to create highly individualized experiences.[13]

- Personalized push notifications or messages based on live customer behaviour, such as location or recent app usage.
- Tailoring discounts or bundles specific to individual customer preferences and behaviours.
- Using augmented reality (AR) or virtual reality (VR) to create personalized environments, such as custom interior designs or virtual try-ons.

Hyper-personalization can be amazing. When you nail it, you're creating experiences that really speak to each customer. It's like having a superpower that helps your brand stand out from the crowd and keeps people coming back for more.

But here's the thing – it's not all smooth sailing. You need some serious tech muscle to make it work, plus you've got to handle all that customer data carefully and ethically. Being upfront about how you're using people's information is super important. And let's not forget that setting up these fancy systems isn't cheap or easy – which is why you typically see bigger companies with deep pockets leading the charge in this space.

From simple greetings to curated playlists, personalization comes in many forms, each building on the last to create richer, more meaningful customer experiences.

As we've seen through Billie's story, when personalization is done right, it becomes a relationship-builder that transforms customer interactions into memorable, loyalty-driving moments.

But I hear you saying, *'Fab, what about other stages of my customer journey, when my customer is, well, not yet a customer?'* Don't you worry, I've got you covered.

Building personalization into the customer journey

Do you think personalization is all about keeping your customers and attracting new ones? Well, think again. Sometimes the most impactful moments of personalization happen when a customer is about to leave.

You've been a loyal customer of a veg box delivery service for years. Every week, a box of fresh, organic produce arrives at your door and it's become a small joy in your routine. But now, life's pulling you in a different direction – maybe you're moving, maybe your circumstances have changed – and it's time to cancel your subscription.

It's bittersweet. You let the company know, half-expecting a generic farewell email or a quick *'Thanks and goodbye'*. Instead, something surprising happens.

A few days later, a package arrives at your doorstep. Inside is a bottle of wine – your favourite one, the one you'd often added to your orders. Along with it is a handwritten note:

> 'Thank you for being part of our journey. We'll miss delivering to you, but we hope this small token reminds you of the good times we've shared. All the best, The Team at Abel & Cole.'

You're floored. It's a gesture so small, yet so meaningful. In that moment, they're more than a company you've done business with – they're a brand that sees you, remembers you and values you.

Bronwen Foster Butler shared on LinkedIn the above story about her experience with Abel & Cole, a B Corp™ known for their veg box deliveries. The bottle of wine she received (one she sometimes ordered) was a small gesture, but it made a huge impact. By acknowledging her loyalty and adding a personal touch, they turned a goodbye into a moment she would remember – and maybe even talk about, as she did on LinkedIn.[14]

This thoughtful farewell was a brilliant example of how personalization can create lasting impressions. By showing appreciation for their customers, even at the end of a relationship, Abel & Cole boosted their reputation and left the door open for future loyalty.

In this section, we'll explore how personalization can be woven seamlessly into every step of the customer journey, ensuring that every interaction strengthens trust, builds emotional connections and leaves customers feeling truly valued.

Awareness stage: Speaking to pain points

The awareness stage is where it all begins. It's your first chance to show customers you get them – their challenges, their goals, their 'why'. Honestly, this ties back to everything we covered earlier in the book about understanding pain points.

Even if you don't have all the fancy tools for hyper-personalization just yet, you can still create a killer first impression by addressing what really matters to your audience. One of my favourite tricks at this stage is tracking behaviours on your website. Think about it: what pages are new visitors exploring? What products are they eyeing? This is pure gold for creating retargeting campaigns that build excitement.

Awareness is all about creating relevance early on, so you're not just another brand shouting into the void. When you make it personal, even in simple ways, customers are far more likely to stick around and see what else you've got.

Awareness quick wins:

- personalized ads tailored to demographic or behavioural data
- content that aligns with a user's search intent or interests

Consideration stage: Building interest

We already know this: by the time someone reaches this stage, they're already curious. Now it's your job to turn that curiosity into excitement. This is where you get to showcase what makes your product or service shine. The question to ask yourself is simple: how can I give buyers a taste of the experience before they commit?

Demos and immersive overviews are brilliant for this – they let your audience try before they buy, which builds trust and confidence. And let's not forget about quizzes! People love a good quiz (guilty as charged) and they're a fun, interactive way to guide potential customers.

We have one for students that helps them decide whether our certification is the right fit – it's a simple tool, but it makes the whole process feel personal and tailored.

At this stage, it's all about creating moments that feel less like 'sales' and more like *'Let me help you make the best decision for you.'* When you do that, your customers will thank you – and they'll probably buy too.

Consideration quick wins:

- retargeting campaigns to follow up on previous interactions
- product recommendations based on browsing history or preferences

Conversion stage: Driving action

Let's talk about Amazon Prime for a second. Love them or not, they've nailed one thing: using free trials to get new customers through the door month after month (even if their tactics can be a bit pushy). It's a genius move because a trial run is the ultimate risk-free way for buyers to experience a product or service without parting with their cash.[15]

But trials aren't the only way to seal the deal. Personalization can play a huge role here too, especially when it's tied to a sense of ownership. How do you increase ownership? You allow customers to put their mark on something – whether it's as simple as adding their name or as creative as customizing the entire product.

Ultimately, the conversion stage is about reducing risk, building trust and making the decision process feel effortless. Whether it's through trials, offers or creative personalization, the goal is the same: helping customers feel confident about saying yes.

Conversion quick wins:

- exclusive discounts or offers for first-time buyers
- personalized services and customizations
- personalized CTAs aligned with the customer's preferences or recent activity

Loyalty stage: Strengthening connections

Loyalty programmes are the secret sauce to keeping customers coming back for more. In fact, they don't just reward behaviour – they make customers feel like they're part of something bigger. This sense of belonging increases ownership, which then fuels loyalty and, ultimately, repeat purchases. It's a simple yet powerful formula: increase ownership, increase loyalty, increase spend.

Take the Costa Club, for example. I'm a proud member and I can tell you – those surprise rewards? I am a sucker for those. Whether it's an unexpected free coffee or a little treat 'just because', they keep the brand top of mind for me.

The beauty of loyalty programmes is in their versatility. They can be as simple as point systems or as elaborate as milestone rewards, but the key is making them personal. When customers see their loyalty being celebrated in a way that feels meaningful, the bond with your brand only grows stronger.

Loyalty quick wins:

- personalized birthday rewards or anniversary discounts
- emails celebrating customer milestones or thanking them for their continued support

Advocacy stage: Turning customers into champions

When it comes to advocacy, one of the most powerful strategies is to turn your customers into co-creators. Whether it's helping to design a product, naming a feature or contributing content, giving your advocates a voice makes them feel like an integral part of your journey (this is how I chose the cover for my first book).

Co-creation taps into a deep sense of ownership, turning already loyal customers into passionate champions. It's not just 'their favourite brand' anymore – it's their brand. And that emotional connection? It's marketing gold, driving word-of-mouth and creating advocates who will proudly spread the word.

Advocacy quick wins:

- reward programmes that recognize top customers
- highlighting loyal customers or user-generated content on your platforms

Every stage of the customer journey presents an opportunity to add personalization, creating moments that leave a lasting impression. Just remember there's no one-size-fits-all approach. Not every brand will have the tools for hyper-personalization or the resources to implement advanced loyalty programmes and that's okay.

What matters is finding ways to meet your customers where they are, showing them that they're more than just another name on a list. Truthfully, a little goes a long way.

REFLECTION TIME
Personalize the journey

Ready to take your personalization game to the next level? Here's your chance to get hands-on and map out exactly how you can weave personalization into every stage of the customer journey.

Start by listing the tools and distribution channels you're currently using for each stage of the journey. Think about everything from ads and emails to loyalty programmes and social media. Be specific – the more detailed your list, the easier it'll be to spot opportunities.

- What tools are you using to raise awareness of your brand?
- What channels or programmes are you using to engage loyal customers and advocates?

Once you've outlined your tools, it's time to think creatively. For each stage of the journey, ask yourself:

1   What's one simple thing I can do to make this more personalized and meaningful?

2   Could I tailor my messaging to a specific pain point?

3   Can I add an element of surprise, like a personalized reward or acknowledgment?

Write down one personalization idea for each tool or channel you've identified. Now that you've got your ideas, take a step back and rank them:

- Which personalization efforts are the most pressing or impactful right now?

- Which ones can wait until I've nailed the basics?

Start with the ideas that will create the biggest impression or solve the most immediate challenges.

Your challenge: once you've mapped everything out, commit to implementing at least one personalized touch this week. Remember, personalization doesn't have to be complicated or overwhelming – sometimes, the smallest gestures can make the biggest difference.

REAL-WORLD EXAMPLE
easyJet and turning data into memories

Imagine opening an email and finding your travel history brought to life. That's exactly what easyJet did in 2015 to celebrate its 20th anniversary. Their Personalized Travel Stories showcased passengers' unique journeys, blending nostalgia with inspiration for future adventures.

Each of the 12 million customers who received an email saw their personal story with easyJet unfold: their first flight, the total miles they'd flown (compared to landmarks like the Nile or the distance to the moon) and even personalized destination recommendations based on their travel history.[16]

It was a seamless blend of looking back and looking forward, creating emails that felt personal, meaningful and – most importantly – memorable.

The response to the campaign speaks for itself really. Open rates more than doubled and click-through rates were 25 per cent higher than easyJet's usual newsletters. Within 30 days, 7.5 per cent of recipients made a booking, with some markets reporting conversion rates nearly 14 times higher than standard promotional emails.[17]

On social media, the campaign reached an estimated 685,000 people, generating over 1.1 million impressions – and the word 'love' was the most frequently used in feedback.[18]

What made the campaign so impactful wasn't just the emotional storytelling but also the clever use of dynamic content. Every element of the email – from copy to images to links – was tailored to the recipient. Using a sophisticated model, easyJet analysed customer travel patterns and generated personalized recommendations for future trips.[19]

The beauty of this approach was how seamless it felt. And yes, you may be thinking that this was a very advanced campaign. Dynamic personalization at this scale requires robust data, sophisticated tools and significant resources – things not all of us can access. But that doesn't mean we can't take inspiration from easyJet's approach.

This campaign shows the power of creativity, especially during big milestones. By leveraging what you know about your customers and tying it to an emotional moment – like a brand anniversary or major achievement – you can create experiences that resonate deeply.

Even if you're not working with millions of data points, thoughtful storytelling and a focus on personal connection can go a long way.

With AI and data analytics getting smarter by the day, brands can now create experiences that feel truly tailored to each customer. It's amazing what's possible – we're talking about experiences that adapt and learn from every interaction. As these tools get more powerful, we need to be extra careful about protecting people's privacy. After all, customers are becoming savvier about their data.

Success lies in balancing technology with authenticity. Winning brands leverage advanced tools while maintaining human connection and understanding. The brands that nail this balance are the ones who prioritize ethical considerations in their personalization strategy. They ask themselves not just *'Can we do this?'* but *'Should we do this?'* and *'How would our customers feel about this?'* It's about showing respect for your audience while still delivering value through personalization.

The pitfalls of personalization

Personalization is powerful, but it's not without its challenges. But when it misses the mark, it can feel awkward, invasive or even tone-deaf. Here are some of the most common pitfalls in personalization and how to steer clear of them:

The privacy–personalization paradox

Customers love personalization until it crosses the line. There's a fine balance between helpful and creepy, and nothing breaks trust faster than a recommendation that feels a little too specific. Over-personalization can make customers feel like they're being watched instead of understood.

Transparency is your best friend here. Be upfront about how you're using customer data and give people control over their information. Focus on personalization that feels contextually relevant – not predictive to the point of discomfort.

Diversity and inclusion gaps

Personalization is only as good as the data and algorithms driving it, which means it's not immune to bias (especially if AI is involved). If your systems fail to account for diverse perspectives, your efforts to personalize could end up excluding or misrepresenting key parts of your audience.

I always talk about building inclusivity into your personalization process, for good reason. Regularly audit your algorithms and involve diverse voices in their development. Personalization should reflect the full spectrum of your customers' needs, values and identities.

Automation vs human touch

While automation is brilliant for efficiency, it's not a replacement for genuine connection. Over-relying on automated systems can strip away the warmth and authenticity that make personalization feel, well, personal. A way to avoid overreliance is to use automation for the heavy lifting – like analysing data or identifying trends – but keep the human touch front and centre. Whether it's a handwritten thank-you note or a heartfelt email, those moments of authenticity are what customers remember most.

Personalization isn't a 'set it and forget it' strategy. It's an ongoing process of understanding your audience, respecting their boundaries and finding ways to connect in ways that feel meaningful and true. Nail that balance and you'll create experiences your customers will never forget – for all the right reasons.

The beauty of personalization lies in its intention. It's about showing your customers that you're listening, that you care and that you're here to make their lives better, one interaction at a time. As clichéd as it sounds, like many things in this book, personalization is a journey, not a destination. Start where you are, with the tools and insights you have. Experiment, learn and most importantly, keep your customers at the heart of everything you do. Because when they feel seen, valued and understood, the impact goes far beyond the next sale – it's the kind of connection that keeps them coming back.

KEY POINTS

- When done right, personalized marketing creates meaningful relationships between brands and customers.

- People value things more when they feel a sense of ownership or personal connection to them.

- Successful personalization balances technological capabilities with authentic human touch.

- Brands must respect customer data and be transparent about how it's used.

- Emerging technologies like Web3 and AI are creating new possibilities for personalized experiences.

- The most successful personalization strategies find the sweet spot between automation and authentic human connection.

Notes

1   Starbucks Archive. On a first-name basis, Starbucks Archive, nd. archive. starbucks.com/record/on-a-first-name-basis

2   *The New Yorker*. The name on my coffee cup, *The New Yorker*, March 2015. www.newyorker.com/culture/culture-desk/the-name-on-my-coffee-cup (archived at https://perma.cc/3LSF-CXPT)

3   *Independent*. Starbucks brings back retro touch with hand-written names on cups, *Independent*, November 2024. www.independent.co.uk/life-style/starbucks-customer-names-cups-sharpie-nostalgia-b2642224.html (archived at https://perma.cc/PP9Q-2XPE)

4   D Kahneman, J L Knetsch and R H Thaler. Experimental tests of the endowment effect and the Coase theorem, *Journal of Political Economy*, 1990, 98 (6), 1325–48

5   D Kahneman, J L Knetsch and R H Thaler. Experimental tests of the endow-
    ment effect and the Coase theorem, *Journal of Political Economy*, 1990, 98 (6),
    1325–48

6   D Kahneman, J L Knetsch and R H Thaler. Experimental tests of the endow-
    ment effect and the Coase theorem, *Journal of Political Economy*, 1990, 98 (6),
    1325–48

7   S Zhao, P Chen, Y Zhu, F Wei and F Liu. Usage, pleasure, price and feeling: A study
    on shopping orientation and consumer outcome, *Frontiers in Psychology*, 2022, 13.
    www.frontiersin.org/journals/psychology/articles/10.3389/fpsyg.2022.823890/full
    (archived at https://perma.cc/7WLK-A8VH)

8   S Zhao, P Chen, Y Zhu, F Wei and F Liu. Usage, pleasure, price and feeling: A study
    on shopping orientation and consumer outcome, *Frontiers in Psychology*, 2022, 13.
    www.frontiersin.org/journals/psychology/articles/10.3389/fpsyg.2022.823890/full
    (archived at https://perma.cc/NC5M-WLEG)

9   M Barris. Cadbury's chocolate-matching campaign sweetens mobile strategy,
    Marketing Dive, nd. www.marketingdive.com/ex/mobilemarketer/cms/news/
    social-networks/19151.html (archived at https://perma.cc/6ACQ-QPR8)

10 McKinsey & Company. The value of getting personalization right – or
    wrong – is multiplying, McKinsey & Company, 2021. www.mckinsey.com/
    capabilities/growth-marketing-and-sales/our-insights/the-value-of-getting-
    personalization-right-or-wrong-is-multiplying (archived at https://perma.cc/
    V63D-LPE8)

11 McKinsey & Company. The value of getting personalization right – or
    wrong – is multiplying, McKinsey & Company, 2021. www.mckinsey.com/
    capabilities/growth-marketing-and-sales/our-insights/the-value-of-getting-
    personalization-right-or-wrong-is-multiplying (archived at https://perma.cc/
    45UV-282Y)

12 B Morgan. 50 stats showing the power of personalization, Forbes, 18 February
    2020. www.forbes.com/sites/blakemorgan/2020/02/18/50-stats-showing-
    the-power-of-personalization (archived at https://perma.cc/XML6-LVJD)

13 A Khandelwal. How does Amazon and Netflix personalization work? VWO
    Blog, 15 November 2004. vwo.com/blog/deliver-personalized-recommendations-
    the-amazon-netflix-way (archived at https://perma.cc/S3E2-XK5M)

14 B Foster-Butler. Best-in-class retention marketing looks like this, LinkedIn,
    nd. www.linkedin.com/posts/bronwen-foster-butler-73a31923_best-in-class-
    retention-marketing-looks-like-activity-7227592287222988801-Rbqu/
    (archived at https://perma.cc/25FC-46YL)

15 B Ross. Psychology of free: Its impact on buying behavior, Emulent Blog,
    6 February 2025. emulent.com/blog/psychology-of-free (archived at https://
    perma.cc/MMF2-AHQ3)

16 Marketing Week. EasyJet launches 'emotional' campaign as it looks to be known for more than value for money, Marketing Week, 25 September 2016. www.marketingweek.com/easyjet-marketing-campaign-beyond-value-for-money/ (archived at https://perma.cc/E2PJ-7RDE)

17 Campaign Live. EasyJet transformed customer data into emotional anniversary stories, Campaign Live, 4 October 2016. www.campaignlive.co.uk/article/easyjet-transformed-customer-data-emotional-anniversary-stories/1414488 (archived at https://perma.cc/DQG7-B2SG)

18 Campaign Live. How easyJet transformed customer data into emotional anniversary stories, Campaign Live, 4 October 2016. www.campaignlive.co.uk/article/easyjet-transformed-customer-data-emotional-anniversary-stories/1414488 (archived at https://perma.cc/64EC-PJ52)

19 Moosend. easyJet transformed email personalization by seeing memories not data, Moosend Blog, 2025. moosend.com/blog/easy-jet-email-personalization-case-study/ (archived at https://perma.cc/XWT4-V2UB)

08

Turning trust into conversions with surprise and delight

> **REMINDER**
>
> Surprise and delight may start as a moment, but its impact can last a lifetime.
> And that's the magic of putting people first.

It's a cold, dreary day and you're curled up on the sofa, feeling miserable. Your nose is stuffy, your head aches and your only companion is a mountain of used tissues. In a moment of self-pity, you take to Facebook, typing: *'Ugh, worst cold ever. Send help!'* You post it, expecting nothing more than a few sympathetic comments or a 'get well soon' GIF.

But then, something surprising happens. A few days later, there's a knock at your door. You open it to find a package addressed to you – a Kleenex Kit. Inside, there's a box of soft tissues, some tea, honey and a handwritten note wishing you a speedy recovery. Suddenly, you feel seen, cared for and connected – all because of a simple post and an unexpected response.

This was the heart of Kleenex's Feel Good campaign. Using Facebook, they tracked users posting about being sick and surprised them with personalized care packages. It was a great example or delivering kindness, comfort and connection when people needed it most. The campaign generated over 650,000 impressions and 1,800 heartfelt customer interactions.[1] But more importantly, it showcased the power of empathy in marketing.

And let's be honest, we've needed empathy more than ever, especially during the pandemic. With in-person everything off the table, brands had to level up their creativity to keep connections alive. For example, Chipotle proved that even a global crisis couldn't stop people from sharing a meal – virtually, of course. They hosted virtual lunch parties on Zoom, complete with celebrity guests, free meal giveaways and just the right amount of *'Let's all pretend we're not in sweatpants.'*[2]

These weren't your average Zoom calls (you know, the ones where you spend more time checking your lighting than paying attention). Chipotle turned them into mini events that made you forget, even for a little while, that you were eating your burrito alone on the couch.

So many campaigns during the pandemic worked because they followed a very simple principle: being human. Brands were showing up when people needed connection the most. Because whether it's a surprise care package or a virtual hangout, those little moments of delight remind us of something we all crave: to feel seen, valued and like we're not doing this whole life thing alone.

But surprise and delight don't exist in a vacuum. They're part of a bigger picture – one that's rooted in principles we've already explored, like trust, connection and even a touch of nostalgia. These are the building blocks of relationships and surprise and delight take them one step further, adding that extra spark that keeps your brand alive in people's hearts and minds.

Trust lays the foundation. It's what gets people to open the door in the first place, to believe that what you're offering is worth their time. Connection? That's the bridge – the human element that turns a transaction into a relationship.

Surprise and delight? It's the unexpected moment that takes all these elements and amplifies them, making your brand not just trusted but unforgettable. And when you're unforgettable, something powerful happens as you stay top of mind.

And it's not just about short-term wins. This approach strengthens the long game too. Each positive experience reinforces trust, deepens the emotional connection and builds a reservoir of goodwill.

So, when it's time for your customer to decide, whether it's choosing between you and a competitor or deciding to upgrade to your latest offering, the choice becomes easy. Why? Because you're already their go-to.

REAL-WORLD EXAMPLE
Dove's Real Beauty campaign

This story started with a simple but bold question: 'What if women saw themselves the way others see them?'

Dove invited real women to participate in a unique experiment. A forensic artist sketched two portraits of each woman – one based on their own description and the other based on how a stranger described them.

The participants didn't see either portrait until both were complete and, yes, the results may surprise you. Dove's Real Beauty Sketches campaign showed something really interesting about how differently women see themselves compared to how others view them.

Dove found that only 4 per cent of women around the world thought of themselves as beautiful.[3] They set out to change that mindset by showing women that they're actually 'more beautiful than they think'. The message struck a chord with viewers and gave many women a much-needed boost in confidence.

The reveal of the two portraits side by side was the moment of surprise – a genuine, unscripted reaction that gave the campaign its emotional punch. Women were confronted with a version of themselves they hadn't recognized before: kinder, softer and more beautiful in the eyes of others.

The magic of surprise and customer-centred storytelling

The difference between how these women saw themselves vs how others saw them hit home in a powerful way. You could really feel the emotion in the room as participants and viewers took it all in.

In fact, Dove used that element of surprise to bring out those genuine feelings. When they revealed those portraits, it wasn't just for show – it created real connections. Instead of coming across as just another corporate campaign, Dove made it personal by putting real people front and centre. That's what made it feel so authentic and relatable.

The campaign really hit home with people – it became one of the most-watched ads ever with more than 180 million views.[4] It got people thinking differently about how they see themselves and started important conversations about beauty standards.

Here's what made this campaign special – it combined surprise, emotion and authenticity in a way that felt natural and personal:

- **It created a 'Wow!' moment:** When those women saw their two portraits side by side, it hit them hard. That unexpected revelation wasn't just powerful in the moment – it stuck with everyone who watched it.

- **It sparked a movement:** By putting real people in the spotlight, Dove got something amazing – thousands of women started sharing their own stories and reactions, which spread the campaign like wildfire.

- **Real people stole the show:** Instead of polished actors, we got to see real women sharing real feelings. That's what made it so easy for everyone to connect with.

This ties directly into the power of user-generated content. The women's raw reactions and heartfelt stories became the focal point, shifting the spotlight from the brand to the customers. Their experiences and emotions were so genuine that they invited millions of others to see themselves in those same moments.

How Dove used the power of UGC in surprise and delight

Even more so, it then inspired more campaigns and ways to build on this conversation and vision, showing how Dove has consistently championed its customers by integrating their voices, stories and creativity into its marketing.

Here are two standout campaigns that show how they used their audience and customers to build emotional connections and amplify a brand's message.

Inspired by a heartfelt letter from a customer about how Dove products had been a staple in her family for generations, the #BeautyStory campaign celebrated the beauty lessons passed down from mothers to daughters.[5]

Dove invited fans to share photos of their mothers along with personal stories of beauty wisdom. These submissions, brimming with emotion and nostalgia, were featured in a gallery on Dove's website and across its social media platforms.

Dove's #ShowUs campaign tackled a much bigger challenge: redefining beauty standards in media.[6]

Partnering with Getty Images and Girlgaze, Dove launched a global initiative to create the world's largest stock photo collection featuring women and non-binary individuals as they truly are – unfiltered and authentic. They invited people to jump on Instagram and share their own unfiltered photos with #ShowUs. As a result, lots of influencers got excited about it too, sharing their stories and getting their followers involved.

So why do people still talk about these examples after years, specifically Dove's Real Beauty? Dove showed they really got their audience and celebrated them and that created a whole community of people who couldn't wait to spread the message. The way they wove surprise into the campaign and put real people at its heart showed just how powerful these unexpected moments can be. What started as a simple surprise turned into something much bigger – creating connections that really lasted.

The psychology of surprise: The Novelty Effect

It's a regular Tuesday morning and you stop by your favourite coffee shop on the way to work. You've ordered the same thing every day for months: a classic flat white. But today, as the barista hands you your cup, they grin and say, '*On the house – we're testing a new caramel vanilla blend. Let us know what you think!*'

You weren't expecting it and it's not your usual order, but as you take a sip, the sweet, velvety flavour catches you off guard – in the best way possible. It's the highlight of your morning and you can't stop thinking about it as you head to work.

That moment was powered by the **Novelty Effect** – our natural tendency to perk up, pay attention and feel a surge of excitement when something new or unexpected comes our way.[7] Psychologically, novelty activates the reward centre in our brains. It's like a little burst of dopamine, sparking curiosity and pleasure. That's why surprise is such a powerful tool – it disrupts the routine, captures our attention and leaves a lasting impression.

Think about it:

- The excitement of opening a subscription box and discovering an extra sample you weren't expecting.
- The joy of finding a handwritten note tucked inside an online order.
- The buzz of your local bakery giving you a free cookie because '*it's a new recipe we're trying out*'.

These moments stick with us because they're unexpected and fresh. They make us feel noticed, appreciated and a little bit special.

Why we can't ignore what's different

Here's the thing about novelty: it grabs us. People are wired to notice things that stand out – the unexpected, the unusual, the downright different. It's why you can't help but double-take at a neon-green car on a road full of grey sedans. Novelty disrupts the ordinary and demands attention.

Take the title of a 2003 book by Seth Godin, for example – *Purple Cow*.[8] The very idea of a purple cow feels absurd – which is exactly the point. Godin uses this metaphor to explain why standing out is essential. The book itself is a testament to its philosophy.

Or consider the book *Freakonomics* by Steven Levitt and Stephen Dubner from 2005.[9] At first glance, a book that combines economics with questions like '*What do schoolteachers and sumo wrestlers have in common?*' shouldn't work. But it does – spectacularly. It approaches complex topics in ways no one else had before, blending curiosity, storytelling and unexpected insights.

Novel ideas challenge the way we think, grabbing our attention with concepts so fresh and unusual that they can't be ignored. When brands harness this same principle, they can turn even the simplest interactions into something unforgettable.

Plus, we see novelty happening again and again as marketers.

Take limited-edition product launches, for example. When something is new *and* scarce, it becomes irresistible. Think of pop-up stores or seasonal campaigns, as the buzz surrounding these events is fuelled by the novelty effect, driving that initial rush of interest and interaction.

Still, there is a pitfall to novelty we have to talk about – it isn't built to last. As soon as the excitement fades, so does the engagement. That's why the most successful campaigns don't just rely on novelty – they layer it with long-term value.

For example, a brand might capture attention with an exclusive product launch but retain customers by offering continuous innovation or interactive experiences that keep them coming back.

In short, the Novelty Effect is great at creating those 'Wow!' moments that make people stop and pay attention. But for brands, the real trick is turning that initial excitement into something that sticks around.

The secret? Mix that novelty with smart, customer-focused strategies. When you combine unexpected moments with genuine value – whether through fresh ideas, stories that touch hearts or personalized experiences – you create something special. It's about finding new ways to surprise and delight your audience while giving them something worth coming back for.

REAL-WORLD EXAMPLE
How Cirque du Soleil redefined novelty

When it comes to standing out in a crowded market, few brands have done it better than Cirque du Soleil. At a time when traditional circuses were struggling to stay relevant, Cirque reinvented the old concept of circus entirely.

By blending elements of circus, theatre, dance and live music, Cirque du Soleil created an entirely new category of entertainment. Gone were the animal acts and sawdust arenas, replaced by high-concept storytelling, mesmerizing acrobatics and a level of artistry that felt more Broadway than big top.

Instead of fighting over the same customers in saturated spaces, brands can harness the novelty effect to carve out 'blue oceans' of untapped opportunity.

Picture a crowded market as a red ocean – filled with sharks fighting over the same customers. Now imagine a wide-open blue ocean, free from rivals, where you can carve out your own space and make the rules. This is known as the **Blue Ocean Strategy**, escaping the bloodbath of competition.[10]

Instead of trying to outperform competitors, Blue Ocean Strategy focuses on innovation. It's about creating new demand by offering something so fresh, so unique, that competition becomes irrelevant. Cirque du Soleil blended theatre and circus; Apple reimagined the phone into a sleek, pocket-sized powerhouse.

But novelty alone isn't enough to sustain growth. Here's where Blue Ocean Strategy really shines – it makes sure these cool new ideas stick around. The strategy is often paired with a framework called the Eliminate–Reduce–Raise–Create Grid.[11] It helps brands figure out what to keep, what to change and what to drop so they stay relevant even after the initial excitement wears off.

- **Eliminate:** Identify and remove elements that no longer add value to your offering.
- **Reduce:** Decrease elements that are less valuable but still necessary.
- **Raise:** Enhance elements that provide significant value.
- **Create:** Develop new elements that add fresh value.

For example, Cirque du Soleil used this approach effectively to redefine circus entertainment by eliminating traditional elements like animal acts while creating new value through artistic performances and storytelling.

This framework helps brands systematically evaluate which features or elements to keep, modify or introduce to maintain relevance after the initial excitement of novelty wears off.

They cut out expensive stuff like animal acts and put all their energy into amazing human performances. This saved them money while making their shows feel more valuable. Sure, tickets weren't cheap, but people were happy to pay for something this special.

And did it work? The numbers to speak for themselves. Cirque du Soleil became huge, putting on shows for more than 180 million people across 400+ cities worldwide.[12] By keeping things fresh and exciting, they proved that the Blue Ocean Strategy really works.

Types of surprise and delight strategies

It's 2012 and the remote town of Bethel, Alaska, is buzzing. A flyer is making the rounds, announcing that a Taco Bell is coming to town. For a place where fast food options are few and far between, this news is huge. Excitement spreads and residents start dreaming of tacos, burritos and cheesy goodness.

But the dream doesn't last. The announcement turns out to be a hoax. There's no Taco Bell coming to Bethel and the disappointment is palpable. For a town with limited access to dining options, it feels like a cruel joke.

That's when Taco Bell steps in.

Hearing about the prank and the town's heartbreak, Taco Bell launches Operation Alaska – an extraordinary gesture that turns disappointment into delight.[13] They load up a truck with 10,000 Doritos Locos Tacos, airlift it into Bethel and bring the ultimate taco party to the town. Residents gather to savour the unexpected feast, their disappointment melting away with every bite. The airlift became a viral sensation, turning a small-town prank into a global story of delight and generosity.

Taco Bell took two core steps that are part of any great marketing strategy: they listened and they acted. They transformed a potential PR nightmare into a moment of magic that strengthened customer loyalty and boosted their brand perception.

Surprise and delight don't need to mean pulling off elaborate stunts (though those can be fun). It's about creating moments that feel thoughtful, unexpected and perfectly tailored to your audience.

Small acts of kindness

Sometimes, it's the little things that matter most. Small, thoughtful gestures – like personalized thank-you notes or unexpected freebies – can turn an ordinary moment into an extraordinary one.

Remember the Kleenex Feel Good campaign? By sending personalized care packages to people posting about being sick on Facebook, they turned a cold, dreary day into one filled with warmth and comfort.[14]

These gestures show that you're listening, paying attention and genuinely care about your audience. And when people feel seen, they remember it.

Experiential marketing

When you want to create a big splash, experiential marketing is your go-to. But instead of traditional approaches, why not put the customer centre stage?

In a previous chapter, we explored the idea of turning traditional press trips into customer press trips. This strategy takes something often reserved for influencers or journalists and extends it to your most loyal customers, giving them an immersive, VIP experience with your brand. Imagine inviting customers to tour your production facility, participate in an exclusive event or co-create content with your team. These moments create deeper connections while generating organic buzz.

Customization and personalization

Nothing says 'We see you' like personalization. As we discussed amply in the previous chapter, personalization can build emotional connections and loyalty like few other strategies. We now know that personalization creates ownership and connection thanks to psychology. It makes customers feel valued as individuals, turning a product or service into something uniquely theirs.

Your local coffee shop might remember that you prefer your latte extra-hot on Monday mornings and iced on Friday afternoons, or you may receive a free workout code on your birthday from your favourite fitness studio. By weaving surprise and delight into your strategy – whether through small gestures, immersive experiences or personalized touches – you create moments that people remember and, even better, love to talk about (oh hello, advocacy).

And in the noisy world of marketing, that's what makes all the difference.

REAL-WORLD EXAMPLE
Alt Marketing School's approach to surprise and delight

At Alt Marketing School, everything revolves around one simple value: making marketing more human. This belief shapes not just the content taught but the way the school engages with its students, teachers and wider community.

For us, every touchpoint (from a welcome email to a classroom session) needs to feel personal, intentional and authentic. Our secret is that we combine surprise and delight with some good old market research.

To truly connect with our community, we place a huge emphasis on gathering data – the right kind of data – to uncover what makes their students and collaborators unique.

- **Sign-up forms:** The relationship starts at the very first step. During sign-up, students are asked to share not just the basics but the little things that make them who they are. Questions like *'What's your power song?'* or *'What are your biggest hopes for this course?'* give the team valuable insights that will shape the student experience.

- **Feedback loops:** By encouraging open communication, the school creates ongoing opportunities for students to share their thoughts. Whether through structured sessions or spontaneous check-ins, this feedback helps refine both the curriculum and the community experience.

- **Milestone tracking:** Special moments like birthdays, anniversaries and achievements are tracked to create opportunities for celebration. The data can easily be obtained at onboarding. This layer of data ensures that even small personal wins are acknowledged and appreciated.

With a foundation of rich audience insights, we can now bring surprise and delight to life through thoughtful, personalized gestures that align with their human-first values.

Here are some of the standout ways we have created memorable moments.

1 Every student's journey begins with **a warm welcome**. Personalized videos, orientation group calls or optional bonus calls are a way of saying, *'We see you. How can we serve you best?'* These personal touches help students feel welcome and supported from day one, making it easier to dive right in and trust the learning process.

2 Sign up and intake forms have been incredibly helpful to customize experiences with surprising touch points. My favourite is celebrating teachers, students and special friends of the school with **virtual birthday cards**.

3 **Cohort power songs** are compiled into a Spotify playlist for the cohort to enjoy and are often incorporated into live sessions. I love to see the response to students recognizing their song coming on throughout the 12 weeks!

We put lots of pride into making our school experience as human as possible, even as a small and lean school and company. By adding these little touches, we build a fiercely loyal group of students and teachers who have become lifelong advocates for Alt Marketing School and its mission to make marketing more human, impactful and fun.

REFLECTION TIME
How can you surprise and delight?

It's your usual Friday evening and you're exhausted after a long week. You decide to treat yourself to your favourite pizza delivery – the one you've ordered from countless times. You pull up the app, place your order and settle in for what feels like the same-old, same-old.

Half an hour later, the delivery driver shows up. But instead of just handing you the pizza, they grin and say, *'This is for you too'*, as they pull out a box of complimentary garlic knots.

'Wait, what?' you ask, pleasantly surprised.

'It's a little something we're offering to regular customers this week,' they explain.

You take the box, a little stunned and head back to your sofa.

When a business offers something unexpected – whether it's a free treat, a handwritten thank-you note or even a simple upgrade – it creates a sense of connection. It says, *'We see you and we value you.'*

May this be your reminder that creating moments of surprise and delight doesn't have to feel overwhelming. It starts with understanding your customers and building on the knowledge you already have.

Here's a simple three-step process to guide you.

1   **Identify special moments.** What milestones or moments matter to your customers? These could be personal dates, like birthdays or anniversaries or even key interactions with your brand – like their first purchase, a loyalty milestone or feedback they've shared. These touchpoints are perfect opportunities to create a meaningful connection.

2   **Choose a gesture.** Think about what small or large gesture would make these moments unforgettable – maybe it's sending a quick thank-you note, giving them a special discount on their birthday or suggesting products you know they'd love. Just make sure whatever you do feels genuine and matches what they want and care about.

3   **Plan for delight.** Once you've identified the moment and the gesture, think about how to execute it in a way that truly delights. It could be adding a touch of creativity, like wrapping their gift beautifully or accompanying it with a personalized message. Focus on making the experience feel special and unique.

Now that you have a framework, here are some prompts to spark inspiration:

- What's one small, thoughtful gesture you could offer your customers today?
- How could you create a unique experience that puts your customers in the spotlight?
- What personalized touch could make your customers feel seen and valued?
- How can you align these moments with your brand values?

Take some time to reflect on these steps and prompts. Remember, creating surprise and delight doesn't have to be all-consuming – it's about thoughtfulness, creativity and connection.

The impact and challenges of surprise and delight

> **TIP**
>
> Every surprise, every act of delight, reinforces the idea that your brand truly understands and values its customers.

Let's talk about something important: while surprise and delight can create amazing connections with your customers, you need to know if it's working. Plus, you want to make sure you're not accidentally doing more harm than good, right? You want to track how well your surprise and delight efforts are performing, but you also need to keep them genuine and meaningful.

So, let's break this down into two simple parts: how to measure success and how to avoid common mistakes that could trip you up along the way.

When tracking, you'll need to look at both the hard numbers and the softer signs. Let's dive into these metrics to help you see exactly how your surprise and delight efforts are making a difference for your brand.

Retention is the holy grail of customer loyalty. Repeat customers are more cost-effective to retain than acquiring new ones and their lifetime value (how much they spend over the course of their relationship with your brand) grows with trust.

- **Retention rates:** Track how long customers stay active after experiencing a surprise and delight moment.
- **Repeat purchases:** Look for patterns of recurring purchases or upgrades. Did that surprise trigger a long-term relationship?
- **CLTV growth:** Compare the lifetime value of customers who experienced surprise and delight efforts vs those who didn't.

Social sharing and word of mouth also matter. When people love a surprise, they talk about it. Social sharing amplifies your reach, turning one happy customer into a brand advocate who introduces you to their network. Word of mouth remains one of the most powerful drivers of trust and acquisition.

- **Social mentions:** Monitor mentions of your brand on platforms like Instagram, TikTok and LinkedIn. Getting help with tools like SproutSocial can be helpful if you are looking at high volumes.
- **User-generated content:** Are customers posting photos, videos or reviews inspired by your efforts?

- **Referrals:** Look for spikes in referral traffic or sign-ups tied to customers who experienced your campaign.

Metrics like retention or shares show what happened, but qualitative feedback reveals *why*. This insight helps you understand the emotional resonance of your efforts and refine future strategies.

- **Testimonials:** Collect direct quotes from customers about how they felt after your surprise.
- **Open-ended survey responses:** Use surveys to ask customers how the experience impacted their relationship with your brand.

Customer engagement is a sign that customers are paying attention. A spike in interactions with your content, emails or events can show that your surprise and delight efforts are making people take notice.

- **Email open and click-through rates:** Do emails tied to your campaign have higher engagement than usual?
- **Platform usage and attendance:** Monitor engagement metrics like course completion rates, live session attendance and participation in community events or special activities.
- **Website activity:** Look for increased time on site, pages viewed or interactions after surprise efforts.

Surprise and delight is about evoking positive emotions, which means we could not end without mentioning sentiment analysis. Sentiment analysis helps you understand how people feel about your brand, showing whether your efforts are building goodwill.

- **Tone of customer reviews:** Analyse reviews or comments to see if words like 'thoughtful', 'unexpected' or 'amazing' come up frequently.
- **Social media sentiment:** Use tools like Hootsuite or Brandwatch to assess whether online mentions of your brand skew positive.
- **Emotional keywords:** Track recurring themes in customer feedback that highlight their emotional response to your efforts with tools like Semrush.

Avoiding the pitfalls: Common challenges and how to tackle them

Surprise and delight strategies can be incredibly effective, but only if they're executed thoughtfully. When done poorly, they risk feeling forced, overwhelming or even alienating – all of which can undermine trust.

Let's talk about how to make sure these surprises work and what to watch out for along the way.

One of the biggest challenges is making your gestures feel real and authentic. I said it before and I will say it again: customers can tell when you're just trying to boost sales rather than genuinely caring about them. Make sure your surprises match who you are as a brand and put your customers' experience first. Focus on showing you really care, rather than just trying to hit those marketing goals.

Another trap is overdoing it. While surprises are meant to stand out, too many of them – or ones that feel overly elaborate – can overwhelm customers. Instead of feeling delighted, they might start to view your efforts as just, well, fake. Simple, thoughtful gestures often go much further than flashy stunts. The aim is to make your customers feel special, not bombarded.

Inclusivity is another critical consideration. Not all surprises resonate universally and failing to account for your audience's diversity can lead to unintended exclusions or missteps. Surprises that assume too much about a customer's preferences or circumstances can come across as tone-deaf. To fix this, make sure your efforts resonate with everyone in your audience – keep your gestures simple and inclusive enough that they work for people from all walks of life.

Finally, let's talk about the execution piece – it can be tricky. You know how it goes – even the best-planned surprise can fall flat if something goes wrong, whether it's miscommunication between teams or just plain bad timing. The key is to be super organized, make sure everyone knows their role and stick to what you know you can deliver. Because at the end of the day, the difference between making someone's day and totally missing the mark comes down to getting those details right.

The joy of building trust through delight

I'll be honest – surprising and delighting our students is one of my favourite things to do and it's something I will never stop doing. It helps us recognize the humanity in every customer interaction and shows that creativity and empathy can build more powerful connections with our audience.

At its core, this approach is rooted in trust. Every surprise, every act of delight, reinforces the idea that your brand truly understands and values its customers. It's a spark that ignites loyalty and advocacy, turning fleeting interactions into long-term relationships.

As you plan your next campaign, ask yourself: *how can I make my audience feel seen, valued and inspired?* Because, in the end, the brands that thrive are the ones that leave their customers with more than just a product or service – they leave them with a story worth sharing.

Surprise and delight may start as a moment, but its impact can last a lifetime. And that's the magic of putting people first.

KEY POINTS

- Trust is created through authentic, thoughtful interactions with customers.
- Success can be measured via customer retention, social sharing, qualitative feedback, engagement metrics and sentiment analysis.
- There must be authenticity in aligning efforts with brand values rather than obvious marketing tactics.
- Delivering meaningful moments must be done without overwhelming customers.
- Ensure your approach is inclusive, considering diverse experiences and backgrounds.
- Execute excellence through careful planning and flawless delivery.
- Regularly refresh strategies to maintain surprise element.
- There can be a long-lasting impact on customer loyalty and brand advocacy when executed properly.

TOOLS

- Social media management software: Sprout Social – sproutsocial.com
- Online visibility management and content marketing platform: Semrush – www.semrush.com
- Consumer intelligence and social media listening tool: Brandwatch – www.brandwatch.com
- Social media management platform: Hootsuite – hootsuite.com

Notes

1 K Ismail. Five successful surprise and delight marketing campaigns, CMSWire, March 2019. www.cmswire.com/digital-marketing/5-successful-surprise-and-delight-marketing-campaigns/ (archived at https://perma.cc/7TK7-QMW8)

2 A Darby. How brands should adjust their content strategy in response to Covid-19, Khoros Blog, 18 March 2020

3 Dove. Real Beauty sketches, Dove UK, September 2015. www.dove.com/uk/stories/campaigns/real-beauty-sketches.html (archived at https://perma.cc/P7DB-3ZXJ)

4 Think with Google. Real beauty shines through: Dove wins Titanium Grand Prix, 163 million views on YouTube, Think with Google, 2013

5 IZEA. Dove's #BeautyStory collects user-generated content, IZEA, 2016. https://izea.com/resources/doves-beautystory-collects-user-generated-content/ (archived at https://perma.cc/BC3W-V95J)

6 BuzzInContent. Dove generates user-generated content for its #ShowUs global campaign through influencer-led amplification strategy, BuzzInContent, 2019. www.buzzincontent.com/story/dove-generates-user-generated-content-for-its-showus-global-campaign-through-influencer-led-amplification-strategy/ (archived at https://perma.cc/3QXZ-4R8C)

7 D M Elston. The novelty effect, *Journal of the American Academy of Dermatology*, 2021, 85 (3), 565–66

8 S Godin (2003) *Purple Cow: Transform your business by being remarkable*, Portfolio, New York

9 S D Levitt and S J Dubner (2005) *Freakonomics: A rogue economist explores the hidden side of everything*, William Morrow, New York.

10 W C Kim and R Mauborgne. Blue ocean strategy, *Harvard Business Review*, October 2004. hbr.org/2004/10/blue-ocean-strategy (archived at https://perma.cc/3FHD-V9S8)

11 Alea Journal. Cirque du Soleil: From street performers to a global phenomenon, Alea Journal, September 2024. aleaglobalgroup.com/2024/09/18/cirque-du-soleil-from-street-performers-to-a-global-phenomenon/ (archived at https://perma.cc/TX37-TBEJ)

12 Alea Journal. Cirque du Soleil: From street performers to a global phenomenon, Alea Journal, September 2024. aleaglobalgroup.com/2024/09/18/cirque-du-soleil-from-street-performers-to-a-global-phenomenon/ (archived at https://perma.cc/TX37-TBEJ)

13 K Ismail. 5 successful surprise and delight marketing campaigns, CMSWire, March 2019. www.cmswire.com/digital-marketing/5-successful-surprise-and-delight-marketing-campaigns/ (archived at https://perma.cc/73MW-E8B9)

14 G Desreumaux. Feel good by Kleenex, WeRSM, 20 November 2014. wersm.com/feel-good-by-kleenex/ (archived at https://perma.cc/65CD-YELA)

09

Retaining loyal customers through feedback

REMINDER

In a world where customers can shop around and share their thoughts with just a few clicks, listening to what they have to say is more important than ever.

It's the start of your workday and as you go through your emails, one jumps out at you, sitting in your inbox.

'Hey, we're reworking our loyalty programme. As one of our valued customers, we'd love your input on what rewards you'd find useful. Got five minutes to share your thoughts?'

You're intrigued. It's not every day a brand asks for your opinion, so you take a few moments to fill out the short survey. You suggest practical perks – discounts on tools you regularly use or access to exclusive resources. It feels good to be heard, but you don't expect much to come of it.

A week later, another email lands in your inbox. The brand has updated their loyalty programme and they've included something tailored just for you: a 15 per cent discount on your favourite design software, directly inspired by your feedback.

You're pleasantly surprised. They listened to your input, acted on it and made the benefits meaningful to you. By asking what you think and doing something with that feedback, the brand turned a simple back-and-forth into a real partnership where both sides win.

Building on trust and empathy

I may sound like a broken record, but in a world where customers can shop around and share their thoughts with just a few clicks, listening to what they have to say is more important than ever. When you gather feedback and do something with it, you're creating a bridge between what your customers want and delivering the kind of value that makes them stick around. Which is why, to me (and in my school), market research and feedback loops are everything.

When people feel like you're listening and making changes based on what they say, they're way more likely to stick around, spend more with you and tell others about your brand. Customers want to share their experiences and insights – but only if they believe it will make a difference. When they see their feedback being taken seriously and implemented? That's when magic happens.

I'll let you in a little secret: people love sharing their thoughts and experiences, but they want to know it matters. And when they see you taking their feedback and doing something with it? That's when you build the kind of loyalty that sticks around for the long haul.

It all starts with a mindset shift, believe it or not. Gathering feedback isn't just about making your numbers look better or fixing what's broken (though yeah, those are good things). Remember how we talked about trust and empathy being super important in marketing? Well, customer feedback is where we get to put those ideas into practice. It's how we turn those big concepts into real changes that make things better for our customers.

I want to challenge you to get curious about why feedback builds loyalty, show you the best ways to collect it and help you turn customer insights into real improvements. You'll see how just listening and doing something with that feedback builds the kind of trust that makes customers not just stick around but become superfans who can't wait to tell others about your brand.

The psychology of feedback and loyalty

You're on the hunt for a new pair of running shoes. After hours of research and scrolling through endless reviews, you finally make your choice. A friend recommended the brand, swearing by their comfort, durability and how they've improved their runs.

Excited, you place your order. A few days later, the shoes arrive and on your first run, they feel great. You think, *'Yep, my friend was right!'*

From then on, every little detail seems to confirm your decision. That small blister you get? You brush it off as a normal break-in period. When you see an online review complaining about the shoes wearing out quickly, you dismiss it. *'That's probably just one unlucky customer,'* you tell yourself.

But when you see positive reviews or hear more praise from your friend, you nod along. *'Exactly – that's why I chose these shoes.'*

This is **confirmation bias** in action. Once you've formed a belief – that these shoes are the best choice for you – your brain filters information to support that belief, ignoring or downplaying anything that contradicts it.

Here's the thing about confirmation bias – it can work both ways for businesses. When customers have good experiences that match what they expect, it builds up their trust and makes them more loyal. But watch out – once customers start having doubts, any negative experience can quickly snowball and make them lose faith in your brand completely.

That's exactly why feedback matters so much – it helps you catch and fix small issues before they turn into big problems. When brands take the time to really listen and make changes based on what customers say, they show they care and build trust in a real, meaningful way.

Confirmation bias: Its role in feedback and loyalty

Confirmation bias is one of those quirks of human psychology that shapes how we see the world – and in this case, how customers perceive, interact with and remain loyal to brands.

It's that tendency we all have to notice information that supports our existing beliefs while conveniently ignoring the rest, but it can be changed and shifted.

Let's say a tech company gets a bunch of complaints about their app glitching. If they ignore those complaints, it only makes things worse – especially if customers already think the app isn't great. But openly addressing the issue – even proactively communicating about the fix – flips the narrative. It tells customers their voices matter, building trust and reinforcing their belief in the brand's commitment to improvement.

Think about how customers interact with feedback.[1] Confirmation bias often acts as a filter, shaping not just what they notice but also how they interpret and share their experiences. A happy customer might go on about how great the packaging looks while completely overlooking a late delivery.

Meanwhile, someone who's not so convinced might turn a tiny issue into a huge deal. This kind of selective attention means the feedback you get might be swinging between extremes.[2]

And here's the interesting part: it's not just about giving feedback, but how people read reviews, too. We all tend to look for opinions that match our own – it's just human nature. This creates a sort of echo chamber effect, where good reviews make happy customers even happier and negative ones make sceptical customers more doubtful. Throw in the way our memory works (we're all guilty of remembering what fits our beliefs and conveniently forgetting what doesn't) and you've got an interesting feedback puzzle to solve.

Interestingly, customers who really like your brand tend to be pretty forgiving about small issues. They're less likely to be swayed by minor issues that might upset someone new. This resistance to change can work in your favour, helping to make your relationship with them even stronger.[3] And here's the ripple effect – customers with strong positive biases are far more likely to share glowing recommendations with others. Word-of-mouth spreads and, before you know it, their belief becomes someone else's first impression.

So, how can you use confirmation bias ethically and effectively? The trick is to lean into what's working and amplify it – and guess what, many of the ways we may do that go back to putting our customers first. Who knew!

- **Consistency is key:** By reinforcing the good experiences customers already believe in – through aligned messaging and thoughtful communication – you keep their trust intact.

- **Highlight benefits that reflect their values:** Make it crystal clear how your product or service just makes sense in their daily life. Nothing beats seeing other happy customers raving about you – when people see others loving what you do, it really helps them feel confident they made the right choice.

- **Building a sense of community:** When customers see your brand as part of their identity or a reflection of their aspirations, the loyalty that stems from confirmation bias becomes even stronger.

Look, when it comes to feedback, you've got to let the numbers speak for themselves. And here's what makes all the difference – being real about it. Just be upfront about what customers are telling you – the good stuff and the not-so-great stuff too.

Transparency: Building credibility through honesty

Transparency isn't just about showing off when things are going well. It's about keeping it real with your customers, especially when stuff doesn't quite go according to plan.

Imagine you're at a restaurant and the waiter accidentally spills your drink. Awkward, right? But then they apologise, bring you a new one and offer you a free dessert. That's the power of owning your mistakes, and it's no different when it comes to any business or brand – plus, who doesn't love free desserts?

Customers don't expect perfection, but they do expect honesty. When you tackle concerns directly and show how you're making things better, customers really appreciate it. It's amazing how being straightforward can turn potential problems into chances to build even stronger relationships.[4]

Which means mastering how to approach negative feedback. It's tempting to gloss over it or pretend it's not there, but please do not do that. Now re-read that sentence again. What really works is tackling it head-on. At the end of the day, people just want to be heard and seen.[5]

- **Keep customers in the loop:** When customers give feedback, let them know it's making a difference. Whether it's an email update, a blog post or a social media shout-out, showing how their input shapes your decisions build trust.

- **Own mistakes:** Mistakes happen – we're all human, and I have said it time and time again in this book. What sets you apart is how you handle them. Acknowledge the issue, explain the fix and follow through. Customers will respect the honesty.

- **Show the process:** Take customers behind the scenes. Share how your team tackles challenges or works on new ideas inspired by feedback. It makes your brand feel approachable and real.

Transparency is a great principle to live by in marketing overall, but even more so with your current customers. Be upfront about what to expect, show them their voice matters and you'll be amazed at how a little openness and recognition can transform any feedback into an opportunity to connect.

Reciprocity: Building loyalty through value exchange

Think back to the last time someone genuinely showed appreciation for something you did. Maybe a colleague went out of their way to thank you, or a friend surprised you with your favourite treat.

Chances are, it made you feel good – and maybe even inspired you to return the favour. That's reciprocity at work again: as we discussed earlier in the book, this simple yet powerful principle drives human connection and, when properly leveraged, strengthens loyalty.[6]

Reciprocity is one of the core reasons feedback is so impactful. It's all about that basic human need for fair give-and-take and genuine connection. When you show customers that you value them and use their suggestions to make real changes they'll stick around longer, tell their friends about you and won't make a big deal out of small hiccups.

For my first book, I wanted the cover to resonate deeply with readers, so I decided to ask them directly. I shared a few design concepts and asked for their input – which one they preferred and why. The response was incredible. Not only did they feel seen and valued, but they also became invested in the book before it even launched.

Even small acts of reciprocity – like a thank-you email, a personalized discount or a shout-out on social media – show customers their voices matter and encourage them to tell you what they want to see. These moments create positive experiences that linger long after the interaction.

And you know what? You don't need deep pockets to make this work. Just keep it real and make sure everything you do has real meaning behind it.

- **Acknowledge feedback:** Respond to customer input with more than a generic thank-you. Be specific – highlight what you've learned and how you're using it to improve.

- **Celebrate contributions:** Recognize customers who go the extra mile, whether by showcasing their stories or offering exclusive perks.

- **Offer personalized rewards:** Use feedback to create offers or benefits that feel tailored to your audience. Personalization shows customers you're paying attention.

Gathering feedback and putting it into action

Feedback is the lifeblood of customer-centric growth, but there's an art to getting it right. Too much feedback and your audience feels overwhelmed. Too little and you miss out on the insights that could transform your strategy.

This is where the **Goldilocks rule** comes in. The human brain thrives on challenges that sit in the optimal zone of difficulty – not too easy, not too hard. As James Clear explains, peak motivation happens when tasks are just at the edge of our current abilities.[7]

The same applies to feedback: make it manageable and engaging for your audience and they'll be motivated to participate.

Types of feedback to gather

Each type of feedback you gather adds a unique layer to your understanding of your audience. When combined, they create a complete picture of their needs, frustrations and aspirations – a roadmap for building better experiences.

DIRECT FEEDBACK: STRAIGHT FROM THE SOURCE

This is the no-frills feedback that comes straight from your audience. Think surveys, focus groups and reviews. These channels allow you to ask specific questions and get actionable answers.

- **Surveys:** Quick, focused surveys let you tap into customer thoughts at scale. Keep them short and targeted to avoid survey fatigue – your customers will thank you.

- **Focus groups:** Perfect for exploring ideas in depth. Whether in-person or virtual, they give you a chance to see real reactions and uncover nuances you might miss in written feedback.

- **Reviews:** A goldmine for insights, especially when you pay attention to recurring themes. What are people loving? What's frustrating them? Use this feedback to pinpoint areas for improvement.

INDIRECT FEEDBACK: WHAT THEY'RE SAYING BEHIND THE SCENES

Sometimes, the most valuable feedback isn't handed to you – you have to find it. Indirect feedback includes the unfiltered conversations happening online or within your own data.

- **Social listening:** Dive into what your audience is saying about your brand on social media. This is where honesty thrives, giving you a real sense of their experiences.

- **Behavioural analytics:** Numbers don't lie. Whether it's tracking website navigation or app usage patterns, this data reveals what's working and what's not, even when users aren't vocal about it.

PROACTIVE FEEDBACK: START THE CONVERSATION

Don't wait for your audience to come to you. Proactive feedback means reaching out and inviting them to share their thoughts.

- **Polls and Q&A sessions:** These quick, interactive methods are easy for your audience to engage with and offer instant insights for you.
- **Beta testing:** Get your audience involved early. By inviting customers to test new features or products, you not only gather valuable feedback but also build anticipation and loyalty.
- **Dedicated campaigns:** Make feedback a feature. Whether it's a social media callout or an email series asking for input, actively showing you value your audience's thoughts builds trust.

Variety truly is the spice of life: when you mix different types of feedback – direct, indirect and proactive – you're really getting the full picture. Just remember to keep things balanced (that sweet spot we talked about with the Goldilocks rule) and you'll keep people interested and willing to share. You'll catch what customers are saying directly, pick up on things they might not be telling you outright and start conversations you wouldn't have had otherwise.

Acting on feedback: Turning insights into action

Collecting feedback is only the first step. Feedback, no matter how insightful, is just noise if it doesn't lead to meaningful change. Customers want to see that their input matters – that it's not only being heard but also being used to make their experience better and that's what builds loyalty. The best way to make this happen is through feedback loops. Think of them as ongoing conversations with your customers that help you keep getting better. When you do it right, these loops create trust and loyalty because customers can see how their input leads to real improvements and they tend to follow a few core steps.

Identify the gems in the data

Not all feedback is actionable and that's okay. The trick is to sift through the noise and find the gold. Look for recurring themes or issues that align with your brand's goals. A single suggestion might spark an idea, but patterns in feedback point you toward where your focus should be.

Start by asking:

- What are the most common pain points?
- Which suggestions align with our priorities or current strategy?
- What feedback could we act on quickly for maximum impact?

Prioritize high-impact changes

Another big truth is that not all feedback is created equal. Some ideas will create a ripple effect of positive change, while others might only scratch the surface. This is where you can really have fun and become the master investigator you were always meant to be.

Quick wins, like fixing small bugs or simplifying user interfaces, show customers you're listening, while bigger projects, like launching a new feature, reinforce your commitment to continuous improvement. When prioritizing, focus on changes that:

- solve widespread issues
- enhance the customer journey in meaningful ways
- align with your company's long-term goals

Communicate the changes

Here's where the cookie proverbially crumbles: let your customers know how their input shaped your decisions. Transparency builds trust and when you show that their feedback led to real change, it strengthens the relationship.

Use channels like:

- product updates to highlight new features or fixes inspired by feedback
- social media to share behind-the-scenes stories about how you acted on user input
- direct communication to send personalized thank-you messages or updates to customers who provided impactful feedback

Don't be shy about celebrating the small wins – fixing even the tiniest annoyance shows your customers you're really listening and that can make a big impact.

Build in public: Sharing the journey

When Howard Schultz launched My Starbucks Idea in 2008, this was the vision: to create a digital version of the coffee shop barista experience, where customers feel heard, valued and connected.[8] The site's transparency builds trust, showing customers exactly what happens to their ideas.

But the magic doesn't stop there. Starbucks has taken ideas submitted by everyday coffee lovers and turned them into real offerings, like Cake Pops, Hazelnut Macchiatos and free Wi-Fi. By 2013, just five years after launch, My Starbucks Idea had inspired over 150,000 submissions, with 277 ideas implemented.[9]

Customers could see their suggestions making a difference, whether it was a big product launch or a small tweak that improved the experience. By listening, engaging and being transparent, Starbucks created a community where customers felt like insiders, shaping the brand they loved, showing a great early example of building in public.

Building in public is a relatively new strategy that invites your audience into the process, and Starbucks was an early example of that. Think sharing roadmaps, letting them test new features or even talking about the challenges you're working through based on their feedback.

Take Notion, for example – they've really nailed this by explaining not just what they're changing, but why they're changing it. That's how they've built such a tight-knit community.

When customers actually see their suggestions turning into real changes, they feel like they matter. And when people feel valued like that, they don't just stick around – they become your biggest cheerleaders.

REAL-WORLD EXAMPLE

Notion: Building a product around customer feedback

Notion, a leading productivity software company, has built its reputation not just on its features but on its commitment to listening to its users. They've made feedback a key part of how they build and improve things, which means every update makes sense for the people using it.

At the heart of Notion's strategy is a robust feedback loop that captures, analyses and acts on user input across multiple channels:

1 **Unified feedback platform:** Notion brings together insights from support tickets, app store reviews, social media and more into a centralized system. By using tools like Enterpret, the team can monitor user sentiments in real time, ensuring no piece of feedback goes unnoticed.[10]

2 **Leveraging technology for insights:** Notion use natural language processing (NLP) to analyse feedback, uncover patterns and identify recurring themes.[11] This approach not only reduces manual categorization but also empowers the team to spot trends and address user needs more efficiently.

3 **Empowering teams with self-service insights:** Feedback isn't siloed at Notion. Product teams can independently query and segment data, streamlining their ability to make informed decisions. This autonomy ensures that user feedback translates quickly into actionable improvements.

Social media is where Notion really shines when it comes to feedback. With their content, they bring their users along for the ride as they develop new features and they take the time to explain why they make even the smallest changes. Whether it's fixing a tiny bug that one person mentioned or rolling out a big feature everyone asked for, they share the news with their community. It's their way of saying *'Hey, we're listening and your input really does make a difference.'*

This process started by really getting feedback from designers and engineers. Instead of just guessing, they dug deep into the actual problems these folks were facing.[12] This hands-on approach kicked off something special – a back-and-forth between Notion and its users that helped them improve quickly. Even now, they keep putting their users first in a few important ways.

- **Feature suggestions and product testing:** They don't just build features in a vacuum – they get users involved in suggesting and testing new stuff, making sure everything works the way people need it to.

- **Transparency in development:** Whether it's a tiny bug fix or a major new tool, Notion tells you exactly why they're making changes. Nothing's too small to mention if it makes the platform better to use.

- **Engagement through iteration:** They're always on social media, keeping everyone in the loop about what's new, what's fixed and what's coming next. It keeps users feeling like they're part of the journey.

By keeping the conversation going and explaining even the little, seemingly trivial updates, Notion's created something that feels less like just another tool and more like something that truly gets what their community needs.

REFLECTION TIME
Listening and learning from your customers

Creating a feedback loop can be one of the most impactful ways of showing your customers that their voices drive change. If you're starting from scratch, follow these steps to build a feedback loop that creates trust and delivers real impact.

Step 1: Define your purpose

Before you start collecting feedback, get clear on your goals – and yes, setting great goals and objectives is one of the most understated skills marketers should cultivate. What do you want to learn from your audience? Are you looking to improve a product, refine a service or identify pain points in the customer experience? When you know what you're looking for, you'll ask better questions and get answers you can use.

Step 2: Choose your channels

Not all feedback channels are created equal. Pick the channels that best suit your audience and align with your goals and consider where your audience is most comfortable engaging with you:

- surveys for quick, structured input
- social media for casual, ongoing conversations
- reviews for unfiltered, detailed feedback
- focus groups or interviews for deep dives into specific topics

Step 3: Make feedback accessible

Let's make sure everyone can share their thoughts easily. Keep your language simple, give people different ways to respond (like writing, talking or even drawing) and be mindful of neurodiverse and disabled customers' needs. The more welcoming you make your feedback process, the better insights you'll get.

Step 4: Analyse the data

Once the feedback starts rolling in, it's time to spot the patterns. Look for recurring themes, identify common pain points and highlight any standout suggestions. Tools like NLP software or a simple spreadsheet can help you organize and make sense of the data.

Step 5: Take action

Feedback is only worth collecting if you're going to do something with it. Pick the suggestions that'll make the biggest difference and make them happen in a way that fits your business. Don't worry if you need to start small – even fixing little things like bugs shows your customers you're paying attention.

Step 6: Close the loop

Let your customers know what you've done with their feedback. Share updates on social media, send emails thanking them for their input or include a 'You asked, we listened' section in your newsletters. Showing customers the impact of their feedback reinforces trust and encourages continued engagement.

Step 7: Keep it going

Here's where I have to break it to you. A feedback loop isn't a one-time effort – it's an ongoing process. Regularly revisit your goals, refine your methods and stay connected with your audience. Think of a feedback loop as an ongoing conversation with your customers that builds loyalty. Just start small, keep things simple and let this back-and-forth grow naturally as your audience grows too.

Creating a safe space for feedback

TIP

Customers don't expect perfection, but they do expect honesty.

Since we talk about loyalty, I'll bring us back to trust, the foundation of good feedback. Your customers need to know that when they speak up, you're really listening and ready to make changes based on what they say. When you create an environment where people feel safe sharing their thoughts, that's when you get the honest feedback that helps you build those lasting customer relationships.

Which leads me to a very important point: set clear intentions. Customers should understand why you're asking for feedback and how you plan to use it. Be transparent about your goals and let them know their input will make a tangible difference.

As you are setting up your feedback loops, keep in mind that everyone communicates differently. Offering various options – surveys, social media polls, email or in-person conversations – encourages customers to share their thoughts in a way that feels comfortable to them.

As feedback starts rolling in, acknowledge it all, whether positive or negative. Show gratitude for their time and thoughts and keep them updated on changes inspired by their input. Closing the loop reinforces trust and encourages ongoing engagement.

Fostering inclusivity in feedback for everyone

Creating a truly inclusive space for feedback goes beyond generic best practices. It's about acknowledging and addressing the diverse needs of your audience, ensuring that neurodiverse and disabled individuals feel just as valued and supported as neurotypical customers.

I had the pleasure of interviewing neurodiverse training expert Tania Gerard for the Alt Marketing School podcast about breaking myths and building inclusive collaborations.[13] Again and again, she went back to the idea of feeling acknowledged – even through something as simple as a 'hello' or a direct invitation to share feedback – can make a huge difference. Without these efforts, brands risk unintentionally excluding a significant portion of their audience.

Tania highlighted the power of safety and acknowledgment in creating meaningful interactions. Neurodiverse individuals thrive when they feel their perspectives are truly valued. Simple gestures like showing gratitude for their input or implementing their suggestions can have a profound impact.

The first step is to simplify communication. Use clear, jargon-free language that is easy to understand. For neurodiverse individuals, straightforward instructions about what you need and why you need it can make a huge difference. As Tania explained, 'Tell us what you're selling and what value it brings to our complex lives.' Clear communication removes barriers and invites authentic engagement.[14]

Offer flexible feedback options, such as anonymous responses, written forms or extended timelines. These adjustments can make it easier for individuals who may find traditional methods intimidating or inaccessible. With that in mind, consider accessibility needs: this could mean providing surveys compatible with screen readers, using dyslexia-friendly fonts or offering alt text for visual elements.

Tania stresses the real goal is to create a judgement-free zone.[15] Encourage honest feedback by making it clear that all input is welcome and will be received with respect. Emphasize that the goal is improvement, not perfection, to help reduce fears of judgment.

As Tania shared, inclusivity and accessibility are foundational to better customer relationships and stronger business outcomes. Go beyond the default audience segments and actively invite input from neurodiverse and disabled customers. Let them know their voices are important and integral to shaping the experience and set a new standard for meaningful engagement that benefits everyone.

Feedback as a path to loyalty

As Bernadette Jiwa put it perfectly, 'Whoever gets closest to their customer wins.'[16] Think about it – when you really listen to what people are saying, act on their suggestions and keep them in the loop about changes, you're doing more than just improving your product. You're building something way more valuable: genuine trust and loyalty from people who believe in what you're doing.

Throughout this chapter, we've looked at how to create a feedback system that works – one that brings people together, includes everyone and keeps things open and honest. Your customers are sharing their real experiences with you – their hopes, their frustrations, what they dream your product could be. When you act based on that and keep them informed, you're showing them that their voice really matters. The most successful brands aren't necessarily the ones making the most noise – they're the ones who are really listening. So, start asking the right questions, make space for everyone to speak up and make feedback a core part of how you do business.

KEY POINTS

- Creating effective feedback loops helps build trust and shows customers their voices drive real change.
- Offer various ways for customers to provide feedback, including surveys, social media, reviews and focus groups.
- Ensure feedback systems are accessible to everyone, including neurodiverse and disabled customers.
- Use simple, jargon-free language and be transparent about how feedback will be used.
- Take meaningful action on feedback received and communicate changes back to customers.
- Foster an environment where customers feel comfortable sharing honest feedback without judgment.
- Consider diverse needs when designing feedback systems, including offering multiple response formats and accommodations.

Notes

1   B Ross. Cognitive bias and marketing: How our minds influence purchasing, Emulent, updated 13 December 2024. emulent.com/blog/cognitive-biases-and-marketing/ (archived at https://perma.cc/368Z-WFUN)

2 G Yeshaswi. What is confirmation bias in consumer research? Entropik, 24 May 2024. www.entropik.io/blogs/what-is-confirmation-bias-in-consumer-research (archived at https://perma.cc/WWX9-7FCU)

3 G Yeshaswi. What is confirmation bias in consumer research? Entropik, 24 May 2024. www.entropik.io/blogs/what-is-confirmation-bias-in-consumer-research (archived at https://perma.cc/FA5X-KCZK)

4 K Donlan. How to build loyalty and trust with brand transparency, Emarsys, 7 June 2024. emarsys.com/learn/blog/brand-transparency-drives-customer-loyalty (archived at https://perma.cc/TQ26-HUK8)

5 C Mărcuţă and MoldStud Research Team. Boost customer trust: The power of transparency in feedback, MoldStud, 11 June 2024. moldstud.com/articles/p-increasing-trust-through-transparency-in-customer-feedback (archived at https://perma.cc/957Z-4FGZ)

6 K Smith. Reciprocal loyalty: The best way to acquire and retain customers, Entrepreneur, 20 October 2014. www.entrepreneur.com/growing-a-business/reciprocal-loyalty-the-best-way-to-acquire-and-retain/238663 (archived at https://perma.cc/S3NV-8C2G)

7 J Clear. The Goldilocks rule, James Clear, 2018. jamesclear.com/goldilocks-rule (archived at https://perma.cc/98UV-MQWS)

8 Harvard Digital Initiative. My Starbucks idea: Crowdsourcing for customer satisfaction and innovation, Harvard Digital Initiative, 2015. d3.harvard.edu/platform-digit/submission/my-starbucks-idea-crowdsourcing-for-customer-satisfaction-and-innovation (archived at https://perma.cc/NE4C-ZN5G)

9 Harvard Digital Initiative. My Starbucks idea: Crowdsourcing for customer satisfaction and innovation, Harvard Digital Initiative, 2015. d3.harvard.edu/platform-digit/submission/my-starbucks-idea-crowdsourcing-for-customer-satisfaction-and-innovation (archived at https://perma.cc/FF9K-VZEP)

10 Enterpret. How Notion is supercharging its product feedback loop using Enterpret, Enterpret, 11 July 2023. www.enterpret.com/customers/notion (archived at https://perma.cc/9CU9-NE5V)

11 Enterpret. How Notion is supercharging its product feedback loop using Enterpret, Enterpret, 11 July 2023. www.enterpret.com/customers/notion (archived at https://perma.cc/J3UA-YXMB)

12 A Ibarra. Top 5 lessons learned from scaling GTM teams at Notion, Asana and Dropbox, SaaStr, nd

13 T Gerard. Interviewed for Alt Marketing School podcast, 2025

14 T Gerard. Interviewed for Alt Marketing School podcast, 2025

15 T Gerard. Interviewed for Alt Marketing School podcast, 2025

16 B Jiwa. Whoever gets closest to their customer wins, The Story of Telling, 16 May 2014. thestoryoftelling.com/closest-to-customer-wins/ (archived at https://perma.cc/DB7J-RFDX)

10

Empowering advocates through shared rituals

> **REMINDER**
>
> The most powerful rituals are those that turn using your product into a special moment.

It's May 1957 and Donald Gilles, a copywriter at the JWT London advertising agency, is brainstorming ideas for a chocolate bar campaign. He scribbles down a line that captures something universal and timeless.[1] The slogan is a stroke of genius, playing on the clever double meaning of 'break' – the physical act of snapping the chocolate bar and the mental pause of taking a momentary rest. It's simple, yet powerful, turning an everyday snack into a ritual that would resonate across generations.

Decades later, that same break is still going strong, surviving the test of time. Nestlé-owned KitKat in Canada took the 'Have a break' philosophy to a new frontier, blending tradition with innovation thanks to artificial intelligence.[2] The campaign was inspired by a discovery from Google DeepMind: *AI performs better when it takes a breather.* Just like humans, it seems, chatbots benefit from a little pause.

To put this to the test, KitKat tasked an AI chatbot with several challenges, from answering trivia to summarizing *Twelfth Night*. At first, the results were good but far from perfect. Then, they added a twist: prompts included the words, 'Have a break and then.' The results were astounding. When the chatbot was 'asked' to take a break before answering, its accuracy improved significantly – jumping from 56 per cent to 78 per cent in the *Twelfth Night* test alone.[3] The digital advert that followed brought this experiment to life, playfully demonstrating that even the smartest AI can benefit from KitKat's timeless advice.

KitKat's magic isn't just in the chocolate or the catchy tagline. It's in the ritual. The act of snapping a KitKat bar has become a symbol of pausing, refreshing and reconnecting, and the brand has made sure to use it across its campaigns over the years. From office workers sharing a KitKat over coffee to families enjoying one on a road trip, the ritual transcends the product, embedding itself in our daily lives.

I love exploring rituals, because to me they go way beyond the concept of habits. At their core, they are intentional acts that carry meaning and reinforce connection. Unlike routines, which often fade into the background, rituals create moments that stand out. They're imbued with significance, reflecting a shared understanding that resonates beyond the act itself.[4] That deliberate framing elevates a simple act into something meaningful.

But why do rituals carry such emotional weight? At their core, they foster a sense of ownership, pride and belonging.[5] When customers participate in rituals, they're becoming part of your brand's story. Whether it's breaking a KitKat or raising a toast, rituals create emotional anchors that make customers feel seen, valued and connected.

This all connects back to what we talked about in Chapter 6 about building brand awareness through belonging. Shared values lay the foundation for community, but rituals really bring people together, turning loose groups into tight-knit tribes. Rituals give people something real and meaningful to connect over, making them feel like they're truly part of something special.

From breaking a KitKat to customizing your next teddy bear, rituals remind us that connection is both simple and profound – and always worth celebrating.

The psychology of rituals and advocacy

It's 1998 and the world is watching as France takes the stage for the FIFA World Cup. In the locker room, the tension is palpable – a mix of nerves, anticipation and the weight of a nation's hopes. Amidst all the prep, Laurent Blanc, the veteran defender, leans over and plants a kiss on the bald head of goalkeeper Fabien Barthez.

To the untrained eye it might seem like an odd gesture, but to the French squad it's sacred. This pre-game ritual means everything to them as it stands for unity, trust and maybe a sprinkle of luck. You see, rituals have this amazing way of bringing meaning to simple actions. They connect us and create stories that stick with people.

Just like Blanc's lucky kiss became part of soccer history, a ritual can grow from a small personal tradition into something bigger – something that brings people together through shared beliefs and celebrations.

For brands, rituals offer a unique opportunity to create meaningful moments that resonate deeply with customers, transforming everyday actions into experiences that build loyalty and advocacy. When people actively engage in a ritual, they feel a sense of ownership over the experience – a phenomenon we explored when talking about personalization in Chapter 6 as the endowment effect.

Let's look at Oreo's famous ritual. You know the one. The one that show-cases the way of eating the all-so-famous cookie has become a tradition that makes people feel like they're part of something. In fact, having a unique brand ritual like this gives you an edge that competitors just can't copy. Now when you hear the slogan, you immediately think Oreo.

When people get to be part of these brand rituals, like making something their own or joining in on these shared traditions, they naturally feel more connected. And when they feel connected? They love telling others about it.

REAL-WORLD EXAMPLE

KitKat's 'Have a break' ritual

At the heart of KitKat's success lies the act of breaking the bar – a deliberate, sensory moment that transforms the act of snacking into a meaningful ritual. By tying the act of snapping the bar to the universal need for breaks, KitKat created a ritual that resonates deeply with consumers, making it both personal and collective. The iconic slogan has cemented a shared ritual that transcends cultures and generations.

The ritual of taking a break has become a springboard for countless KitKat campaigns, each reinforcing the brand's promise to be a companion in moments of pause. KitKat got creative with their office workers, asking them to jump on Facebook and share why they desperately needed a break.[6] The lucky winners got a box of KitKats delivered right to their desk – a simple but effective way to make that break ritual feel real and special.

In another creative campaign, KitKat tackled our always-connected lifestyle by setting up 'No Wi-Fi zones' with signal blockers on benches.[7] It was a clever way to get people to unplug for a bit and enjoy a peaceful moment with their KitKat – showing how the classic break ritual still works perfectly in our digital age.

KitKat's shared ritual has also inspired a wealth of user-generated content, further embedding the brand into everyday life. With their Instagram championing those taking a break for a snack, for example, KitKat highlighted diverse ways people take breaks, which incorporated user-submitted content or stories about unique break moments.[8]

KitKat knows exactly how to use social media to their advantage – they get their fans excited about sharing their own break moments online, which naturally turns regular customers into people who love talking about the brand.

As you reflect on the KitKat example, notice how it follows some core rules of rituals in marketing:

1 **Keep it simple:** Look at KitKat – they took something as basic as breaking a chocolate bar and turned it into a moment that means something to people everywhere. Think about what simple actions could become special moments for your brand.

2 **Make it mean something:** Your ritual needs to connect with how people really feel. What emotional moments could your brand be part of?

3 **Stay fresh but true:** KitKat shows us how to keep up with the times without losing what makes them special. Don't be scared to try new things – just make sure you keep the heart of your ritual intact.

It's easy for anyone to take part in this ritual and, because it means something special to people, it's stayed popular across different generations. From office workers sharing a KitKat over coffee to families enjoying one on a road trip, the ritual transcends the product, embedding itself in our daily lives.

Social identity theory: Strengthening the 'us'

You're at a convention, surrounded by excited fans in costumes. Suddenly, across the crowd, one raises their hand in a strange gesture – fingers parted in the middle – and says one of the most memorable lines in TV and cinema. Almost immediately, someone else makes the same sign back and says those words too. When their eyes meet, they both smile – they just get it, you know?

To an outsider, it seems small, almost insignificant. But this simple act – the Vulcan salute – is far more than a hand gesture and emoji. Rooted in *Star Trek* lore and inspired by Leonard Nimoy's Jewish heritage, it has become a symbol of belonging. It says, '*We're in this together*.'[9]

This is **social identity theory** in action. The salute strengthens the 'us' by uniting fans under a shared symbol, turning individual followers into a community.[10] You know how we all like to feel like we belong somewhere? Well, social identity theory tells us that's exactly what happens when we're part of a group we really connect with. Sports fans all wearing their team's colours on game day, or coffee lovers who have 'their' drink at their favourite café. The most powerful rituals are those that turn using your product into a special moment.

Consistency principle for advocacy

The **Commitment and consistency principle** suggests that people are more likely to advocate for a cause or brand they've consistently engaged with. Rituals encourage repeated participation, transforming customers from passive consumers into active participants.[11] By tapping into social identity, you can create a sense of community around their brand. This can be achieved through targeted ads or messaging that highlight shared values, interests or experiences among your target audience.

Think about how different communities have their own special ways of connecting – like how *Star Trek* fans do the Vulcan salute. Your audience probably has their own rituals too.

Just look at gamers – they've got their own special emotes, gestures and victory dances that everyone in the community knows and loves. Similarly, many food brands have successfully tapped into how people consume their products. Think of Corona's lime ritual or the specific way people eat certain candies or snacks.

When identifying potential rituals for your brand, look for:

- existing behaviours that your audience already performs naturally
- opportunities to add meaning to everyday actions
- ways to make the experience more shareable and social

Remember that the most successful rituals feel natural and authentic to your audience's existing behaviours and values. They should emerge from and reinforce the community's shared identity, rather than feeling forced or artificial.

Building shared rituals: What makes a ritual work?

Saying a person's name is one of the best ways to grab their attention. Coca-Cola tapped into this psychological truth with its campaign surrounding sharing, turning an everyday, mindless purchase into a personal experience. By replacing its logo with common names, Coca-Cola transformed a habitual transaction into an exciting, participatory ritual.[12]

It all started in Australia. Coca-Cola noticed young adults weren't feeling that special connection with the brand anymore.[13] They came up with this brilliant idea – they'd swap out their famous logo on bottles with 150 of Australia's most popular first names, making each drink feel personal and unique.

Coca-Cola's research revealed an interesting challenge: while their iconic brand status resonated with young consumers, there was a disconnect in how the brand communicated with them. This was particularly evident in Australia's culture, where being too corporate or distant could alienate customers.

The solution was brilliantly simple – by featuring first names on their packaging, Coca-Cola found a way to make their marketing more personal and approachable.[14] Suddenly, customers were searching for their names, their friends' names or even a fun twist that felt meaningful. People who had never considered reaching for a Coke were now engaging with the brand in a new way. The result was spiked sales, social sharing and a sense of connection that turned a simple bottle into a must-have moment.

This is the power of a well-crafted ritual – it makes an experience personal, meaningful and worth repeating. But what separates a ritual that sticks from one that fizzles out? Let's break down the essential elements of an effective shared ritual.

Meaningful: Reflect your brand's core values

The best rituals are infused with meaning. They resonate because they connect to something bigger – a shared purpose or value that aligns with your brand's identity. To create a meaningful ritual, consider what your brand stands for and how a ritual could amplify that message in a way that feels authentic.

Simple: Easy to understand and replicate

Complexity is the enemy of participation. A ritual should be simple enough for anyone to engage with, yet compelling enough to create an impact.

Coke's campaign was a masterclass in this. The concept was as straightforward as it gets – swap out the brand logo for a name and let people find (or gift) their perfect bottle. No elaborate instructions, no barriers to entry – just a simple twist that made the experience personal.

Starbucks has mastered this balance with its custom drink ordering system – a ritual that's easy to replicate but feels personal and rewarding. Simplicity ensures the ritual is accessible, encouraging more people to participate and adopt it as part of their routine.

Repeatable: Build habits and emotional bonds over time

For a ritual to create lasting impact, it must be repeatable. Frequency matters, because each repetition strengthens the emotional connection between the participant and the brand.

Coca-Cola recognized this and expanded the sharing campaign over multiple seasons, adding new name variations, digital personalization options and even allowing customers to vote on which names should be included.[15] Each iteration reinforced the ritual and ensured it remained fresh while still feeling familiar.

Social: Encourage community and sharing

Rituals thrive on connection. Designing rituals that can be shared or experienced collectively amplifies their impact. Think of sports teams with pre-game chants or festivals with unique traditions that attendees take part in together. Social rituals foster a sense of belonging and create opportunities for customers to share their experiences with others, whether in person or online. This amplifies your brand's visibility and encourages organic advocacy.

For example, more than 500,000 photos were posted on Instagram using the #ShareaCoke hashtag, increasing user engagement. In Australia, the campaign increased Coke's share of the market by 4 per cent and reversed a decade-long decline in sales. In the US, it boosted sales by over 2 per cent, reversing more than 10 years of declining consumption, proving that rituals can truly build advocacy after all.[16]

Building a shared language: Reinforcing rituals through words

> TIP
>
> Great rituals are about building relationships, which is at the core of customer-driven strategies. The ones that build superfans for life.

Think about shared language like the special words and phrases that naturally go along with your rituals. It's basically the way your community talks about their shared experiences – like having your own special way of saying things. When people know and use these words, they feel like they truly belong. It makes everything feel more special than just buying and using a product.

Shared language also plays a role in breaking the 'default thinking' of your audience, as illustrated by the **Einstellung effect** – the psychological tendency to stick with familiar solutions even when better ones exist.[17]

Brands can use this to their advantage, by shaking up how people think by using fresh language that makes their solution feel like the obvious choice. Remember Blockbuster, by any chance? Those were the days of going to the shop, renting your new favourite movie to watch with your friends and then making sure you brought it back in time to avoid late fees. Then Netflix arrived. Instead of talking about 'renting movies' like everyone else, they started talking about 'unlimited entertainment delivered to your door'.

By using phrases like 'no late fees', 'unlimited movies' and 'stream instantly', they completely changed how people thought about watching movies at home. Suddenly, the old way of doing things felt outdated and inconvenient, breaking the 'default thinking' that was built over decades by Blockbusters – and we know how that turned out for them.

Creating a tribe through insider language

We explored the connection between language and community in Chapter 6, where we discussed how brands cultivate community by fostering a sense of inclusion. When people share a special way of talking about something, it helps them feel like they truly belong to that brand's community as it becomes the natural way fans and customers talk about what they love.

Few brands exemplify the power of shared language better than LEGO. The LEGO community thrives on unique terminology, rituals and traditions – from the satisfying *click* of bricks snapping together to the universal experience of stepping on a rogue piece in the middle of the night.[18] LEGO enthusiasts become *builders* and their shared language reflects this. They use terms like MOCs (My Own Creations) for original builds and AFOLs (Adult Fans of LEGO) to describe their lifelong passion. This insider terminology fosters a deep sense of community, making LEGO the cultural phenomenon it is today.

The beauty of LEGO's shared language is that it extends beyond the company itself. Fans have created their own lexicon, reinforcing their sense of identity and ownership. When a brand gives customers a language to rally around, it transforms passive consumers into active participants.

Your brand's shared language

To craft your own shared language, consider these steps:

1 **Tie it to rituals:** Align your language with specific rituals or actions to create a seamless connection.

2 **Make it inclusive:** Ensure it is accessible and easy to adopt for new customers while still feeling meaningful to loyal advocates.

3 **Encourage usage:** Use the language consistently across campaigns, social media and customer interactions to reinforce its significance.

Just like how LEGO fans can't help but make that satisfying 'click' sound when they connect bricks, or how Netflix viewers all know what 'Netflix and chill' really means, shared language combined with rituals creates those special moments that turn regular customers into passionate advocates.

When building a shared language, be aware of the potential challenges. You want your shared language to be unique to your community yet still welcoming. Avoid overly complex terminology that might alienate newcomers. Make sure your language is easy to understand and adopt. Be mindful of cultural sensitivities and ensure your language doesn't inadvertently exclude certain groups or create barriers to participation.

When introducing new terms or phrases, explain their meaning clearly. You can even consider creating a glossary or resource that new community members can reference. Be open to how your community naturally adapts and shapes the language. After all, the goal is to create a shared vocabulary that brings people together rather than creating insider/outsider dynamics.

REAL-WORLD EXAMPLE
Build-A-Bear personalized customer journey

It's a drizzly afternoon and a young girl and her mum step into a Build-A-Bear store. The girl wanders through the store, her eyes lighting up as she chooses her bear – soft, golden and just right.

She picks out her bear and gets to work – stuffing it just right, dressing it up in a sparkly outfit and even recording a sweet 'I love you!' message that makes it extra special. Then, it's time for the 'Heart Ceremony'. With a tiny red heart in her hand, she makes a wish, presses it to her bear and gives it a big hug before tucking the heart inside. Here's her bear: crafted with her hands, her wishes and a little extra magic.

This moment perfectly captures Build-A-Bear's philosophy: to add a little more heart to life. The brand's dedication to creating personalized experiences has turned it into a global phenomenon.

Look back at your brand: is there an opportunity to add small, meaningful moments that connect emotionally with your audience? What rituals or processes could make your product or service feel more personal and engaging?

Build-A-Bear's in-store experience is the perfect example of a shared ritual: customers get to stuff their bear, choose outfits and accessories and participate in the heartwarming Heart Ceremony. Every detail reinforces a sense of ownership and emotional connection.[19]

As customer expectations evolve, Build-A-Bear has extended its personal touch into the digital space. Platforms like the Bear Builder and a 3D virtual workshop make the magic accessible from anywhere.[20] Behind the scenes, Build-A-Bear uses smart tech to make everything work like magic. They've got interactive displays in their stores and cloud systems that remember what customers like – all to make sure every visit feels just right for each person who walks through their doors.

By combining connection, ritualized experiences and smart technology, Build-A-Bear has created a customer journey that's equal parts memorable and magical.

Customer-centric philosophy

At the core of Build-A-Bear's strategy is a simple but powerful question: how can we serve our customers while staying true to our brand? CEO Sharon Price John shared three key questions for every business decision, questions we can all learn from:[21]

1 Is this on brand?

2 Does it serve customers?

3 Is it backed by data?

Every decision comes back to this mission – making sure personalization truly shapes how customers experience the brand. When you're building strategies around your customers, this kind of dedication really makes a difference.

As marketers, we can learn from their commitment to adding a little more heart to every interaction. The question is: how will you add yours?

REFLECTION TIME

What rituals can you create?

The best rituals look effortless, but there's a lot of thought behind them, just like any good recipe. They're built on what we know about how people think, act and connect with each other. The best rituals don't require customers to learn something new – they elevate behaviours that already exist. Look for moments where customers naturally engage with your brand and ask:

- What is something customers already do when interacting with your brand?
- Are there repeatable behaviours that could be turned into a meaningful ritual?
- How do customers naturally use or personalize your product?

Making it personal and repeatable

Rituals become powerful when they're easy to repeat and feel uniquely personal. Think about how your ritual can become part of a customer's daily, weekly or seasonal habit.

- How can customers make it their own?
- What small but intentional action could make it feel like more than a habit?

Sharing your ritual with others

Rituals become even more meaningful when they extend beyond the individual. Consider ways your ritual encourages social participation, either online or offline.

- Does it invite customers to interact with one another?
- How might customers share their experiences in a way that amplifies the ritual?

Reflecting your brand's core values

For a ritual to stick, it has to feel like a natural extension of your brand. A great place to start is make sure it aligns with what your brand stands for.

- What feeling or message do you want the ritual to reinforce?
- Does it feel organic, or does it feel forced?

Introducing and evolving your ritual

Look, even the best rituals need time to mature and age well, just like the perfect wedge of Parmesan. You'll want to test things out and make tweaks along the way. The key is to roll out your ritual in a way that feels natural and easy for customers to pick up.

- What feedback can you gather to see if it's working?
- How can you adapt and evolve it over time to keep it relevant?

Rituals don't need to be fancy or complicated. What matters is that they're meaningful. When you create a simple action that people can do again and again, it naturally grows into something special that keeps your customers coming back for more and eager to tell others about it.

Amplifying rituals for advocacy: Strategies and pitfalls

Shared rituals have the power to transform customers into passionate brand advocates. When done right, these rituals create memorable experiences that customers naturally want to share with others.

It stands to reason that when people can make a ritual their own, adding their personal touch or tweaking it to fit their style, it becomes a natural part of their day. It could be as simple as letting them customize how they do things, put their own spin on it, or even help shape how it grows.

Take what we do at Alt Marketing School, for example. We have this thing called the 'gratitude train' at the end of each cohort session. It started when students spontaneously began thanking each other in the chat for their insights and support. Now it's become this awesome tradition – students kick it off themselves, creating this beautiful moment of connection. New students pick it up right away, keeping this culture of support going strong.

There's a lesson in here: when people feel like they truly own a ritual, it stops being just another thing a brand wants them to do. It becomes their thing. And when people feel that ownership, they're way more likely to keep doing it and tell others about it too.

Creating shareable moments

Look at Build-A-Bear's heart ceremony – it's a perfect example of how to do this right. Parents naturally want to capture that special moment when their child makes a wish and gives their new friend its heart.

Or Coca-Cola's sharing campaign: they made something as simple as putting names on bottles turn into a social media phenomenon, with over 500,000 Instagram posts using their hashtag.

Rituals catch on when people want to share them. You can't force it. The best ones just feel natural to share because they're either visually appealing, emotionally meaningful or tied to moments people love to capture. When people start sharing these experiences – whether it's face-to-face, in their group chats or on social media – it creates this amazing snowball effect. Others see it, want to join in and the ritual grows stronger.

Remember: the goal is not to go viral (even if it can be a great bonus) but create something people genuinely want to talk about. In fact, rituals are the perfect UGC moment, as people love to join in when they see others are already taking part.

Take Müller yogurt, for example. In their 2023 campaign, they asked their fans to share their unique ways of eating their yogurt online.[22] Some people mix in fruit, others swirl it with honey, but everyone has their own style. It turned into this fun community thing, with people sharing their creative ideas and inspiring others to try something new.

When brands share real stories of customers taking part in their rituals (through reviews, social posts or community highlights) it creates this amazing ripple effect.

Overcoming challenges in creating rituals

Here's the thing about rituals – not all of them stick around. Even the ones that look natural today probably took some trial and error to get right. And if a ritual feels forced or doesn't really connect with what your customers care about? It's probably not going to last.

Think about it – a ritual should feel like it naturally fits with your brand and how people already interact with it. The minute it starts feeling gimmicky, people tune out. You want to build on what people are already doing – like taking breaks, celebrating wins or sharing moments – and just make it a bit more special.

Great rituals should feel timeless, but that doesn't mean they can't evolve. The trick is finding that sweet spot between keeping what makes the ritual special while making sure it stays relevant as times change.

I already mentioned this, but I do not think it can be reiterated enough: a ritual that's meant to bring people together can leave some folks feeling left out. Maybe it's too expensive, too location-specific or just doesn't fit with everyone's culture. The best rituals are ones where anyone can join in their own way.

- Can everyone take part in your rituals?
- Can they make it their own?
- Is it easy for newcomers to understand and participate without feeling like they're missing years of inside jokes or unspoken rules?

The goal is to create rituals that feel inclusive from day one, not exclusive to long-time members.

Finding shared moments wherever you go

My husband and I have an unspoken rule when we go for our weekly shop. One person (usually yours truly) braves the crowded aisles and wrestles with the shopping cart. And then one person (pretty sure I do not need to spell out who that is) magically appears the moment snacks come out of the bags.

We all know how it goes, right? These little moments and unspoken rules of who does what – they're part of what makes a household tick.

That's exactly what Cadbury tapped into with their clever Made to Share campaign. They took their 40-square Dairy Milk bar and divided it up based on these everyday family dynamics. The bigger share goes to 'who did the shop', a decent chunk for 'who carried the bags in' and just a tiny bit for 'who raided them'.[23] It's such a simple but brilliant way to recognize those little acts of give-and-take we all know so well. These special edition bars turned an everyday moment into something worth sharing and talking about. Extra brownie points, as it fits perfectly with what Cadbury's all about – spreading joy and generosity.

The smartest marketers don't try to force their way into people's lives. Remember, great marketing is about direction, after all. Great marketers become part of the natural flow of their audience's daily life – the inside jokes, the shared moments, the little traditions. Whether it's how you take your morning coffee or celebrate small wins, the best brand rituals don't feel like marketing at all. They just feel natural. Because when you get right down to it, great rituals are about building relationships, which is at the core of customer-driven strategies. The ones that build superfans for life.

KEY POINTS

- Rituals create strong communities and drive brand advocacy when they feel natural and meaningful to customers.

- Effective rituals must be easy to repeat and feel uniquely personal to customers.

- Successful rituals encourage interaction between customers and create shareable moments.

- The most successful rituals are those where customers feel ownership and can personalize the experience.

- Using real customer experiences helps reinforce rituals and inspires others to participate.

- The most effective rituals become natural parts of customers' daily experiences.

Notes

1   *Eslogan Magazine.* The history of KitKat slogan: Have a break, *Eslogan Magazine*, April 2021. en.esloganmagazine.com/history-of-kit-kat-slogan-have-a-break/ (archived at https://perma.cc/G87G-KHLV)

2   Contagious. Have AI break, have a KitKat, Contagious, 2024. www.contagious. com/iq/article/have-ai-break-have-a-kitkat (archived at https://perma.cc/8WRA-YPXN)

3   Contagious. Have AI break, have a KitKat, Contagious, 2024. www.contagious. com/iq/article/have-ai-break-have-a-kitkat (archived at https://perma.cc/A6BY-UNMA)

4   N M Hobson, J Schroeder, J L Risen, D Xygalatas and M Inzlicht. The psychology of rituals: An integrative review and process-based framework, *Personality and Social Psychology Review*, 2017, 1–25

5   A M Graybiel. Habits, rituals, and the evaluative brain, *Annual Review of Neuroscience*, 2008, 31, 359–87. www.researchgate.net/publication/5297571_Habits_Rituals_and_the_Evaluative_Brain (archived at https://perma.cc/5MU6-XM9M)

6   J Davidge. How KitKat breathes life into its 'Have a break' strapline, The Marketing Society, 2013. www.marketingsociety.com/the-library/how-kitkat-breathes-life-its-have-break-strapline (archived at https://perma.cc/Y6FN-WW9E)

7   J Davidge. How KitKat breathes life into its 'Have a break' strapline, The
    Marketing Society, 2013. www.marketingsociety.com/the-library/how-kitkat-
    breathes-life-its-have-break-strapline (archived at https://perma.cc/XV9R-S28F)

8   The Brand Hopper. A deep dive into marketing strategies of KitKat, The Brand
    Hopper, April 2024. thebrandhopper.com/2024/04/25/a-deep-dive-into-
    marketing-strategies-of-kitkat/ (archived at https://perma.cc/A3FE-JWZU)

9   L Nimoy. How Leonard Nimoy's Jewish roots inspired the Vulcan salute, Star
    Trek, 17 July 2021. www.startrek.com/en-un/news/the-jewish-ritual-that-led-
    nimoy-to-create-the-vulcan-salute (archived at https://perma.cc/Y4HH-TR3R)

10 Newcastle University. Social identity theory, Newcastle University Open Lab,
    nd. open.ncl.ac.uk/academic-theories/9/social-identity-theory (archived at
    https://perma.cc/2QXQ-9HUL)

11 R Cialdini (1984) *Influence: The psychology of persuasion*, Harper Business,
    New York

12 The Coca-Cola Company. How a groundbreaking campaign got its start 'down
    under': Share a Coke, The Coca-Cola Company, 25 September 2014. www.
    coca-colacompany.com/about-us/history/how-a-campaign-got-its-start-down-
    under (archived at https://perma.cc/HV7P-GRBZ)

13 The Coca-Cola Company. How a groundbreaking campaign got its start 'down
    under': Share a Coke, The Coca-Cola Company, 25 September 2014. www.
    coca-colacompany.com/about-us/history/how-a-campaign-got-its-start-down-
    under (archived at https://perma.cc/59CU-FJXJ)

14 The Coca-Cola Company. How a groundbreaking campaign got its start 'down
    under': Share a Coke, The Coca-Cola Company, 25 September 2014. www.
    coca-colacompany.com/about-us/history/how-a-campaign-got-its-start-down-
    under (archived at https://perma.cc/V6U9-TF3L)

15 The Coca-Cola Company. How a groundbreaking campaign got its start 'down
    under': Share a Coke, The Coca-Cola Company, 25 September 2014. www.
    coca-colacompany.com/about-us/history/how-a-campaign-got-its-start-down-
    under (archived at https://perma.cc/K6QM-9BPX)

16 StoryBox. Coca-Cola Share A Coke: Campaign ad results, stats and analysis,
    StoryBox, 11 April 2024. storybox.io/coca-cola-share-a-coke-ad-campaign/
    (archived at https://perma.cc/V6M9-3V4W)

17 Interaction Design Foundation. What is the Einstellung effect? Interaction
    Design Foundation, 27 October, 2021. www.interaction-design.org/literature/
    topics/einstellung-effect (archived at https://perma.cc/3RED-LBZ9)

18 J V Knudstorp. LEGO CEO Jørgen Vig Knudstorp on leading through survival
    and growth, *Harvard Business Review*, January 2009. hbr.org/2009/01/lego-ceo-
    jorgen-vig-knudstorp-on-leading-through-survival-and-growth (archived at
    https://perma.cc/WSM2-N6ZG)

19 B M Morgan. Build-A-Bear CEO Sharon Price John talks CX strategy, Blake Michelle Morgan, 2023. www.blakemichellemorgan.com/podcast/listen-to-build-a-bears-ceo-talk-about-her-customer-experience-strategy (archived at https://perma.cc/2K58-WGRA)

20 D Berthiaume. Build-A-Bear transforms store for customer engagement, Chain Store Age, 17 January 2024. chainstoreage.com/build-bear-transforms-store-customer-engagement (archived at https://perma.cc/63PJ-ND8R)

21 Merkle. Build-A-Bear case study: Building a guest-led loyalty experience, Merkle, nd. www.merkle.com/en/work/case-studies/building-a-guest-led-loyalty-experience.html (archived at https://perma.cc/X3SM-VRZR)

22 LBBOnline. Müller urges fans to share their rituals to 'love every bit' in masterbrand campaign, LBBOnline, 2023. lbbonline.com/news/muller-urges-fans-to-share-their-rituals-to-love-every-bit-in-masterbrand-campaign (archived at https://perma.cc/2DA7-XBZS)

23 LBBOnline. Cadbury celebrates everyday generosity with limited edition 'Made to Share' Dairy Milk bars, LBBOnline, 2025. lbbonline.com/news/cadbury-celebrates-everyday-generosity-with-limited-edition-made-to-share-dairy-milk-bars (archived at https://perma.cc/RSQ3-SUGY)

11

Experimentation

How testing drives results

REMINDER

Marketing is a game of probabilities, not guarantees.

I am usually a pretty good baker, but there was a time I completely ruined a baked gift. I was making something special for a friend's graduation, one of those homemade, from-the-heart treats that's meant to say, 'I appreciate you.' I followed the recipe *to the letter*. Or at least, I *thought* I did. But when she took the first bite, her face said it all: something was very, very wrong.

Turns out, instead of 50 grams of sugar, I had added 500 grams. What was supposed to be a warm, delicious, celebratory treat had turned into a sickly-sweet sugar explosion. To this day, we still laugh about it.

And the harsh truth is that if I had tested the recipe first, even with just a small batch, I would've caught my mistake before it became a full-scale, inedible catastrophe.

Is there a marketing lesson in here somewhere? Of course there is. You can have the best strategy, the most well-researched campaign and all the confidence in the world that your approach will work. But if you don't test it first, you're running the risk of making a mistake that could have been *easily* avoided.

This is what separates good marketers from great ones. The best marketers are not only investigators, but also scientists. They test new ideas, track what works, learn from what doesn't and continuously refine their strategies. This mindset of continuous learning is what turns marketing from a guessing game into a scalable, data-driven process that delivers results.

In this chapter we're going to break down exactly why experimentation is non-negotiable in marketing, how to set up tests that drive meaningful results and the key mindset shift that separates marketers who guess from marketers who grow. Because, trust me, no one wants to be the person who adds 500 grams of sugar when 50 would do just fine.

The psychology of experimentation: Why we resist testing

If we *know* that experimentation leads to better results, why don't more marketers embrace it?

On paper, testing makes perfect sense: why would anyone want to gamble on a campaign without validating what works first? And yet, so many brands still rely on gut instinct, past experiences or just plain old 'this has always worked for us' thinking instead of structured testing.

It's not because they don't *want* better results. It's because, whether we realize it or not, our brains are wired to resist change. Psychologically, we crave certainty. We like to believe that our instincts are correct, that our years of experience make us immune to errors and that if something isn't broken, it doesn't need fixing.

This mindset is comfortable, but it's also dangerous: because in marketing, the moment you stop testing, you stop learning. Research by Kahneman and Tversky[1] highlighted just how deep this resistance runs. Their studies on the psychological principle called **loss aversion** found that individuals required significantly greater potential gains to offset perceived losses. For example, when presented with a coin flip bet, most people wouldn't accept unless the potential winnings were at least twice the amount they could lose.

The experiment Kahneman and Tversky ran involved asking people if they would accept a bet based on the flip of a coin. If the coin came up tails the person would lose $100 and if it came up heads, they would win $200. The results of the experiment showed that on average people needed to gain about twice as much as they were willing to lose to proceed forward with the bet. This shows how we instinctively avoid risk, even when the odds are in our favour.

Now, apply that thinking to marketing. If a campaign is performing *reasonably well*, the fear of making a change and potentially losing even a fraction of that success often outweighs the potential of significantly greater gains. Instead of iterating and optimizing, many businesses stick with 'good enough' because the idea of losing what they already have feels worse than the idea of gaining something better.

The fear of testing comes in different forms. Sometimes, it's the worry that making changes might backfire and break something that's already 'good enough'. Other times, it's the overconfidence that tells us we don't need to test because we already *know* what works. And often, it's just the pull of habit, following the idea that if we've always done something a certain way, it must be the right way.

When you change your mindset (and start making this a practice) experimentation is stacking the odds in your favour. It allows you to refine your approach using real data instead of gut instinct. The smartest marketers out there don't test because they're doubting themselves. They test because they know there's always room to make even their best ideas even better.

Understanding the fear of losing

You're at a coffee shop with a colleague. It's one of those rare afternoons where things feel relaxed and you're chatting about weekend plans. Suddenly, the conversation shifts to an opportunity they've been mulling over: a new job offer.

'It's more money,' they admit, stirring their latte, 'and the role is exciting, but... what if it doesn't work out? What if I leave what I have now and regret it?'

You nod, understanding completely. They're thinking about the comfort of what they already have: the familiar routine, the supportive team, the sense of stability.

It's a classic example of **loss aversion**, the psychological principle that we fear losing what we already have far more than we value potential gains.[2] Even when the new opportunity offers clear benefits, the risk of losing what's familiar feels overwhelming. It's why we hesitate to upgrade our phones, fearing the new one won't feel the same. It's why we hold onto clothes we no longer wear or stick with service providers we've outgrown.

Now, think about how this plays out in marketing. Let's say your current ad campaign is performing *okay*, not amazing, but not terrible either. The rational choice would be to experiment with a few tweaks that could potentially double engagement or conversions. But instead, many brands avoid testing altogether because of the fear that *any* change might cause performance to drop. This is loss aversion in action. Marketers aren't necessarily resistant to improvement, they're resistant to *risk*. But here's the irony: not testing is the bigger risk.

The good news is that, in a way, we train ourselves to see those risks and tackle them head on. These are my three go-to shifts I recommend you explore as well.

1 **Reframe the risk:** Instead of seeing testing as a gamble, view it as an insurance policy against bigger mistakes. Small, controlled experiments prevent larger failures down the line.

2 **Run low-stakes tests first:** If making a big change feels too risky, start with micro-experiments. Test a subject line before overhauling an entire email campaign.

3 **Focus on learning, not just winning:** I tell my students this during every single class. Even if a test 'fails' you gain valuable data. You're eliminating what doesn't work and getting closer to what *does*.

By refusing to experiment, you're choosing to stick with what you know, even if it's underperforming. You're trading potential growth for the comfort of familiarity. And in a world where consumer behaviour, algorithms and trends change constantly, staying still is a guaranteed way to fall behind.

The 'I knew it all along' trap

Ever looked at a successful marketing campaign and thought, '*Well, obviously that was going to work*'? That's **hindsight bias** talking.

Hindsight bias is the false belief that we 'knew all along' how something would turn out, even when we had no way of being certain at the time.[3] It's the reason we look at past successes and assume they were inevitable, rather than recognizing the decisions, iterations and, yes, experiments that led to them.

In marketing, hindsight bias can be dangerous. It convinces us that we already 'know' what works, leading us to avoid structured testing altogether. After all, if we believe we're already making the right calls, why bother experimenting?

But here's the maybe not so comfortable truth: even the best campaigns weren't obvious winners at the start. Think about some of the most iconic marketing successes, whether it's a viral social media trend, a record-breaking email open rate or an ad that resonated globally. Most of these weren't perfect on the first attempt. They were tested, refined and optimized before becoming the success stories we now take for granted.

This bias also explains why, after a campaign fails, people often claim *they saw it coming*. But if that were true, wouldn't they have prevented it in the first place? The reality is, hindsight makes everything seem more predictable than it was, making us overconfident in our assumptions and less likely to test future ideas.

It's a close cousin to confirmation bias, which we explored in Chapter 9: the tendency to only look for information that supports what we already believe. Both cognitive traps lead marketers to stick to what *feels* true rather than what's backed by data. And the ever-changing marketing world, that's a dangerous place to be. The beauty is that hindsight bias can help you run better experiments, which is what I always encourage our students to do.

---

1 **Document your predictions:** Before launching a campaign, write down your expectations. What do you *think* will happen? When you look back later, compare your predictions with actual results. This forces you to acknowledge gaps in foresight.

2 **Acknowledge past surprises:** No matter how experienced you are, you've likely been surprised by results before. Reminding yourself of these moments helps counteract the illusion that outcomes are predictable.

3 **Test even when you're 'sure':** If you believe a campaign idea is a guaranteed success, challenge yourself to test one small variation anyway. You might be right, but you might also uncover something even better.

Remember, just because something has worked in the past this doesn't mean it's still the best approach. Regularly ask: *'If we were starting from scratch today, is this how we'd do it?'*

If this still makes you close to physically sick, instead of making experimentation feel like a 'big risk', normalize small, continuous improvements. Testing doesn't have to mean an entire overhaul, in fact it can start with something as simple as tweaking a headline.

The comfort zone trap

TIP

In marketing, what worked yesterday won't always work tomorrow.

I am a child of the 1990s, which means I love a good candid analogue photo. My mum has dozens of albums of pictures from my grandparents, as well as childhood collections from my brother and me.

There is something magical in some of those pictures. Most likely it's the Nostalgia effect talking here! However, as much as nostalgia can be great for our campaigns, resistance to change, as already mentioned in this section, can be destructive (and has been) for many brands.

Let's take photography, for example. In 1975, an engineer at Kodak invented the world's first digital camera.[4] You'd think this would have been a game-changer for the company, right? Instead, Kodak's leadership dismissed the invention, fearing it would cannibalize their film business. They doubled down on what had always worked (physical film), ignoring the fact that customer behaviour was shifting.

Fast forward a few decades and Kodak's reluctance to evolve led to its downfall. By the time they finally embraced digital photography, companies like Canon, Sony and Apple had already taken over.[5] What was once an industry leader becoming a cautionary tale of what happens when brands resist change.

Ever heard the phrase, 'If it ain't broke, don't fix it'? That's status quo bias in action. In marketing, we often assume that if something has been working well enough, there's no need to change it. **Status quo bias** is the tendency to prefer things as they are, simply because they're familiar.[6] It's easier to stick to what's familiar than to introduce uncertainty. But in a world where customer behaviour, platforms and algorithms are constantly evolving, clinging to the past is holding your strategy back.

Here's the problem: what worked yesterday won't always work tomorrow. Think of major brands that dominated their industries but failed to evolve, like Kodak; or Blockbuster, which had the opportunity to innovate alongside Netflix but instead doubled down on the status quo.

The same logic applies to marketing strategies. A campaign that once delivered incredible results might be gradually losing effectiveness without you even realizing it. If you're not testing and evolving, you're likely falling behind simply because your competitors *are* experimenting and adapting. Keep an eye on changing customer behaviours and market shifts. Marketing is a game of probabilities, not guarantees, and experimentation stacks the odds in your favour.

Types of marketing experiments (and when to use them)

It's 1968 and Spencer Silver, a 3M scientist, accidentally creates a weak adhesive while trying to develop a strong one for the aerospace industry. Initially seen as a failure, the adhesive sits unused for years – until 1974, when Art Fry, another 3M employee, has a problem: his bookmarks keep falling out of his hymnal.[7] Fry connects the dots. Using Silver's adhesive, he develops the first version of what would become Post-it Notes. But the journey is far from over.

When 3M tests the product in 1977 under the name Press-n-Peel, it flops: customers don't understand how to use it. Most companies might have scrapped the idea, but 3M tries again with a bold experiment. In 1979 3M launched a marketing campaign known as the Boise Blitz. They distributed free samples to businesses in Boise, Idaho.[8] After the experiment, 90 per cent of recipients say they'd buy the product. By 1980, Post-it Notes launched nationwide, becoming a global sensation. Today, over 50 billion are sold annually.[9]

The story of Post-it Notes is proof of the power of persistence and experimentation in marketing, but also a reminder that not all experiments are created equal. A big part of testing stands in choosing the right type of experiment for the right situation. Think of experiments like detective work: you ask questions, gather clues and uncover insights that help you make better choices. Just like a detective uses different tools for different cases, we'll use different testing methods depending on what we want to learn.

Let's break down the most valuable types of marketing experiments, when to use them and how they can help you make decisions based on real data, not just hunches.

A/B testing: The classic showdown

We have seen this example often, the one for ecommerce brands testing the effectiveness of calls-to-action (CTAs) from 'Buy now' to 'Get yours today' to boost sales. By running an A/B test, they can measure which variation drives higher conversions without making assumptions.

With A/B testing, you can see which one works better instead of just guessing. A/B testing is perfect for tweaking these specific elements and it's a great way to start if you're new to testing things out.

When to use it:

- You're optimizing a webpage, ad or email and want to improve conversions.
- You're debating between two different headlines and want to see which resonates more.
- You want to test a *single* element at a time to measure its impact.

If you want to test one small variable at a time, A/B testing (also known as split testing) is your best friend. It involves creating two different versions of something (an email subject line, a landing page headline, a CTA button colour) and testing which one performs better.

Multivariate testing: The power of combinations

This one is for the over-achievers. Say you're running a software company and want to give your homepage a fresh look. Instead of just changing one thing at a time, you test new headlines, images and CTA buttons all at once. Multivariate testing shows you exactly which mix of these changes gets people to sign up.

When to use it:

- You're making multiple updates to a landing page and want to see how they work together.
- You're experimenting with several different ad variations and want to understand which *combination* of elements is most effective.

While A/B testing lets you try out one thing at a time, multivariate testing is like juggling multiple changes at once. It helps you see how different elements work together and influence each other. This kind of testing is perfect when you want to understand how different pieces work together, just keep in mind you'll need plenty of website visitors to get reliable results.

Incremental testing: Measuring true impact

Social media managers can sometimes see incremental testing in action on their Facebook ads. They split their audience into two groups: one group sees the ads and the other doesn't see them at all. Then they look at how many people from each group end up converting. If both groups convert about the same, it means those ads probably aren't doing as much as they thought.

This kind of testing helps brands catch when they're giving too much credit to campaigns that might not actually be moving the needle.

When to use it:

- You're running paid ads and want to prove they're truly influencing conversions.

- You want to measure the impact of organic vs paid marketing efforts.

- You suspect that a certain channel (e.g. social media) is getting too much credit for conversions.

Lots of marketing ideas look good at first glance (they come from your excellent brain after all), but you've got to ask yourself: would these sales have happened anyway? That's where incremental testing comes in handy as it helps you figure out what's working vs what just looks like it's working.

Look, each experiment has its own special job, but they're all trying to do the same thing: turn your guesses into solid facts. Just starting out? A/B testing and user feedback are your best friends, they're simple but super effective. When you're ready to level up, that's when you can dive into multivariate and incremental testing to really fine-tune your marketing.

REAL-WORLD EXAMPLE
How a simple experiment generated $100 million

Back in 2012, Microsoft Bing was constantly refining its search experience and ad performance.[10] One employee suggested a simple tweak: why not pull text from the first line of an ad and incorporate it into the headline? The idea was promising, but like many low-priority suggestions, it was shelved.

Until one engineer decided to test it.

Someone on the team realized that this change was simple enough to implement and ran an A/B test. The test split users into two groups, one seeing Bing's standard ad format and the other experiencing the new headline variation. They wanted to see if people would click more on these new-style ads. What happened next was unexpected.

The results: A $100 million shift

The new ad format boosted revenue by 12 per cent right off the bat, which set off some internal alarms because the jump was so unexpected.[11]

When they investigated, they found that this tiny change was bringing in an extra $100 million a year just in the US, and customers didn't mind the change one bit.[12]

This shows the power of experiments as we have been presenting them already so far:

- **Testing beats assumptions:** What was initially considered 'low priority' turned out to be a massive revenue driver. If they had relied on gut instinct instead of data, this opportunity would have been lost.

- **Incremental improvements scale:** No dramatic overhaul was needed. A single, well-executed tweak led to a multi-million-dollar impact.

- **A culture of experimentation:** Bing's success with A/B testing helped solidify a culture of data-driven decision-making, influencing not just internal strategy but also best practices across industries.

When it comes to experimenting in your customer journey and strategy, you don't need to reinvent the wheel to see major improvements. Small, data-backed optimizations can compound into massive gains.

Designing a great experiment: The scientific approach

I've spent dozens of hours on useless marketing experiments. They felt productive in the moment, but afterwards I realized I didn't learn anything I could act on.

You can avoid this mistake. Now, before I run any experiment, I ask myself one simple question: '*What am I going to do with this information?*'

Pretend you're done with the experiment and have the results on hand. Think about what you'd do with them. Avoid nice-to-know, vague statements like '*This will help us gain more insight about our audience.*' You could say that about anything. It's a low bar. You don't need more FYIs. You need actionable insights that will inform what you do next.

Here are the five steps we use when we run experiments at Alt Marketing School.

Step 1: Identify the problem you're trying to solve (or the strategy you want to test)

Before you test anything, define the specific issue or opportunity you want to address.

Questions I asked myself in the past included:

- Are conversions lower than expected?
- Is engagement dropping on a particular channel?
- Do you suspect a pricing tweak could increase sales?

Or maybe you want to test drive a new strategy before going all in. Instead of rolling out a new idea across your entire marketing funnel, you can run a quick test first to see if it works.

Examples:

- You want to experiment with interactive content (like quizzes) to see if it boosts engagement.
- You're considering launching a higher-priced premium version of your product but want to test demand first.
- You're exploring a new social media platform and want to see if it's worth continued investment.

A vague goal like *'We want to optimize our website'* isn't useful. A clear goal like *'We want to increase email sign-ups on our homepage by 10 per cent'* is.

The best experiments start with a focused question that leads to a decision, whether that's solving an existing issue or validating a brand-new opportunity.

Step 2: Form a hypothesis

This step may sound tedious (and oh so Virgo of me), but it can make all the difference when clarifying the *why* behind any experiment. A hypothesis is a simple cause-and-effect statement:

'If we do X, we expect Y to happen.'

For example, *'If we shorten our lead capture form from five fields to three, we expect to see a 15 per cent increase in sign-ups because users will experience less friction.'*

Your hypothesis should be based on logic, past data or user behaviour and not just gut instinct (even if we love that as well).

Step 3: Select your variables

Especially when getting started, a good experiment isolates one key variable at a time. Otherwise, you won't know which change influenced the results.

Think of it like baking (and be reminded of my terrible baking attempt at the beginning of this chapter): if you change the flour, sugar and oven temperature all at once and the cake turns out terrible, you won't know which change ruined it.

Examples of variables to test:

- **messaging** (e.g. testing two different email subject lines)
- **design** (e.g. changing the cooler of a CTA button)
- **timing** (e.g. sending an email in the morning vs evening)

Before going for multivariate testing, get familiar with simple tests. Control what stays the same so you can measure only the impact of what's changing.

Step 4: Measure and analyse results

Before we talk about measuring, a word to the wise. Take your time with your experiments (we like to test ours for at least 30 days, even the small ones). One of the biggest mistakes in experimentation is calling results too early. If you stop too early, you might get fooled by random ups and downs in your data.

Make sure you've got enough responses to make your results meaningful (that's what we call statistical significance). After all, you don't want to jump to conclusions just because a handful of people did something – you need bigger numbers to be sure.

Once your test has run its course, look at the data objectively.

- Did the change lead to an improvement?
- Was the difference large enough to be meaningful?
- Are there any unexpected side effects?

Your conclusion should always answer the question: *What do we do next?*

Step 5: Take action based on what you learned

We are almost at the finish line (well done you, I knew you could do it!). Now that you have got data, you have results and you have (hopefully) some answers, it's time to take action. Here's what to do with your experiment results:

- **Double down on what works:** When something's working well, roll it out across your marketing. Simple as that.

- **Cut what doesn't:** If something flops, don't just shrug it off. Ask yourself why – maybe your guess was wrong, or something else is going on.
- **Iterate and refine:** Sometimes you'll get hints rather than clear answers. That's fine – just tweak things and try again.

This way, you won't waste time on experiments that don't help you make better decisions.

Making sense of your results

Running an experiment is only half the battle. The real work starts when you're looking at those results, scratching your head, wondering what they're telling you.

It's tempting to get excited about a sudden spike in conversions or give up when a test doesn't go your way. But not every up and down in your data means something, and even 'failed' experiments can teach you valuable lessons. What sets great marketers apart is their ability to look at results with clear eyes and avoid the common traps that can mess with good decision-making.

One of the biggest mistakes is stopping an experiment too early. If you run a test for just a few days and see a 20 per cent increase in conversions, you might feel tempted to call it a success. But without enough data, that jump could just be random noise. If you don't have enough data, you might be making decisions based on coincidence rather than actual customer behaviour. Once again, depending on the impact of the experiment (how big is the change, how innovative is the idea, how cold is your audience) you want to look at 30 to 90 days for each of them.

Another huge culprit is false assumptions. Just because two things happen at the same time doesn't mean one caused the other (fancy names for this is causality and correlation). Let's say your conversions went up while testing a new landing page: it might not be the new design that did it. It could be seasonal trends, maybe an influencer mentioned you or even changes in social media algorithms.

Want to avoid jumping to wrong conclusions? Make sure to compare your test results with a control group (your past results, data and KPIs) and check whether you can get the same results more than once. Think about it – if you can't recreate that success in another test, it was probably just luck rather than something that works.

Let's talk about another tricky part of experimenting, which is what to do when your results aren't what you hoped for. It's really tempting to just toss out a test that didn't work and pretend it never happened. But failed experiments still provide valuable insights. When your hypothesis misses the mark, it's telling you something valuable about your audience, messaging or how users behave. Instead of thinking '*Well, that was a waste*', try asking: *What can we learn from this and how can we make our next test better?*

Finally, many marketers have to battle against internal resistance. People often resist experimenting because they're worried about changing something that's 'already working'. But, as we've seen, sticking with the status quo can be the bigger risk. The best way to overcome this hesitation is to shift the conversation. Instead of framing testing as a gamble, position it to reduce risk by making incremental, informed improvements.

Ultimately, the goal of experimentation isn't just to prove what works, but to refine your decision-making process over time. Even the best marketing teams get things wrong. What sets them apart is that they are not afraid to keep testing and tweaking their approach based on what the actual data shows them, not just what they hoped would happen.

REFLECTION TIME
What's your first experiment?

Now it's your turn. Instead of just reading about experimentation, let's design one together.

A well-structured experiment doesn't have to be complicated; it just needs a clear goal, a testable hypothesis and a way to measure success. Use the following prompts to shape your first (or next) marketing experiment.

Think about a problem you want to solve or a new strategy you want to try. Ask yourself:

- Is there a part of your marketing that could be performing better?

- Have you been relying on assumptions instead of testing them?

- Is there a new approach, tactic or channel you've been considering but haven't validated yet?

Once you answer those questions, it's time to form your hypothesis! And to do that, you can use the handy framework: '*If we do X, we expect Y to happen because Z.*'

For example: *'If we add customer testimonials to our checkout page, we expect conversion rates to increase because new buyers will feel reassured by social proof.'*

Decide on the format of your experiment:

- **A/B test:** Testing two variations against each other.
- **Multivariate test:** Testing multiple changes at once.
- **Incremental test:** Comparing performance to a control group.

For example, *'We'll run an A/B test with 50 per cent of visitors seeing the checkout page with testimonials and 50 per cent seeing the original version for two weeks.'*

Here's where the proverbial cookie crumbles: it's time to measure whether the change worked. Pick one clear metric that reflects success or failure.

- If you're testing a website change, track conversion rates or bounce rates.
- If you're testing email subject lines, monitor open rates and click-through rates.
- If you're testing a new ad creative, measure engagement and cost per conversion.

For example, *'Success means at least a 5 per cent increase in checkout conversion rates compared to the past 30 days.'*

You are almost there! However, before starting the experiment, ask yourself:

- If the test works, what will I do next?
- If the test fails, how will I use the insights?

Remember, you want to steer away from vague outcomes like *'This will help us learn more about our audience.'* Instead, focus on specific next steps. For example, *'If the test is successful, we'll roll out testimonials across all key conversion pages. If the test fails, we'll explore different placements or messaging for social proof before testing again.'*

Think like a scientist, market like a pro

TIP

In marketing, the moment you stop testing, you stop learning.

Being a great marketer means being curious and being willing to step out of your comfort zone. Sometimes the best discoveries happen when you're brave enough to try something new, even if it takes you down an unexpected path. Just like in 1930s, when a squishy, dough-like substance has been invented, with the purpose of cleaning wallpaper. At first, that's all it is – a practical, unremarkable product.[13] Then a worker saw kids having fun with it, squishing and shaping it into all sorts of things. That's when the light bulb went off. They tweaked the recipe, added some fun colours and a nice smell, and Play-Doh was born in the 1950s.

Over the course of this book, we have been following the journey our audience and customer takes and in our case even shapes our strategy. Hopefully, many of the ideas, tactics and even strategies explored got you already excited to implement new experiments in your existing work. Experiments can help you take all of those ideas (the blessing and the curse of idea people like me) and build on structured, intentional tests that reveal what works. And when you discover something that *does* work, the final step is knowing when and how to scale it up.

Which is exactly why I could not finish this chapter without mentioning it. Not every successful experiment should be implemented immediately or at full scale. Just because an A/B test shows a 15 per cent lift this doesn't mean it will hold up in different conditions or with a wider audience. Before going all in, guns blazing, ask:

- **Was the improvement significant and repeatable?** Run follow-up tests to confirm the results aren't a one-off fluke.

- **Does it align with long-term strategy?** Just because a certain ad style converts well now doesn't mean it fits your brand vision. Ensure changes are sustainable.

- **Are there unintended trade-offs?** A test might increase conversions but negatively impact another key metric, like customer retention. Always look at the full picture before scaling.

When a test consistently delivers strong results across multiple scenarios, that's your green light to roll it out, whether that's a new ad format, a refined landing page or a messaging shift. But don't stop testing just because something's working. Keep experimenting!

So, as you move forward, don't just execute. Experiment. Test. Iterate. And if you're ever tempted to launch a campaign without testing first, just remember what happens when you add 500 grams of sugar instead of 50. A little testing now can save you from some awkward situations later.

KEY POINTS

- Regular testing helps validate assumptions and improve marketing outcomes.

- Every experiment needs a clear hypothesis, measurable metrics and defined timeframes.

- Don't stop tests too early or confuse correlation with causation.

- Failed experiments provide valuable insights for future strategies.

- Successful tests should be validated multiple times before full implementation.

- Continue testing and refining even when something works – there's always room for improvement.

Notes

1 D Kahneman and A Tversky. Prospect theory: An analysis of decision under risk, *Econometrica*, 1979, 47 (2), 263–91

2 U Schmidt and H Zank. What is loss aversion? *Journal of Risk and Uncertainty*, 2005, 30 (2), 157–67. www.jstor.org/stable/41761190 (archived at https://perma.cc/K5U3-GJS8)

3 Britannica. Hindsight bias, Encyclopædia Britannica, nd. www.britannica.com/topic/hindsight-bias (archived at https://perma.cc/VL67-JT6L)

4 Kodak. Chronology of film, Kodak, nd. www.kodak.com/en/motion/page/chronology-of-film/ (archived at https://perma.cc/7WUQ-WQXJ)

5 Analogue Wonderland. The rise and fall and rise of Kodak film, Analogue Wonderland, nd. analoguewonderland.co.uk/pages/about-kodak (archived at https://perma.cc/JC63-H5AT)

6 W Samuelson and R Zeckhauser. Status quo bias in decision making, *Journal of Risk and Uncertainty*, 1988, 1 (1), 7–59. www.jstor.org/stable/41760530 (archived at https://perma.cc/FS97-8SDX)

7 C Skonord. Post-it Notes: An employee idea that was originally a mistake, Ideawake, 19 February 2021. ideawake.com/post-it-notes-employee-idea-that-was-originally-mistake/ (archived at https://perma.cc/8E7K-Z2MJ)

8 D Kahneman and A Tversky. Prospect theory: An analysis of decision under risk, *Econometrica*, 1979, 47 (2), 263–91

9 N Glass and T Hume. The 'hallelujah moment' behind the invention of the Post-it note, CNN, 4 April 2013. edition.cnn.com/2013/04/04/tech/post-it-note-history/index.html (archived at https://perma.cc/QLB4-TC63)

10 Bing Blogs. Large scale experimentation at Bing, Bing Search Quality Insights, 8 August 2013. blogs.bing.com/search-quality-insights/August-2013/Large-Scale-Experimentation-at-Bing (archived at https://perma.cc/T7HW-T96L)

11 R Kohavi and S Thomke. The surprising power of online experiments: Getting the most out of A/B and other controlled tests, Harvard Business Review, September–October 2017

12 R Kohavi and S Thomke. The surprising power of online experiments: Getting the most out of A/B and other controlled tests, *Harvard Business Review*, September–October 2017. hbr.org/2017/09/the-surprising-power-of-online-experiments (archived at https://perma.cc/U2WN-ZZR8)

13 R Despres. 15 of the coolest accidental inventions, HowStuffWorks, 1 January 1970. science.howstuffworks.com/innovation/inventions/15-of-the-coolest-accidental-inventions.htm (archived at https://perma.cc/VTM3-RYLT)

12

Measuring success
and adapting to change

REMINDER

The best marketers don't track more data. They track better data.

Have you ever owned a fitness tracker? Only asking because I have owned plenty over the years and maybe because I am a type A individual, well, the progress motivation works on me. Plus, science backs me up. Just like those fitness trackers, seeing your progress can really motivate you to keep going.[1] They show you how you're doing and help you stick to your goals. Of course, they work better for some people than others (it really depends on how you use them and make them part of your daily life).

Let's say you also wear some sort of tracker and as you check your steps and notice you're averaging about 3,000 a day, far from the 10,000 goal you've always heard about. But instead of shrugging it off, you decide to make a small change. You start adding a 10-minute walk after lunch. The tracker buzzes with encouragement, showing you've hit 5,000 steps. The next week, you park further away at the grocery store. By the end of the day, you've cracked 8,000 steps.

The data backs this up, too – when people wear activity trackers, they naturally move more. In fact, most people end up taking about 1,235 more steps each day, which works out to roughly 40 extra minutes of walking.[2] A month later, you're hitting 10,000 steps regularly and it doesn't feel like a chore anymore. By tracking your progress, you have been inspired to act, as it showed you that progress is possible when you pay attention to the numbers and adjust your habits.

'What has this got to do with marketing, Fab?' you may be asking.

It's an important lesson: what gets measured, gets managed. Metrics like engagement rates, traffic or conversions can teach so much to the patient marketers who take the time to measure their efforts.

- A spike in clicks on a new campaign? Double down on what's working.
- A dip in email open rates? Test new subject lines or send times.
- High-performing content? Repurpose it for other platforms.

When you let data guide your decisions, even small tweaks can make a big difference.

It's just like our fitness tracker example: once you start paying attention to the numbers, you'll naturally find ways to improve and grow.

What gets measured, gets managed (but only if you act on it)

Data is everywhere. Marketers track clicks, conversions, engagement, impressions, followers, open rates: you name it. But most of that data just sits there. It's collected, analysed, placed in a neat little dashboard... and then? Nothing changes.

Repeat after me: data is only as valuable as the action it inspires. After all, if it's not influencing decisions, shaping strategies or helping you refine your approach, why track it at all?

And yet, marketers still fall into the trap of tracking data without purpose. We fixate on dashboards, obsess over engagement rates and present reports that look impressive, but what are they *actually* telling us?

So no, this chapter is not just about metrics. It's about dispelling some myths, clarifying intentions and taking action.

Data should be meaningful and tied to action: if it's not driving decisions, why measure it?

Numbers alone don't tell a story, context does. A dip in engagement or an increase in website traffic means nothing without understanding *why* it's happening.

Measurement is as much about celebrating success as it is about learning what works and what doesn't, so you can refine, pivot and improve. Instead of collecting data for the sake of it, we're going to reframe it as a tool for learning, adapting and making better decisions, which, as always, puts our customers at the centre of our decision-making.

Bringing back OKRs:
How to align measurement with your strategy

I am a plant owner with most likely what you'd call a pale green thumb, which means I often opt to care for plants that are relatively easy to keep alive. And plants behave very similarly to goal setting in marketing.

Like with my plants, if I don't focus on tracking the right metrics in marketing, growth won't happen. Just as watering alone isn't enough for a plant that needs better sunlight or soil, focusing on the wrong metrics won't lead to marketing success.

Tracking the right things (whether it's sunlight and nutrients for plants, or meaningful metrics for marketing) can bring real growth. Not all metrics matter equally and, no, I am not going to start talking about vanity metrics (well, just yet).

On the one hand, if you are drowning in data without seeing real impact you may be tracking too much. And if, on the other hand, you are feeling overwhelmed even starting to track anything, your goals can help you get started.

Here's where objectives and key results (**OKRs**) come into play. Great OKRs will link every number you track back to something bigger.

Let's say your goal for the next quarter is to build a community through retention. In that case, you may not want to prioritize growth metrics (likes, etc.) over engagement. Instead, look at things that really matter – how people engage with your content, how they participate in discussions and whether they're spreading the word about you.

And if you're aiming to boost conversions? Don't just count clicks. Look at the whole picture: track how people move from first finding out about you to becoming customers. What makes them take that final step?

The vanity metrics myth: No metric is useless

Vanity metrics have become a favourite villain in marketing. The idea is simple: certain numbers (like social media likes or followers) are 'vanity' because they *look good* but don't *mean much*.

Look, it's true that not every metric is going to lead straight to making money. But the real issue isn't about vanity metrics at all. It's about tracking stuff that doesn't match what you're trying to achieve. Here's my unpopular opinion: no metric is useless if you understand why you're tracking it.

The mistake isn't measuring reach, impressions or followers, but measuring them in isolation, without connecting them to something deeper.

In my experience, a metric only becomes 'vanity' if it's presented without context. Consider these two scenarios:

1   A company tracks Instagram followers and reports on month-over-month growth, with no further analysis. It looks impressive, but it tells them nothing about engagement, conversions or business impact.

2   Another company also tracks Instagram followers but uses it as an indicator of community growth before launching an event. They correlate follower increases with UGC and RSVPs, seeing a direct link between audience expansion and event participation.

Same metric, yet two very different levels of insight.

Vanity metrics become meaningful when:

- they serve as an early signal of success (e.g. rising engagement before an uptick in conversions)
- they support long-term goals, even if they don't drive immediate revenue
- they are used in combination with deeper performance metrics to tell a fuller story

Look, vanity metrics aren't really the bad guys here. The real problem is when we track numbers without really knowing why or how they fit into our bigger picture. When you use them right, even those surface-level numbers can tell you a lot about how aware people are of your brand, how they're behaving and where things are headed.

Metrics only matter if they help you make smarter decisions. If you're tracking something on your dashboard but never using it to take action, maybe it's time to ask yourself why you're tracking it at all.

Gut-check test: Are you measuring the right things?

Collecting data can already feel overwhelming. But knowing what to do with it? That's where things get messy. Too often, we report on numbers without questioning *why* we're tracking them in the first place. A dashboard packed with engagement rates, CTRs and follower counts might look impressive, but if those metrics don't lead to smarter decisions, they're just taking up space.

It's time for a gut-check test – something I encourage our students to do as well. Before adding another metric to your tracking list, pause and think about the *why* of your metrics. Every data point you track should have a reason for existing. If you can't trace it back to a business objective, it's likely just noise.

Gut-check: Can I clearly explain how this metric ties back to an OKR, or am I tracking it just because it's there?

Even more so, not all improvements mean progress. A 50 per cent increase in website traffic sounds great – until you realize those visitors are bouncing after five seconds. More email subscribers might look like growth, but if they're not engaging with your content, are they really helping your business?

Data needs context. If a metric goes up, down or sideways, you should be able to answer:

- What does this mean for my strategy?
- Does it lead to deeper engagement, stronger relationships or more conversions?
- If it changes, does my strategy need to shift?

If a metric changes but doesn't influence your next move, it's not worth tracking.

Gut-check: If this metric went up by 30 per cent tomorrow, what would I do differently? If the answer is 'nothing', stop measuring it.

Finally, an unspoken truth is that some data is just easier to collect. Social media platforms hand out engagement metrics like candy. Google Analytics will give you endless reports on website visits. These numbers are *accessible*, but that doesn't mean they're *useful*.

On the flip side, harder-to-measure insights (like customer sentiment, qualitative feedback and true conversion drivers) often require more effort but provide far richer direction.

Take a B2B company focused on increasing customer retention. It's tempting to track new conversions and assume that high numbers mean customers are happy. But what's more valuable? Looking at NPS scores to learn why certain customers stay, which services they engage with most and what pain points cause others to leave.

Gut-check: Am I prioritizing easy-to-track data over meaningful insights that would drive action?

Look at your last performance report or dashboard. Identify the top five metrics you're currently tracking and put them through the gut-check:

- What OKR does this metric tie back to?
- If this number improves, what action will I take?
- Am I tracking this because it's valuable or because it's easy?

If a metric doesn't have a clear purpose, contributes no actionable insight or exists just because it's available, consider whether it should be there in the first place. The best marketers don't track *more* data. They track *better* data. You heard it here first.

Breaking down measurement across the customer journey

> TIP
>
> Data is only as valuable as the action it inspires.

If you're scratching your head about what to track or how to tie metrics to your customer goals, don't worry, I have a framework that will help you out. It's designed to help you measure stuff that matters as customers move through their journey.

We're talking real insights into how people think and act, not just numbers on a spreadsheet. The right data depends on where your audience is in their journey. What matters at the awareness stage won't be the same as what matters at conversion or retention.

While following standard practices is great, sometimes you need to think outside the proverbial sketched lines. That's where our gut-check test comes in handy. If a metric isn't telling you anything useful, it's totally okay to switch things up and track something that better reflects what your customers are doing. Remember, it's not about following a strict playbook of KPIs, but making sure the numbers you're tracking help you make better decisions.

As a refresher, **KPIs** are the numbers that tell you if you're on track to hit your goals. They're like a report card that shows how well you're doing at achieving what matters most.

The awareness stage

At the awareness stage of your customer journey, for example, the goal isn't immediate sale but getting on your audience's radar and ensuring they *remember* you. People are discovering your brand for the first time, so the focus is on visibility and recall.

Key metrics are often identified as:

- **Brand awareness:** Are people recognizing your brand when they see it? (Quantifiable through share of voice, brand recall surveys, PR mentions.)
- **Impressions and reach:** Are the right people seeing your content?
- **Engagement (early stage):** Are people stopping to interact (likes, shares, comments)?
- **New website visitors:** How many first-time visitors are checking you out?

Going off script here (I am a marketing rebel, after all), not every brand benefits from high reach, especially if quality engagement matters more than scale.

If your audience is niche, you might prioritize depth over breadth, tracking how deeply a smaller audience engages rather than how many people see your content.

Just don't fall into the trap of expecting conversions too early. Measuring purchases at this stage makes no sense – people aren't ready to buy yet. Instead, keep your eye on how many folks are discovering your brand for the first time. That's what really matters at this stage.

The consideration stage

Once people know about you, the next question is: are they engaging deeper? As a refresher, the consideration stage is about moving from passive awareness to active interest and the all-so important place where customers start weighing their options.

Key metrics:

- **Time on site and pages viewed:** Are people exploring your content, or are they bouncing immediately?
- **Content engagement:** Are they reading blog posts, watching videos, engaging with emails?
- **Lead generation:** Are they opting into your newsletter, downloading resources, signing up for webinars? (Quantifiable through subscribers' growth, attendees' numbers.)

Some businesses do better with one-on-one conversations rather than public posts. If you're selling something that requires a big investment decision, you might want to pay more attention to those DM conversations, email responses and how deeply people are diving into your content, rather than just counting likes and comments.

So, make sure you're clear about what metrics matter at each stage and don't fall into the trap of skipping consideration metrics. Remember: you want to give yourself as many chances as possible to measure (and show) successful relationship building.

The conversion stage

At this point, the customer has shown interest. This is where things get real: and I'm talking about that magical moment when someone's ready to act. Maybe they're about to hit that 'buy' button or sign up for your service. Your main job? Make it super easy for them to say 'yes' by removing any roadblocks in their way.

Key actionable metrics:

- **Conversion rate:** What percentage of engaged users convert?
- **Cost per acquisition:** How much are you spending to gain each new customer? (Quantifiable through ads spend and results, for example.)
- **Sales funnel drop-off points:** Where are potential customers hesitating or leaving?
- **Time to conversion:** How long does it take for a prospect to go from first touchpoint to purchase?

Never forget to put your investigator's hat on. If you only track total sales without analysing the why you will miss key insights in the long run. If your conversions aren't where you want them to be, try digging deeper. Look at where potential customers might be getting stuck or what's making them hesitate. Sometimes you'll need to go back to good old market research to figure out what's really going on.

The customer journey doesn't stop at conversion. Hopefully, by this point in the book, you are fully on board with the idea that retention is just as important as acquisition.

The loyalty and advocacy stage

Adding metrics for loyalty and advocacy can really change the way you present success all round.

Here's where you may also have to start educating clients, teams and manager to buy into these results. They can get so caught up chasing new customers that they completely forget about the ones they already have.

Key metrics:

- **Repeat purchase rate:** How many customers come back – what is your churn rate?
- **Customer lifetime value:** How much revenue does a single customer bring over time?
- **Referral and advocacy participation:** Are customers recommending you to others? (Quantifiable through testimonials and reviews.)
- **Community engagement:** Are customers engaging with your brand beyond just purchasing? (Think user-generated content or even employee-generated content.)

Some businesses thrive on *brand love* more than repeat purchases. If you're in an industry where customers don't buy frequently (e.g. high-ticket products), it makes more sense to track how much people are talking about you, recommending you to others or staying connected with your brand, even when they're not shopping.

When you align your metrics with where your audience is in their journey, you stop chasing the wrong numbers and start measuring what truly drives growth.

How to present data and make it actionable

You're at a team meeting and it's time to present last month's marketing report. The numbers aren't great: website traffic dipped, conversion rates are down and engagement on social media has dropped. You feel the tension rising as you prepare to share the bad news.

You have two choices. Choice one, dump the problems on the table: *'Traffic is down 20 per cent, engagement dropped and conversions are lagging. We're not sure why.'*

The room goes silent and your team looks worried. Now, instead of discussing solutions, everyone is stuck in problem mode.

Or frame the report with solutions.

'Traffic dipped 20 per cent, but our email campaigns performed well. If we focus more on targeted email outreach, we can drive qualified leads back to the site. Engagement is lower on social, but we saw an increase in video interactions, so let's test more short form content this month.'

The difference is that instead of presenting problems, you're leading with solutions. This is one of the core lessons I have learned during my agency and CMO work over the past 10 years.

The harsh truth is that every report tells a story and when the numbers don't look good, that story should focus on *what's next*, not just what went wrong. Because, in the end, you should not be afraid to talk about the 'negative' (losing followers, or the traffic drop) because what your team/client really wants to know is what this data tells us and how we're going to fix it.

Data is only as useful as the story it tells. The problem is that too many marketing reports are just a bunch of numbers thrown together without any real meaning. Sure, your dashboard might tell you engagement dropped 20 per cent, but if you can't explain *why* that happened or *what we should do about it*, those numbers aren't helping anyone.

Compare these two statements:

'Engagement dropped 20 per cent last month.'

'Engagement dropped 20 per cent last month, largely due to a decline in reach on Instagram. This coincided with changes to the algorithm that deprioritized certain content formats. To adapt, we should shift focus to video-first posts and test new formats to regain visibility.'

The second statement gives you the full picture: what happened, why it happened and what we're going to do about it. Without these details, you're just looking at numbers that don't really tell you what to do next.

- What's the one thing the audience needs to know?
- Why should they care about this trend or shift?
- What should the team do with this information?

Actionable insights vs raw data

Not all numbers are equally useful. A common mistake in reporting is focusing on what's *easy* to track rather than what's *useful*.

For example, saying

'Website traffic increased 30 per cent'

is raw data.

Saying

'Website traffic increased 30 per cent, largely from organic search, due to improved rankings on high-intent keywords. This suggests our SEO efforts are paying off and we should double down on content in these areas'

Before you start freaking out, here's what you need to remember: while the tools, platforms and tactics evolve, the fundamentals of human behaviour don't. No matter how much things change, people still want to feel connected, to trust who we're dealing with and to belong somewhere.

They want brands that understand them, experiences that feel personal and interactions that feel meaningful. The challenge for marketers is to stay rooted in these timeless principles while adapting to new opportunities.

Filtering out the noise and focusing on what matters

Every few months, a new trend pops up claiming to be *the* future of marketing.

One minute it's AI writing everything for us, then it's the metaverse, then BeReal comes along and now everyone's worried about TikTok getting banned. With all this happening, you might feel pressured to try everything just to keep up.

But the best marketers are the ones who know how to filter out the noise, focus on what matters and refine instead of restart. They see change as an opportunity, not a threat. Instead of scrambling to keep up, they ask:

- How does this new tool, platform or behaviour fit into what I already know about my audience?
- Does this align with my strategy, or is it just a distraction?
- Will this genuinely improve customer experience, or is it just a shiny new thing?

When you approach marketing with this mindset, change becomes a part of the process. You're making *intentional* choices about where to spend your time and effort.

The brands that last play the long game

If you want proof, look at the brands that have stood the test of time. Despite all the changes around them, they thrived because they stayed customer centric. Their platforms may have changed. Their tactics may have evolved. But their core principles remained the same. And when in doubt, they asked their audience for guidance.

Think of how Apple has approached its strategy over the decades. Campaigns like #ShotoniPhone have encouraged users for years to share their stories and photos taken with Apple devices, fostering a sense of turns it into an actionable insight.

Think of analysing data like being a detective, as you've got to ask the right questions to get to the bottom of things. When you see a number trending up or down, don't just nod and move on. Get curious! What's that number really telling you about how your audience behaves? How does it fit into your bigger marketing picture?

Most importantly, what can you do with this information? It's all about turning those numbers into a story that shows you what to do next.

Reporting shouldn't just be a retrospective task. A great report should inform what happens next. Every report should lead to a discussion about action.

A simple three-step framework to make sure data translates into next steps:

1 What happened? Summarize the key trend.

2 Why did it happen? Provide context and contributing factors.

3 What should we do next? Suggest a data-driven adjustment.

In practice, it may look a little bit like this:

> 'Website traffic increased 30 per cent this quarter. After analysing the data, we found that blog posts with actionable tips and tutorials drove the most visits. Moving forward, we'll focus on creating more educational content and optimize our top-performing articles to maintain this growth trend.'

Presenting and adapting data for different audiences

CTRs, CLV and too many acronyms to count. The truth about many reports is that they can end up looking like word salads. Reports will look different depending on what you want to highlight, but also who you are presenting your data too. Not everyone needs the same level of detail. A CEO, a marketing director and a content strategist all care about performance, but they'll want the data presented differently.

- **Executives want the big picture.** High-level insights, trends and business impact. Keep it clear and strategic.
- **Marketing managers want key performance drivers.** What's working, what's not and where to adjust strategy.
- **Specialists want granular insights.** Specific data on engagement, conversion rates or ad performance to refine their work.

Talking about your audience, I see upskilling and expert marketers often make another big mistake. They may have learned to talk the *customers' language* but they forget to talk their clients' language. This is through knowledge bias, often referred to as the **curse of knowledge**, a cognitive bias that happens when individuals with specialized knowledge assume others share the same level of understanding (something I fought a lot with as a teacher).[3]

A great way to avoid knowledge bias is to provide quick, digestible explanations for any data point that might not be universally understood. For example, instead of simply saying: *'Our CTR dropped by 20 per cent last quarter'* reframe it for clarity:

> 'Our click-through rate (CTR), which measures how many people clicked on our content after seeing it, dropped by 20 per cent last quarter. This suggests that either our messaging isn't engaging enough or that we're reaching the wrong audience. We'll be testing new ad creatives and refining targeting to improve results.'

If presenting data to clients, senior stakeholders or teams outside of marketing, consider:

- adding short definitions for key metrics that may not be familiar.
- explaining why a specific metric matters and how it connects to business goals.
- providing visual context like graphs, side-by-side comparisons or trends over time to make the data easier to digest.

At the end of the day, data can tell different stories depending on who you're talking to. The key is knowing your audience and tailoring your message to what matters to them. And hey, when the numbers aren't looking great, it's tempting to get stuck on the negatives. But remember marketing is all about adapting. Every piece of data, even the not-so-great stuff, gives us a chance to get better.

REFLECTION TIME
What are you measuring (and why)?

Let's take a moment to review what you're measuring. Are your metrics really telling you what you need to know, or are they just numbers on a page? Here are some questions to help you figure out whether your data is helping you make better decisions or if it's just creating more noise.

Let's start by identifying your top three metrics – and whether they tell you something useful. Look at your current reports or dashboards. What are the top three numbers you track the most? For each one, ask:

- What is this number telling me?
- Does it align with my broader marketing goals?
- If it changed tomorrow, would it impact my strategy?

If a metric isn't shaping your next move, it might be time to replace it with one that does. Be wary of this common mistake though, as some data points are easier to collect than others, but, as we mentioned in this chapter, convenience doesn't equal importance.

Are you tracking these metrics because they're meaningful, or just because they're available? What's a harder-to-measure insight that would provide real value?

Think about it – things like customer feedback, how people feel about your brand and the way they use your product often tell you much more than just looking at engagement stats. Sometimes you need to look beyond the numbers to get the real story.

If you feel you have the right metrics at hand, next you want to dive deeper than surface-level data. For each metric, explore its impact:

- **Am I tracking the next step?** For example, if engagement is up, am I also measuring how it's leading to conversions or deeper interactions?
- **Am I correlating metrics?** For example, if my email open rate is improving, am I also tracking whether it's leading to higher click-through rates or sales?

Now, it's time for a gut-check: if a key metric doesn't align with where the customer is in their journey, it might be misleading rather than useful.

First, identify which stage of the journey you are focusing on for each metric: awareness, consideration, conversion or loyalty. Don't stop here, however. Be inquisitive and explore the connection of each metric:

- **Does my metric make sense for that stage?** If I'm tracking awareness, should I be looking at brand recall and reach rather than sales?
- **Am I focusing on the right moment, or skipping ahead?** If I want to build engagement, am I measuring participation, or am I expecting conversions too soon?

Remember, your metrics only matter if they help you make smarter decisions. Look at your recent reports: have they led you to try something new or change your approach?

Finally, here's the real test: can you look at your current data and spot at least one thing you could do differently tomorrow?

If you're scratching your head trying to figure out how to use your data, maybe it's time to shake up what you're measuring and how you're using it.

Using metrics as a growth tool, not a performance checklist

TIP

The brands that win aren't the ones that track the most, but the ones that learn the fastest.

Back when I was a personal trainer, I had these super dedicated clients who'd show up religiously every week, giving it their all, but somehow weren't seeing the results they wanted. These were the really committed ones, you know, the type with clear goals in mind.

The issue wasn't their dedication, but it was their approach to tracking progress. Some focused too much on the number on the scale, ignoring strength gains and endurance improvements. Others tracked everything (calories burned, steps taken, gym sessions logged) but had no strategy to adjust based on what was working. The solution did not lay in more burpees, or better macros. It stood from something that goes beyond fitness: measuring with purpose.

I helped my clients focus on the right metrics for their goals, whether it was increasing strength, improving stamina or hitting personal bests. Rather than getting hung up on every little number, we kept track of what showed progress and tweaked things as needed. That's exactly the mindset we need for marketing metrics too.

As marketers, too often we just collect data and create reports without doing anything with them. As explored in this chapter, metrics should help us make better decisions, not just show what we've done in the past. Every number we track should have a purpose. If something goes up or down, we should know exactly what to do about it.

Think about it: when engagement drops, we need to figure out why.

1 Is our content not hitting the mark?

2 Did our audience's behaviour change?

3 Are there outside factors at play?

And if we suddenly get more website traffic, we shouldn't just celebrate the numbers – we should ask ourselves who these new visitors are and what they're doing on our site.

When to adapt vs when to stay the course

I am not going to sugar-coat it: metrics can be a bit tricky to interpret. Just because your numbers dip for a day or two doesn't mean everything's falling apart. And on the flip side, a sudden spike in traffic doesn't always mean you've struck gold. Sometimes these ups and downs are just normal fluctuations or caused by things outside your control.

Data only becomes truly useful when you look at the bigger picture. You need to understand the patterns over time, how seasons affect your numbers and what other factors might be influencing your results.

As you are reviewing your efforts periodically (every 90 days is a good practice) reflect on whether it's time for a change.

- **Is this shift part of a long-term trend or just short-term volatility?** A drop in engagement for one week might be nothing, but if the decline continues for months, it's time to investigate.
- **Are external factors influencing the data?** Seasonality, platform algorithm changes or industry shifts might explain the trends you're seeing.
- **Have I given this strategy enough time to work?** Some marketing efforts (like community building or SEO) take time. If you pivot too quickly, you might miss long-term growth potential.

The best marketers go beyond performance by tracking progress. That means evolving measurement strategies as goals change, industry landscapes shift and customer behaviour adapts.

- Your metrics should evolve as your strategy evolves. What you tracked a year ago might not be relevant today.
- Start learning from data. Insights should shape your next move, not just explain the last one.
- If your data isn't helping you make better decisions, rethink what you're measuring. Every metric should contribute to clarity, not confusion.

Marketing that shows results, like fitness, is about knowing *why* things work (or don't) and being ready to switch things up when needed. When you measure things the right way, you've got a super powerful tool for growth in your hands.

Because in the end, the brands that win aren't the ones that track the most, but the ones that learn the fastest.

KEY POINTS

- Metrics should be meaningful and actionable, not just easily available – focus on data that drives decisions.
- Adapt your measurement strategy as your goals and industry landscape evolve.
- Avoid knowledge bias by providing clear context and explanations when sharing data with different audiences.
- Look beyond surface-level metrics to understand the complete customer journey and correlations between different data points.
- Use data as a learning tool to improve strategies, not just as a performance checklist.
- Consider external factors and long-term trends when deciding whether to adapt or maintain current strategies.
- Success comes from learning and adapting based on insights, not just collecting more data.

Notes

1   C Bäccman and E Wästlund. The use of fitness-trackers and the role of motivational intermissions to maintain healthy behaviors: An explorative case study on runners, *South Florida Journal of Development*, 2022, 3 (6), 6629–50. ojs.southfloridapublishing.com/ojs/index.php/jdev/article/view/1909 (archived at https://perma.cc/T4LN-D82A)

2   H Godman. Do activity trackers make us exercise more? Harvard Health Letter, 1 October 2022. www.health.harvard.edu/exercise-and-fitness/do-activity-trackers-make-us-exercise-more (archived at https://perma.cc/2D66-K9FC)

3   K Jones. The curse of knowledge: A cognitive bias all teachers should be aware of, Evidence Based Education, 14 November 2023. evidencebased.education/the-curse-of-knowledge-a-cognitive-bias-all-teachers-should-be-aware-of (archived at https://perma.cc/66BX-5EY7)

Conclusion

Better marketing for marketers

REMINDER

The key to future-proof marketing isn't knowing what's coming next. It's knowing what's timeless.

A few years back, I was standing in front of a room filled with hundreds of marketers, doing a talk about human marketing practices. As I started my session, instead of diving straight into tactics and strategies, I asked them a simple question, having them submit their choice through their phones:

'If you could choose just one word to describe what marketing is missing right now, what would it be?'

One by one, words started coming in. Some were expected (trust, creativity, authenticity). But as I scanned the responses, one word kept appearing over and over again.

Kindness.

It caught me off-guard at first. Kindness? In marketing? But the more I thought about it, the more it made sense.

Because marketing, first and foremost, needs to be *better* for marketers. The people behind the strategies, the content, the campaigns – they're looking for kindness. From each other. From clients. From audiences.

That moment shaped something in me. It changed how I think about marketing, but more importantly, how I show up in this space. Now, whether I'm teaching a class, recording a podcast or speaking on YouTube, I end with the same message:

'Be kind to yourselves and others.'

It might sound like it has nothing to do with marketing, but it has *every-thing* to do with it. Because when marketers feel supported, when they feel valued, when they are given space to create without fear, well, *that's* when marketing gets better. Not just for us, but for the people we serve. And maybe, just maybe, kindness is the missing piece we've been overlooking all along.

Making marketing better for marketers

Marketing should be better for marketers.

I've said this before and I'll say it again: marketers go through a lot and we don't talk about it enough.

We are the ones constantly showing up: talking to customers, nurturing them, guiding them and holding their hands through every stage of their journey. We absorb the good, the bad and the downright exhausting. We create, optimize, engage and we're expected to do all of this while navigating ever-changing trends, shifting platforms and an endless list of demands from leadership or clients.

And the hard truth is that we're rarely told to do *less*, but *better*. Instead, marketers are often asked to do *more*: more content, more strategies, more output, more results.

What if the real shift in marketing isn't just about putting customers first, but putting marketers first *alongside* them? Because if we don't take care of ourselves, if we don't create sustainable, strategic and enjoyable ways of marketing, then what's the point? Better marketing is about creating a way of working that doesn't drain us, that doesn't make us feel like we're constantly sprinting just to keep up. Marketing should be smart. It should be intentional. And yes, it should even be fun.

This chapter is about moving forward with a better, more human approach to marketing. One that works for customers but also works for *you*.

The reality of marketing today: What's next?

Marketing these days is like trying to hit a moving target. New platforms pop up, algorithms do their thing and yesterday's hot trend becomes today's old news. Just when you think you've got it figured out, everything changes.

No wonder so many marketers feel like they're always trying to catch up.

community and authenticity around the brand.[1] Not only does this campaign show off what iPhone cameras can do, but it also creates this great sense of community as people feel like they're really part of something when their photos become part of Apple's marketing. Whether through print ads, keynote speeches or digital campaigns, they've always prioritized simplicity, innovation and emotional connection. The tools have changed. Their core message hasn't.

The same applies to smaller, niche brands that have built dedicated communities. They don't panic every time a new algorithm change rolls out because their customers are looking for *connection* over *content*.

The key to future-proof marketing isn't knowing what's coming next. It's knowing what *never changes*. Marketing will always be about understanding people. The marketers that win won't be the ones chasing the latest gimmick, but the ones who keep their focus where it's always belonged: their customers.

THE BIGGEST LESSONS (BUT MAKE IT PRACTICAL!)

We've covered a lot in this book. But, like I repeated throughout, knowledge without action can only take you *so far*. The best marketing is lived, tested, tweaked and refined in real time. So instead of a traditional recap, let's distil the biggest lessons into something actionable.

The marketing plan is your blueprint

Strategy before tactics. Always. The most successful marketers aren't the ones chasing every shiny new trend, but the ones who take time to build a solid plan and really get to know their audience. Feeling lost? Take a step back and look at your strategy. That's what it's there for.

Look at your current marketing approach. If you could change one thing to make it simpler or more effective, what would it be? It could be stopping an unnecessary task, doubling down on what's working, or shifting focus to strategy instead of tactics. Decide on that one change and take action.

Know your audience deeply

Put your audience at the forefront of your decisions, which means get as close to your customers as possible. After all, assumptions don't build great marketing strategies. Knowing *who* you're speaking to is just the start. You need to understand *why* they buy, what motivates them and what keeps them up at night. When in doubt, go back to customer psychology, pain points and behaviour.

Open your inbox or social media messages and find one real customer comment or question. What does it tell you about their needs, frustrations or desires? If you're making marketing decisions without actual customer input, you're guessing it's time to start listening instead.

Trust is the currency of modern marketing

With a great brand comes great responsibility. In fact, every interaction (whether it's content, customer service or an ad) is either building trust or breaking it. Transparency, authenticity and reliability win in the long run, even if they don't give you the quickest conversion.

Write down one promise your brand makes to its customers. It could be about quality, service, values or experience.

Now ask yourself: *'Have I clearly communicated this promise across my marketing?'*

If not, find one place (your website, social media or email sequence) where you can reinforce it today.

Personalization and belonging create connection

Marketing is about making people feel *seen*. When customers feel like they belong, they stick around. Personalization goes beyond using a first name in an email. Great personalization makes each customer feel valued through processes, systems and the right tools.

Identify your latest customer, client or audience member (someone who recently followed you, signed up for something or made a purchase). Do one personalized touchpoint for them.

It could be a short video, a customized follow-up email or a simple voice note saying thank you. No automation, no templates – just a human-to-human moment.

Surprise and delight turn customers into advocates

People remember how you make them feel. The small, unexpected moments (whether it's a handwritten note, an Easter egg in your content or an exclusive perk) are what turn customers into fans.

Advocacy is earned through these moments. Choose one small but unexpected way to surprise your audience this week. It could be a bonus resource, a personalized thank-you message or an exclusive tip just for your community. The key is to make it feel personal, not transactional.

Data and experimentation are non-negotiable

Gut instinct is a great starting point, but the best marketing is *measured, tested and optimized*. If you're not looking at what's working (and what isn't), you're just guessing. Experiment, track, learn and iterate. That's how marketing stays effective.

Pick one marketing metric you rely on (engagement, conversion, retention, etc.). Now, ask yourself: *'What's one small test I can run to improve it?'* Try tweaking a subject line, testing a new call to action or adjusting your timing: just change one thing, track it and see what happens.

Marketing is a conversation, not a broadcast

Customers today want to be part of the conversation. The best marketers get this. They create dialogue, build rituals and make space for real engagement. Gone are the days when marketing was a one-way street. Now, it's all about building genuine connections that keep people coming back. Instead of just posting content this week, ask your audience something. It could be a question, a poll or a direct invite to share their thoughts.

At the end of the day, customer-driven marketing is about making marketing *better for everyone*. More thoughtful. More sustainable. More human.

REFLECTION TIME
What kind of marketer do you want to be?

Great marketing becomes a reflection of who you *are* as a marketer. The way you show up, the choices you make and the strategies you build all shape how people experience your work.

So, here's the question: *What's the one word you want your marketing to embody?*

Not something vague like 'successful' or 'effective'. But a word that *means* something to you. A word that captures the kind of marketer you want to be, the way you want people to feel when they interact with your work, the impact you want to leave behind.

- Maybe your word is **bold**, because you want your marketing to challenge the norm, push boundaries and stand out.
- Maybe it's **empathetic**, because you want your work to centre around deep understanding and human connection.

- Maybe it's **thoughtful**, because you value intentionality over urgency and strategy over speed.
- Or it's **curious, playful, fearless, disruptive** or **trustworthy**.

Struggling? You can always ask others about how they perceive your work, content or communication. If someone were to describe you marketing style, which word would they use?

Or how do *you* want to feel when you get marketed to? Just like choosing a word that captures your marketing philosophy, looking back at marketing that worked on you can teach you a lot about what you want to do in your own work.

Think about times when:

- you got a marketing email that made you smile
- a brand did something that pleasantly caught you off guard
- you came across content that felt real and spoke directly to you

These experiences can help shape the kind of marketer you want to be and inform how you want your audience to feel when interacting with your work.

Whatever this word is, it becomes your compass. When faced with a decision (whether it's launching a campaign, refining a message or even choosing which trends to follow) you can ask yourself: *Does this align with the kind of marketer I want to be?*

Before we close (even the best things come to an end), take a moment to write down the word that best represents your marketing philosophy. Then, expand on it:

- Why does this word resonate with me?
- How do I want this word to show up in my work?

Start creating a filter for your choices. Marketing is filled with distractions, expectations and conflicting advice. But when you know the kind of marketer you want to be, you start making decisions with clarity and confidence.

Final thought: Marketing should be fun (yes, really!)

TIP

Marketing is about momentum. It's not just what you learn: it's what you do with it.

Somewhere along the way, marketing got serious. Overloaded calendars, aggressive KPIs, endless data dashboards; it's easy to forget that, at its core, marketing is about creativity, connection and problem-solving. It's about understanding people and making something that speaks to them. And that should be *fun*.

That doesn't mean it's always easy. Marketing has its fair share of challenges: tight deadlines, shifting algorithms and the constant pressure to do more. But the best marketers find ways to bring their unique skills and strengths into the process. They approach problems like puzzles, not chores. Just like the maddest of scientists, they experiment, test, play.

If marketing ever starts to feel like an endless cycle of stress and guesswork, pause. Go back to the basics. Use these questions as a compass:

- Who am I trying to help?
- What problem am I solving?
- How can I make people's lives better?

At its best, marketing is an opportunity to create, to connect, to tell a story worth listening to. The best marketers a bring passion, joy and curiosity to their work. Because when marketing is fun (for you and for your audience) it shows.

A final challenge: Take action now

Before you go, I just want to say **thank you**.

Thank you for showing up. For challenging your beliefs. For being willing to rethink, refine and try something new.

Marketing isn't easy. It's messy, unpredictable and constantly evolving. But the fact that you're here, reading this, means you care enough to do it *well*. To make it better: not just for your customers, but for yourself.

Marketing is about momentum. It's not just what you *learn*: it's what you *do* with it. So before you close this book, before you get caught up in the next task, the next deadline or the next big idea, commit to taking action. Right now. Not next week. Not when things 'calm down'. Now. Pick *one* idea from this book (just one, you cheeky overachiever) and implement it this week. It doesn't have to be big. It doesn't have to be perfect. It just must move you forward.

Still not sure where to start? Try one of these:

- Refine one piece of messaging to better align with your audience's needs.
- Build one small moment of personalization into your marketing.

- Audit your customer journey for one place to add trust or connection.
- Test a small experiment: change a subject line, shift your call to action, tweak your timing.

Or, if you really want to solidify what you've learned, share your biggest takeaway with someone else. Teaching is one of the best ways to internalize learning. Whether it's a teammate, a peer or your audience, talk about what resonated with you the most (and maybe, just maybe, recommend this book to them).

And don't forget to tag me at @fabgiovanetti on social and access your special workbook and marketing plan template at altmarketingschool.com/book

Better marketing doesn't happen all at once. It happens through small, intentional steps, repeated over time. So, whatever comes next, keep going. Keep learning. Keep experimenting. Keep finding ways to make marketing work for *you*, not just the other way around.

Because better marketing starts with marketers who refuse to settle for *just okay*. With rebels who dare to put their customers first in their strategy. And that's exactly who you are.

Note

1   Benamic. Promotional perfection: Apple's 'Shot on iPhone' campaign using user-generated content, Benamic, 2019. www.benamic.com/blog/promotional-perfection-apples-shot-on-iphone-campaign-using-user-generated-content (archived at https://perma.cc/8PHT-73RU)

INDEX

The main index is filed in alphabetical, word-by-word order. Acronyms and 'Mc' are filed as presented; numbers are filed as spelt out.

Looking for another book?

Explore our award-winning
books from global business
experts in Marketing and Sales

Scan the code to browse

www.koganpage.com/marketing

From 4 December 2025 the EU Responsible Person (GPSR) is:
eucomply oÜ, Pärnu mnt. 139b – 14, 11317 Tallinn, Estonia
www.eucompliancepartner.com

www.ingramcontent.com/pod-product-compliance
Lightning Source LLC
Chambersburg PA
CBHW071550210326
41597CB00019B/3187